Beyers Naudé: Pilgrimage of

BEYERS NAUDÉ
Pilgrimage of Faith

COLLEEN RYAN

DAVID PHILIP · Cape Town
Wm. B. EERDMANS · Grand Rapids
AFRICA WORLD PRESS · Trenton, N.J.

First published 1990 in southern Africa by David Philip Publishers (Pty) Ltd, 208 Werdmuller Centre, Claremont 7700, South Africa.

Published 1990 in the United States of America by Wm. B. Eerdmans Publishing Co., 255 Jefferson Avenue, SE, Grand Rapids, Michigan 49503; and Africa World Press, 15 Industry Court, Trenton, New Jersey 08638.

© 1990 Colleen Ryan

All rights reserved

Printed in South Africa

ISBN 0-86486-156-7 David Philip
ISBN 0-8028-0531-0 Wm. B. Eerdmans
ISBN 0-86543-190-6 Africa World Press

Printed by Creda Press, Solan Road, Cape Town

Contents

	Foreword by Frank Chikane	vii
	Preface	viii
1	The Banning of Beyers Naudé, 19 October 1977	1
2	Born into Afrikaner Nationalism	4
3	The Shaping of a Young Nationalist, 1921–1939	12
4	Early Ministry: Living with Apartheid, 1939–1954	30
5	Awakening and Sharpeville, 1955–1960	40
6	Cottesloe, December 1960	53
7	The Storm after Cottesloe, 1961–1962	63
8	Leaving the Fold: The Christian Institute Established, 1963	73
9	Broederbond Exposés, 1963	86
10	A New Ministry Unfolds, 1963–1965	96
11	Years of Struggle at the Christian Institute, 1966–1968	110
12	The Challenge of Black Consciousness, 1969–1972	124
13	State Pressure Intensifies, 1972–1974	148
14	The Confrontation Grows, 1975–1977	167
15	The Death of the Christian Institute, 1977	186
16	Seven Lean Years, 1977–1984	193
17	Pilgrimage of Faith	204
	References	210
	Index	225

Photographs following p. viii

Foreword

It is with a deep sense of humility that I write this foreword about the man I first heard of in the turbulent years of the mid-1970s, and whom, during the intervening years, I have grown to respect and love. Beyers Naudé's life, in his own words, has been a 'pilgrimage of faith'. His unshakeable faith in God and his belief in the fundamental principles of justice taught by Jesus Christ have guided him through his own Damascus to repentance and beyond. It was from his position as a leading intellectual figure within the laager of the Afrikaner theological, political and social establishment that Dr Naudé fired his first salvos of challenge to the apartheid government. The price he paid for this cost him dearly: he was vilified, persecuted and ostracised by his own people and denied the right to minister in his own church.

1963 marked the beginning of a new existence for him within a different community: an existence of solidarity and acceptance within an ecumenical community, a resisting community and eventually a black community. His work in the Christian Institute placed him at the forefront of the ecumenical movement; as General Secretary of the South African Council of Churches, he emerged as one of its leaders.

It is to his great credit that as a white South African, he occupies the unique position of being regarded by black South Africans as one of their leaders, despite never having been formally elected to office in the liberation movements. His courageous resistance to apartheid, both within the country and abroad, his defence of the oppressed, and his accessibility to those in need, have contributed to his stature as a leader and as a revered symbol of resistance.

I believe that this book is a fitting tribute to the man who in his own lifetime has become one of the greatest sons of South Africa. He is a patriot who has struggled, with deep humility and love for his compatriots, for the realisation of his vision of a new South Africa.

His conversion, followed by nearly three decades of courageous opposition to apartheid and an unrelenting struggle for justice, has provided a powerful legacy of hope: a legacy which demonstrates for black South Africans the capacity of Afrikaners, and of whites, to change, and the potential for a non-racial future in our beloved country.

The Rev. Dr Frank Chikane
General Secretary of the South African Council of Churches

Preface

Many people have helped in providing material for this book. My first and deepest thanks go to Beyers Naudé who spent many patient hours with me. His approach was always clear, direct and honest. I am also very grateful to Ilse Naudé for her support and warmth. I started out on this project a stranger to the Naudés and ended feeling a privileged friend.

My thanks also go to the many people who willingly sacrificed their time and were interviewed for this book. Some excerpts of these interviews appear in this work, and though many, many others do not appear, ideas and thoughts were gleaned from all of them.

Several other people, both in South Africa and overseas, deserve special mention: Bert and Veronica Berkhof for their help and hospitality in the Netherlands, Bob Bilheimer and Worldwide Documentaries for the use of their interview material, Rune Forsbeck and the Swedish Ecumenical Council for the encouragement and their research grant, and Peter Randall for the use of his material.

I am also indebted to those who read my manuscript and offered valuable criticism: Brian Brown, Horst Kleinschmidt, Wolfram Kistner, Margaret Nash, Beyers and Ilse Naudé, Peter Randall, Zenaide Vendeiro and Charles Villa-Vicencio. My thanks go also to Frank Chikane for his foreword and to Russell Martin for his thorough editing. I am also deeply grateful to my husband, Neill, and my mother, Phyllis, for their unwavering support.

While this book was being prepared for publication, in February 1990, the South African government announced the lifting of restrictions on many organisations. Vast attention was justifiably focused on the legalised African National Congress, Pan-Africanist Congress and the South African Communist Party. By contrast, the lifting of the bans imposed in 1977 on the Christian Institute, seventeen Black Consciousness organisations and *Pro Veritate*, *The World* and *Weekend World*, went largely unnoticed. In spite of these promising changes, the blows suffered over the years will take a long time to heal. I merely cite one physical example: the researching of this book was complicated by the difficulty in acquiring documentary evidence. At the time of writing, the vast quantity of archival and personal material seized from the Christian Institute by the police in 1977 still remains lost and unaccounted for.

1 The Naudé family photographed with Ouma van Huyssteen in Graaff-Reinet

2 Beyers (seated) with his parents and brother Joos, photographed shortly after the brothers' ordination, 1940.

3 Beyers and Ilse with Liesel and (from left) François, Hermann and Johann, 1953

4 & 5 Beyers and Ilse at a reception to welcome them to the Aasvoëlkop church, 1959. With them (below) are D. du Plessis (head of South African Railways) and Dr Piet Meyer (head of the SA Broadcasting Corporation) and their wives.

6 Beyers Naudé, shortly after the launch of the Christian Institute, 31 December 1963. *(The Star)*

7 Fred van Wyk, first administrative director of the Christian Institute. (Photo: Danie van Zyl)

8 Albert Geyser, who leaked Beyers's copies of Broederbond documents to the press. *(The Star)*

9 Beyers and other ministers at an African Independent Churches Association conference held in Soweto in the 1960s. (Photo: Danie van Zyl)

10 Delegates to the SACC conference at Hammanskraal, August 1974, which adopted the historic resolution on conscientious objection. From left: Beyers Naudé, Rev. Philip Russell, Rev. Maurice Ngakane, John Rees and Dr Manas Buthelezi. *(The Star)*

11 Subpoenas served on Brian Brown, Beyers Naudé and Horst Kleinschmidt to appear before the Schlebusch Commission, 1973. *(The Star)*

12 The final scene in the drama outside the SACC headquarters in Khotso House, when police tried to break up a meeting being held inside, 11 June 1986. (Photo: Alf Kumalo, *The Star*)

13 Ethel Kennedy presents Beyers with the Robert F Kennedy Human Rights Award on his first trip to the United States after his unbanning, 1985.

14 Ilse Naudé, September 1984.

15 Beyers on the day he was unbanned, 27 September 1984. *(The Star)*

16 Beyers preaching in Johannesburg, 17 March 1988. *(The Star)*

17 Beyers and Frank Chikane, his successor as general secretary of the SACC, 1987.

1
The Banning of Beyers Naudé, 19 October 1977

The shrill ringing of the telephone jolted Beyers Naudé out of his sleep on Wednesday, 19 October 1977. It was 5.30 a.m. as he hurried into his small study to still the piercing noise. He heard a woman's voice. She did not identify herself, but said in a whisper: 'They are raiding us. Be prepared. The end has come.' The phone was silent. He had been expecting such a call for weeks, and he felt afraid.

He quickly woke his wife, Ilse, and told her the security police were moving in to destroy the Christian Institute. They dressed and, as Ilse hurriedly made coffee, he tried desperately to contact friends and colleagues for news of what was happening. They locked the house and quietly moved out of their driveway in the well-to-do suburb of Greenside in the north of Johannesburg. In silence, Beyers drove his Peugeot along the familiar route to the city's business area of Braamfontein where the Christian Institute had its offices.

As they approached Diakonia House they realised the building was under siege. Police vans were parked outside and plain-clothes and uniformed policemen crowded the entrance to the building. In the foyer Beyers saw a sea of familiar faces – mostly workers from the Christian Institute – and then a policeman separated him from his wife. Senior staff members of the Christian Institute were allowed to go up to their offices, but all other personnel were told to wait in the hall downstairs. Finally, Beyers was escorted to his office. A security policeman informed him that the Minister of Justice, Mr Jimmy Kruger, had declared the Christian Institute an unlawful organisation. All its assets and documents were to be confiscated by the state. He sat down behind his desk for the last time, and watched, in a daze, as scores of policemen searched every room. Every book and document was carefully marked and packed into boxes. Each desk, chair, filing cabinet and typewriter was marked too and moved out of the offices, and then loaded onto waiting trucks in the alley behind Diakonia House.

Beyers was not allowed to leave his office or to use the telephone. For four hours he watched these mechanical proceedings as unanswered questions raced through his mind. He asked himself: 'Does this mean the end of everything that

I have stood for? Has every sacrifice I have made been in vain? Has the witness of the Christian Institute been for nothing?' He sat and thought about the events of the morning which had started with a telephone call from Helen Kotze, wife of Theo Kotze, the Christian Institute's regional director in Cape Town. He worried about what was happening to his staff downstairs, about the people who worked in the CI's regional offices, in the Cape and Natal. He thought of Ilse who had suffered so much since he had taken office as director of the CI in 1963. How would she take this shock? How would his four adult children and their families react?

Finally, all the CI's belongings were taken away. At noon, two security policemen walked into the echoing, empty room where Beyers Naudé was waiting.

One of them, a Colonel Van Rensburg, said to him: 'I would like to hand you a document.'

'Yes, what document?' Beyers asked.

'I regret to state that you have been banned and this document contains the requirements of the banning order. Will you please sign it?' The policeman handed him three copies of a document signed by the Minister of Justice and dated 11 October 1977. It declared that in terms of the Internal Security Act his rights and movements were to be restricted for five years.

He signed the banning orders, put the copies in his briefcase – the only possession which the police had not taken – and left his office. Walking down the passage he looked deep into the eyes of the policemen who were standing around, but they would not return his gaze. As he left the Christian Institute's office for the last time, he prayed silently: 'Thank You, God, for Your goodness in allowing me nearly forty years of ministry in Your service.'

Outside the building, a phalanx of reporters and photographers had gathered, and one stepped forward and asked him: 'Is it true that you have been banned?'

'Yes, for a period of five years.'

'Do you have any comment?' the reporter asked.

'Yes, I have much to say, but you can't quote me,' Beyers replied and walked away. Ilse had already been taken home by a friend, and so he drove home alone, thinking about the enormity of his banning order and the closure of the Christian Institute. He had been ordered to cease all his work. He would have to report to the local police station every Wednesday morning. He could not be quoted in the press, he could not write anything for publication, he could not meet socially with more than one person at a time, he could not leave the magisterial district of Johannesburg without permission, he could not enter any school, university or other educational institution, or any place where material was being prepared for publication. Suddenly, at the age of 62 he was a 'non-person', he had been condemned to 'civil death'.

Ilse was waiting at the front door. She embraced him, took his hand, and said: 'I am sorry, Bey.' There was a long silence and it was their last quiet moment for many weeks. The phone started to ring incessantly, and their children and friends began arriving at their home as the news spread. But Beyers knew that the action against himself and the CI was only a small part of a massive clampdown by the Nationalist government on anti-apartheid activists and organisations.[1]

On that 'Black Wednesday' security police conducted similar raids on seventeen Black Consciousness organisations which had been declared unlawful, and closed down the black-readership newspapers *The World* and *The Weekend World*, as well as the Christian Institute's journal, *Pro Veritate*. Several other white staff members and one former staff member of the Christian Institute were banned, while more than 70 leading Black Consciousness figures, many of whom were already serving banning orders, were detained without trial. The crackdown came sixteen months after the start of mass black revolt in South Africa, sparked by uprisings in Johannesburg's sprawling black township, Soweto. Thousands of youths had left the country, hundreds more caught up in the unrest had been shot, many had been detained and Black Consciousness leader Steve Biko had died of head injuries while being detained without trial by the security police.

It was only much later that Beyers had a chance to reflect on the events of that day, which he regarded as a turning point in his life. How had it happened that he – a white Afrikaner brought up to believe in the mission of his people to rule South Africa – had ended up confined to his house by his own *volk*? He had started out so promisingly as a minister of the largest and most important of the three Afrikaans Reformed churches, the Nederduitse Gereformeerde Kerk. His rise through the ranks had been rapid until, in mid-life, he had begun to question the race policies of his church and government.

After 23 years, he had given up his position as minister of the NGK to form the Christian Institute with the support of a small group of moderate Afrikaners who were opposed to their church's support for apartheid. Beyers and his colleagues had hoped to convince their brothers gradually of the errors of their ways. But the CI failed to move the Afrikaner establishment and increasingly came to identify itself with the oppressed people of South Africa. By the mid-1970s the CI, under his leadership, had moved rapidly away from its moderate position; its unequivocal support for blacks fighting to end white rule and its criticism of the unjust economic order in South Africa frightened off many of its white supporters and infuriated the authorities. Government pressure on Beyers Naudé and the CI began to increase. A commission was appointed to investigate the CI's activities and found it to be a danger to the state. Beyers was charged and convicted for refusing to give evidence before this commission, and his organisation was barred from receiving foreign funding. Most of the CI's black staff members were banned and then, finally, its leading white members were banned too and the entire Institute was closed down.

In the loneliness of his office on the morning of 19 October 1977, Beyers asked: 'Was it all in vain?' But even on that, the bleakest day of his life, he believed he knew the answer. The Christian Institute might have been destroyed, its staff silenced, but its truth would remain.

2
Born into Afrikaner Nationalism

Christiaan Frederick Beyers Naudé was born a privileged Afrikaner, a member of the white tribe which has played such an important role in the modern history of South Africa. For the first 45 years of his life he was fiercely loyal to his people and the nationalist cause. He rejoiced when the National Party came to power in 1948 and did not question when they introduced apartheid, which was to create such hardship and suffering for the black majority.

Afrikaner leaders had expected opposition to apartheid: from the outside world, from some English-speaking white South Africans, and from blacks. But an important part of their success had been to forge unity within their own ranks. Members of the Afrikaner *volk* were discouraged from questioning a system which they were told was sanctioned by God to ensure their nation's continued survival.

One of the early Afrikaner heroes, Piet Retief, had spelt out the fate of Afrikaner dissenters more than 160 years before in a manifesto explaining why Dutch-speaking farmers, the Boers, were leaving the British-ruled Cape Colony to seek new lands in the interior of South Africa. Outlining what the Boers would do once they had resettled, Retief declared: 'We make known that when we shall have framed a code of laws for our future guidance, copies shall be forwarded to the [British] colony for general information; but we take this opportunity of stating that it is our firm resolve to make provision for the summary punishment of any traitors who may be found amongst us.'[1]

Beyers Naudé was himself to come up against this harsh and punitive attitude towards those who weakened or betrayed the cause of the Afrikaner. When he broke with the Afrikaner establishment in church and state over their race policies, he was regarded as a traitor and treated as such. But even though his *volk* turned their back on him, he never lost his deep love for the Afrikaans language and never became ashamed, nor tried to deny, that he was an Afrikaner. His family was long rooted in South Africa and his father had been closely associated with the emergence of Afrikaner nationalism.

Jozua François Naudé, Beyers's father, was born on 20 March 1873 in Middelburg, Cape, a small farming town in the Karoo. The eldest child in a large family, he was named after his father, who was a teacher and the town's catechism master. His parents were conservative, religious Afrikaners, faithful members of the Nederduitse Gereformeerde Kerk, or Dutch Reformed Church, who brought up their children in accordance with the strict Calvinist and evangelistic traditions of their faith. Every day there was family worship and on Sundays the whole family attended church.[2]

Jozua's family sometimes travelled the hundred kilometres to Graaff-Reinet, the most important town in the Karoo, and on significant occasions attended services, held in Dutch, in the town's impressive Groote Kerk. The Graaff-Reinet church was dominated by the Murrays, a family of ministers of Scots extraction who made an important contribution to the development of education at the Cape and who were zealous evangelists. As a result of their influence, the NGK became an ardent evangelistic church and laid great stress on the importance of personal conversion and the spreading of the gospel.

When Jozua was a schoolboy, English, the sole official language in the Colony, was also the only medium of instruction in schools. It was in this language that he was mainly educated, but his first love was always his own mother-tongue.[3] After completing school, he attended the Normal College in Cape Town where at the age of 20 he qualified as a teacher. His first post was in the small village of Riebeek West[4] and during this time, while visiting the Van Huysteen family at Wittedrif, near Plettenberg Bay, he met his future bride. Adriana Johanna Zondagh van Huysteen was only 15 years old at the time, but their meeting led to a lengthy courtship and eventual marriage.

Sharp contrasts have often been drawn between Jozua Naudé, the zealous Afrikaner nationalist, and his son Beyers, held up as one who 'betrayed the *volk*'. In spite of the differences in the causes they ultimately espoused, there were many similarities between father and son; both were deeply religious, with strong convictions and a sense of justice, not afraid to go against the stream and to risk criticism when they felt their principles were at stake. Jozua displayed great energy and drive, and piled on himself numerous commitments and responsibilities – a characteristic people would also recognise in Beyers.

Jozua was strongly committed to the NGK's evangelism and fervently believed in the need to spread the gospel. He also agreed with the view then emerging that God had created the Afrikaner nation, like the Israelites of old, for the purpose of spreading His Word, and for keeping the Christian faith alive on the dark continent of Africa. But for Afrikaners to fulfil their destiny, their language and culture had to be set free and allowed to develop.

Towards the turn of the century, Jozua Naudé settled in the Transvaal Republic and took up a post as teacher in a church school in the Reef mining town of Germiston. Thousands of others, attracted by the discovery of gold and the development of the gold-mining industry, were also pouring into the Republic. It was a time of rising political tension in South Africa. President Paul Kruger of the Transvaal stubbornly refused to allow the Uitlanders, the mainly English-speaking immigrants to the gold fields, the right to vote. On this pretext Britain, determined to bring the strategically and economically valuable territory within the British sphere of influence, provoked a war. Jozua had become a naturalised citizen of the Republic shortly before the outbreak of hostilities in October 1899. He fully supported the Boer cause and showed no hesitation in giving up his job as headmaster of his small church school to take up arms. Being an active lay preacher, he also served as unofficial pastor to the Boer forces during the war.

Jozua spoke infrequently to his children of his wartime experiences, but what he said made a profound impact. His son Beyers learnt how Britain had set out to crush the two independent Boer Republics in South Africa, Transvaal and the neighbouring Orange Free State, and how they had stopped at nothing to accomplish this. He heard of the bravery and courage of the Boer generals and their commandos, of the suffering and hardship experienced by their families. He was told how the British, to prevent Boer women from giving food and support to the Boer forces, herded thousands of them, with their children, into hastily constructed concentration camps – in which some 26 000 died; and of the scorched-earth policy adopted by the British forces in a desperate effort to end the war.

Jozua Naudé contributed to the war in several ways. In the first place, he was considered a brave soldier; he believed the Afrikaners were fighting a just war and had no qualms about shooting the enemy. But on Sundays, or when the Boer forces had an opportunity to rest, he would become their minister and comforter. He kept detailed notebooks throughout the war, some of which he buried and later dug up and used when he wrote a book in Dutch on his own experiences and on the campaigns of his close wartime friends, generals Jan Kemp and Christiaan Frederik Beyers.[5] As the war dragged on, Jozua realised that the struggle of the Afrikaner *volk* would not be an easy one, but he believed that ultimately his people would triumph. He described this vision in his book. One day, riding alone through the veld on his horse, he stopped to rest at a little waterfall on the Tugela River. As he watched the trickling water he thought deeply about the long battle which lay before the Afrikaner people. Upstream, the river was merely three little rivulets meandering through a shallow riverbed but, as the streams neared the waterfall, they flowed into a big rock pool, and then, joined as one, tumbled powerfully down. It suddenly struck Jozua that just as the waterfall had only become a force when the separate streams had been joined, so, too, the Afrikaner people would only triumph when they were united as one.[6]

By 1902 the war was going badly for the Boers and the plight of Boer civilians and soldiers had become desperate in many parts of the country. Surrender had become inevitable, and in May the Boer generals began to negotiate a peace with the British authorities. The formal treaty, in which the Transvaal and Free State surrendered their independence, was signed on 31 May 1902, but not before a bitter debate among the Boers. On 29 May, some 60 Boer representatives met at Vereeniging in the Transvaal to choose between unconditional surrender or continuing with the war. The argument raged for three days, and gradually the delegates were won over to the position of the Transvaal leaders, who felt that the continued existence of the Boers as a people depended on the cessation of the war.[7] However, a handful of delegates vowed not to lay down their arms. One of these *bittereinders* was Jozua François Naudé. On 30 May, the night before the delegates were to take a final vote on the treaty, the leading Boer general and future prime minister, Jan Smuts, took Jozua aside. Pacing up and down between the delegates' tents, General Smuts pleaded with the influential pastor to accept the peace, but Jozua would not hear of it. From that day Jozua regarded Smuts a traitor to the Afrikaner cause.[8] The next day, when the vote was taken in the conference tent, 54 delegates voted to accept the peace and only 6 voted against it. When the defeated Boers were ordered to hand in their arms, Jozua ignored the order and kept possession of a Mauser which he had taken from a British soldier during the Battle of Colenso. He kept the rifle after he entered the church. Years later, after his death, his eldest son, Jozua, handed the firearm to a museum.[9]

The war and the ultimate defeat of the two Boer Republics deeply affected Jozua Naudé. Before the war, he had regarded himself as a 'colonial Transvaler' and felt a slight distance between himself and the Afrikaner Republicans, but by the end of the struggle this had disappeared and he believed a spirit of unity had emerged among Afrikaners throughout South Africa.[10] Profoundly moved by the bitter fight which his people had waged for their freedom, he dedicated the rest of his life to the struggle to regain their independence. In the ashes of bitter defeat, the flames of Afrikaner nationalism were smouldering. Jozua typified a new breed of fiercely patriotic Afrikaners, who were beginning to come together in a common cause. Their goal was the elimination of British power on the southern tip of the African continent and its replacement with exclusive white Afrikaner power. But in the early 1900s victory was still a long way off.

Jozua and Ada's correspondence had been interrupted by the war, but the relationship resumed when he moved to Stellenbosch in the Cape to study for the ministry. Six years younger than her husband, Adriana van Huyssteen had grown up in the Knysna district of the Cape, the youngest of three children of conservative parents. Determined that all their children would be well educated, they sent Ada hundreds of kilometres away to the Huguenot College in Wellington, where she received her education in English. Artistic and musical, she acquired a second-class teacher's certificate at the age of 23 and then taught for a few years. Like the rest of her family, she was a devout member of the NGK, and by marrying a minister of the church she was following a family tradition; her brother had become a *dominee*, while her sister had also married an NGK minister.[11] Ada appears to have been a highly strung young woman. Like her husband, she believed in the justness of the Afrikaner's cause and was given to expressing strong nationalistic sentiments.[12] Their courtship continued through the early days of Jozua's academic career and they were married in a double wedding ceremony, together with Ada's sister and brother-in-law, on Christmas day 1906.[13]

Jozua completed his theological studies at the NGK's Theological Seminary in Stellenbosch in 1909. He had received calls from several congregations and decided to accept an invitation to become superintendent of the Goedemoed work colony, established by the church in the Orange Free State as a refuge for poor, dispossessed white tenant farmers, or *bywoners*, as they were commonly known. In January 1910 the couple moved to the remote, undeveloped settlement close to the banks of the Orange River and remained there for eighteen months. Jozua was deeply moved by the poverty of his congregation, which he realised formed but part of a national crisis facing the Afrikaner people. In the aftermath of war and in a rapidly industrialising South Africa, many Afrikaners had been unable to survive on the land, and had begun pouring into the towns in search of work. In 1911 Jozua accepted a call to the struggling NGK community in Roodepoort, a mining town on the Witwatersrand, where the campaign for Afrikaner rights had begun in earnest.[14]

In the previous year, the four former British colonies of the Cape, Natal, Orange Free State and Transvaal had come together in the Union of South Africa. The black majority were deprived of political rights, but white Afrikaners were promised the same rights as their English counterparts. But deep differences still existed, not only between English- and Afrikaans-speakers, but also among Afrikaners, who were split between the politics of conciliation and the politics of ethnic nationalism. Bitterness among the Afrikaner people came to a head in 1914 when South Africa had to choose whether to remain neutral or to join the side of the Allies in the First World War. The South African government under the leadership of generals Louis Botha and Jan Smuts decided to stand with Britain. To Jozua Naudé and other Boer patriots, siding with the old enemy was unthinkable. When in September 1914 the South African government ordered the army to invade the neighbouring German colony of South West Africa, many Boer generals in the Defence Force opposed this step and thought the time was right to loosen the ties of British control and declare an independent Afrikaner republic. Leading military men, including General Koos de la Rey and Jozua's close friend General Beyers, led the revolt. Beyers resigned his post in the Defence Force and began to lobby support for the rebels. The insurrection lasted a few months, but was finally crushed by loyal government troops. Some of the rebel leaders surrendered, one was executed and General Beyers himself was drowned while attempting to evade capture by crossing the Vaal River. Jozua Naudé grieved over the loss of his friend and the blood that had been spilt between Afrikaners.

It was during the turmoil of the First World War that Ada Naudé became pregnant again. As she prepared to give birth to her second son (and fourth child) in the Roodepoort parsonage in May 1915, violence once more broke out on the Witwatersrand, sparked by the German sinking of the British liner, the *Lusitania*. The attack set off a wave of anti-German sentiment abroad and in South Africa. Ada testified that on 10 May, the night Beyers was born, a gang set fire to German shops nearby; a bright orange glow from the burning buildings lit up the room in which she gave birth to her son.[15] At least one house was burnt down and three shops were destroyed in Roodepoort; the wave of attacks reached a climax three days later when mobs burnt, destroyed or damaged shops, restaurants, cinemas and homes belonging or suspected of belonging to Germans in Johannesburg and other towns around the country.[16] It was into this violent world that Jozua and Ada's younger son was born. Jozua decided that instead of giving the infant the family names Matthys Petrus, which were the names of his father-in-law, he would call him Christiaan Frederick Beyers, in honour of his close friend. When his son was older, Jozua gave him a small Dutch Bible which he had given to General Beyers during the Anglo–Boer War. It was a possession young Beyers came to treasure, and he kept it all his life.[17]

De Volkstem newspaper reported on the unusual names given to the baby and his parents received numerous letters of support and good wishes for their son's future.[18] The parents had shown a penchant for the unusual in naming some of their other children. They named their first daughter Ligstraal (Ray of light), because she symbolised a light in their lives after the disappointment of losing their first set of twins as well as Ligstraal's twin sister at birth. They called their second daughter Hymne, indicating a song of praise, but when their first son was born, they chose the traditional names Jozua François. They named their next daughter Adalena Tricharda, to mark her baptism in the town of Louis Trichardt, followed by Vryheidster (Star of freedom), to commemorate the ending of the First World War.[19] When their fifth daughter was born in Graaff-Reinet, they named her Reinet (while the assistant minister named his new-born son Graaff). The last-born was christened Lirieka (Lyrical), at the suggestion of the famous Afrikaans poet, C. J. Langenhoven, who was a family friend.[20]

Beyers and his brother and sisters grew up in a home where broader community and political issues were often discussed. As a *dominee* Jozua commanded great respect in the community, and people streamed to him with their problems. He was also involved in the struggle for the recognition of his own language at a time when English was still favoured in the courts, in schools, in the civil service and business, and when Dutch, and not Afrikaans, was the official language of the NGK. At successive synods Jozua put forward the case for Afrikaans. He pointed out that Afrikaans, not Dutch, was the language of the people and that the time had come for the church to recognise it. The arguments made by him and others eventually won the day and in time it was accepted that Afrikaans should have the same status as Dutch in the church.[21]

Jozua was also determined to push for the rights of his people in schools. When the Naudés' eldest child reached school-going age, there was no exclusive Afrikaans or Dutch-medium school in the town, so they taught her at home. When the authorities began planning a new school for the town, Jozua spearheaded a campaign to have it declared an Afrikaans school. However, the education authorities refused this demand, and so Jozua began an informal Afrikaans school on church property. Ada, already fully preoccupied with five young children and pregnant once again, served as principal and teacher at the small school. Having no one with whom to leave her youngest – still a baby – she had to tie the child, who was beginning to crawl, to a tree near the church door so that she could give classes. She continued teaching until three days before the birth of her sixth child.[22]

The school language battle was finally won in July 1918 when the new Roodepoort Afrikaans school was opened, the first school in the Transvaal where the medium of instruction was exclusively Afrikaans – an important victory for the nationalist cause. But Jozua, moved by the economic plight of his fellow Afrikaners, many of whom felt inferior to English-speakers with their better skills, jobs and homes, was not satisfied with the pace of progress made by the nationalist movement. He met frequently with other young leading Afrikaners to discuss the numerous problems facing their people. From these discussions emerged the Afrikaner Broederbond (Brotherhood of Afrikaners).

The impetus for the Broederbond came from a meeting called by the National Party in Johannesburg in April 1918. It was to have been addressed by the future prime minister and then Cape leader of the party, Dr D. F. Malan, but it broke up in chaos when a pro-Smuts mob arrived. They smashed up the hall, and fighting broke out in the street between the rival groups. A few of the young nationalists present were particularly angered and frustrated, and decided the time was right to form a pro-Afrikaner organisation. About two months later at a private home in the poor Afrikaner suburb of Malvern, Johannesburg, an organisation of 'Young South Africa', later called the Broederbond, was formally established.[23] It was to be a service organisation 'for the reconciliation of all Afrikaners in a single brotherhood – an organisation in which Afrikaners could find each other in the midst of great confusion and disunity and be able to work together for the survival of the Afrikaner people in South Africa and the promotion of its interests'. Jozua Naudé was elected its first president.[24] In 1920, a constitution was adopted and it was decided that the Broederbond should become a secret body. From these small beginnings there grew an organisation which was to have considerable influence on South African political events. It became one of the prime movers behind the burgeoning nationalism among Afrikaners, and nurtured and championed the policy of apartheid to ensure the survival of the Afrikaner. Highly selective about who could join, the Broederbond cultivated the cream of Afrikaners within its ranks, so that in time the top echelons in Afrikaner politics, in the church, in schools, hospitals, provincial administrations, Afrikaner business – in fact, every walk of life – were members. As it reached its zenith in the 1950s and 1960s, practically all important government posts went to Broeders, so that it often became hard to say whether the government selected the Broeders or the Broeders selected the government.

At the same time as the Broederbond was being formalised, Jozua accepted a call to a small town in the eastern Transvaal, Piet Retief, where the family lived for about two years. For Ada particularly, it was a happy period. Her husband was away from the mainstream of political activity, and she enjoyed having more time with him in the home.[25] Her children were also happy, and Beyers was fast catching up to his elder brother, Jozua, who was a quiet child often plagued by poor health. Beyers appears to have been a bright, high-spirited child. He loved outdoor activities and played with the many little Zulu-speaking children who lived in the black 'location'. His mother later said that by the time the family left the town, her younger son spoke better Zulu than he did Afrikaans, but knowledge of the language soon faded from his young mind.[26]

Piet Retief held few challenges for a minister as committed and ambitious as Jozua. He barely hesitated when he received a call from Graaff-Reinet, by then one of the most important inland towns in the Cape, to take up the position of senior minister. His wife and children did not want to leave Piet Retief. For Ada, it was a hard blow. She enjoyed the pace of life and climate of Piet Retief and she knew that in Graaff-Reinet her husband would be more occupied than ever with his work. But for Jozua there was much still to be done in the service of the Afrikaner, and that settled the argument.[27]

3
The Shaping of a Young Nationalist, 1921–1939

On a mid-winter's day in 1921 the young Beyers Naudé and his family arrived by train at the coastal city of Port Elizabeth and changed trains to travel to the inland town of Graaff-Reinet, some 250 kilometres away. The wind and the greenery of the coast soon gave way to the still, semi-desert terrain of the Karoo. In spite of its harshness, Beyers Naudé would come to love this country.

As they neared Graaff-Reinet the landscape grew increasingly rugged until clusters of tiny, uniform houses tucked into the hills came into view. These were the dwellings of the town's servants and workers, most of whom shared the language and religion of the white townsfolk but were set apart by the colour of their skins. Then the eager family saw the main town of Graaff-Reinet. Tucked into the horse-shoe bend of the Sundays River and surrounded on all sides by the Sneeuberg, the neat shops and houses were dominated by the tall and imposing NGK church.

Jozua Naudé was happy to be back in the area of his youth and felt as if he was coming home.[1] He had lived in these hot, dry farmlands as a poor, uneducated boy but was now returning as a distinguished minister. It was in Graaff-Reinet that he was to make great strides in advancing the nationalist cause and win recognition for Afrikaans both in the church and in the classroom.

Beyers was unaware of his father's ambitions as he shared in the chores of the large parsonage, or *Pastorie,* provided for the family. The house was not as imposing as Reinet House, the old Murray parsonage next door. But with its large front garden, verandah surrounding most of the dwelling, and high ceilings, it had a character of its own. Much larger than the ordinary houses in the town it had six bedrooms, enabling even as large a family as the Naudés to provide Beyers and his brother with a room of their own. The living areas were equally spacious, with a frontroom or *voorkamer* reserved for special occasions, another two large rooms used as the family's dining and study areas as well as for important church functions, and an enormous kitchen. The house had a large backgarden where vegetables were cultivated and the cow and chickens were given place, and at the side was a shady grapevine.[2]

The Naudé children were considered more privileged than most and did not want for necessities. But there was never money for luxuries, and they were expected to be thrifty and to help with the domestic chores. Beyers and his brother were required to work in the garden and milk the cow, and both acquired practical skills through helping with small jobs in and around the house. As the parsonage was only a block away from the Sundays River, the boys spent much of their spare time swimming or else exploring the koppies surrounding the town. When they were a little older, Jozua allowed his two sons to accompany him on pastoral visits, or *huisbesoek,* to local farms. The boys loved these trips, enjoying the sheep-shearing and other farming rituals. When Beyers and his brother were teenagers, they bought bicycles which they rode endlessly through the flat streets of the town. Hunting became another teenage passion, and during school holidays Beyers loved to visit school friends on neighbouring farms to shoot game.[3]

The young Beyers was of average build, with blue eyes and thick sandy hair which he wore very short and parted in the middle. Healthy, energetic and sociable, he was, in physique and personality, different from his older brother Jozua, nicknamed Joos, who was quiet, introvert and often plagued with illness.[4] Ada kept Joos out of school for a year because of ill health and, from their third year of school, the two brothers were in the same class. In this way, the boys almost became 'twins', with Beyers taking the leading role, both at school and in their games. Indeed, Beyers felt a sense of responsibility for his older brother. Their close relationship as children continued into young adulthood, when they went to university together. Notwithstanding the inevitable sibling quarrels, the brothers were very fond of each other.[5]

Beyers did not take his schoolwork particularly seriously, but he had an ability to learn and absorb facts easily and was usually among the top three scholars in the class. He loved reading, particularly the Dutch books which his sisters brought home from university. During his school years, he did not read much in English but his parents, who spoke excellent English, encouraged their children to become fluent in this language.[6]

Jozua and Ada shared two ideals which dominated the Naudé home: they had a deep, unshakeable faith in God and felt strongly about the future of their *volk*. Adhering to old-style pietism, every morning and evening they held *huisgodsdiens,* or Bible reading and prayer, and the children had to attend at least one church service on a Sunday. In accordance with the NGK's strict interpretation of Calvinism, Sunday was the Lord's day, a day of rest. Ada Naudé did not even approve of knitting on a Sunday, and the family motor car was driven only in emergencies. The use of alcohol and cigarettes was forbidden, and the children were not allowed to go to 'bioscope' or to dances. The Naudé children were also brought up to be obedient to their parents and to show respect for their elders at all times.[7]

In the traditional Afrikaans way, the roles of the sexes were very clearly defined in the Naudé household. Beyers and his brother were taught to regard males as somehow more important than females, and the Naudé girls were expected to perform domestic chores for their brothers, such as mending and washing their clothes and ironing their shirts. It was also natural that in a family where there were so many more girls than boys, the focus was often on Beyers and young Joos.[8]

Ada always tried to keep a little distance between her family and the other children of the town. Her two sons were not allowed to play contact sports like rugby, but in his teens Beyers became so insistent that Ada reluctantly allowed him to play.[9] The Naudé children were aware of their father's high status and of a certain class distinction existing between themselves and other families of the town. While most Afrikaner children were brought up in the Calvinist faith, the Naudés' rigorously conservative homelife added to the children's sense of isolation.[10] As teenagers, they were discouraged from forming relationships with the opposite sex. All these constraints made for a protected homelife during Beyers's formative years.

Growing up in this confined environment, the children turned to each other for companionship and recreation, and they enjoyed the family's musical evenings. Their parents had a passion for singing; Ada especially wanted her children to learn music, so when her father died she invested her inheritance in a Steinway grand piano. All the children learnt to play the instrument with varying degrees of success. Beyers also played the violin, while his brother studied the cello. After evening service the family would join in singing their favourite hymns, listen to the elder daughters play a duet, or sing *volksliedere* (folk songs) together.[11]

Every December, when the mid-summer heat brought the town to a virtual standstill, the Naudé family escaped to Port Elizabeth for their annual holiday. The family could not afford to hire a cottage and so they camped, first near New Brighton beach and later at The Willows, where the sea was safer for the children. Year after year the family made the pilgrimage to the sea, hauled their equipment out of storage, and set up camp. But the annual trip to Port Elizabeth was not all leisure. Money was still very short, and Ada used the annual vacation to shop at the summer sales. For days, she and the children would join the queues of poor people hunting from shop to shop in search of cheap clothing.[12]

During the Depression years thousands of families in Graaff-Reinet and on the surrounding farms lived in dire poverty. The poorest class of all were the landless 'Coloured' (or mulatto) and African people of the town, but there were many white Afrikaner families also living at this time below the breadline. In a society where racial barriers were already firmly in place, Jozua Naudé and his wife concerned themselves mainly with the welfare of their white flock. On many occasions the Naudé family provided overnight shelter to poor white tenant farmers, who had been forced off the farms by the drought and depression. They would pack their few belongings onto oxwagons or donkey carts, leave the barren farms and trek to Port Elizabeth in search of jobs. As a child, Beyers was moved by the hopelessness of these people, and as an adult he came to feel the same empathy for the impoverished black people of South Africa. He said of his contact with poor whites: 'Through that experience my social consciousness was formed: of hunger, of poverty, of people in situations of dire distress, of the helplessness of people who experienced forces or events over which they were powerless, either to control or to direct; this left a very deep impression on my mind.'[13]

Widespread poverty was only one of the problems that Jozua Naudé had to face during his early years at Graaff-Reinet. He was still determined to win recognition for the Afrikaans language in the NGK, and his actions caused deep dissension and ultimately a split in his congregation. Jozua wasted no time in demonstrating his feelings to his congregation by delivering his induction service in Afrikaans instead of the conventional Dutch. Basing his sermon on a passage from Acts, he told the congregation that he felt God had called him to Graaff-Reinet for a special purpose.[14] Beyers never forgot that day in church, and although he did not appreciate the significance of the use of Afrikaans, he clearly remembered the indignation it evoked. One woman, a member of the Murray family, registered her disgust at the start of the service by storming out of the church, and she was reported to have said: 'To think that he is going to use kitchen Dutch in my father's pulpit. I'd rather send my child to a Roman Catholic church than let him listen to his kitchen Dutch.'[15] Although it was not the first time Afrikaans had been spoken from the pulpit it was still the exception, and by delivering his opening service in Afrikaans, Jozua Naudé had effectively challenged the pre-eminence of the Dutch language in the NGK.

Jozua attracted both praise and protest for his stand, and soon his opponents drew together to respond to the challenge which the 'backward'[16] parvenu from the Transvaal had delivered. A formal complaint was delivered to the church council; this heralded the start of a struggle between two factions, which came to a head six years later when 600 members left to establish a rival church in the town. Soon the dispute became more than a simple conflict over the use of a church language. As the battle raged on, with complaints and charges being made to higher church authorities, petitions launched, investigations conducted, and accusations and counter-accusations made, it became clear that the clash had acquired a political dynamic. Jozua's opponents supported the prime minister, General Smuts, and his South African Party, which promoted conciliation with Britain, while he and his own supporters were mainly fervent nationalists who backed General Hertzog and wanted to see an end to British influence in South Africa.

Jozua Naudé was also determined to establish an Afrikaans school in the town. When the family arrived in Graaff-Reinet, there were two schools in existence, one for boys and one for girls, both using the medium of English. Jozua and Ada resented the fact that their daughters had to be educated in English, and made them stand outside during Bible classes rather than receive their religious instruction in this language. Soon after his arrival Jozua formed a committee of Afrikaans parents which called on the principal of the girls' school to adhere to the new education ordinance allowing high-school children the option of mother-tongue instruction. The demand provoked a great controversy and finally led to the resignation of the principal. At the same time English parents, who were deeply prejudiced against Afrikaans and were alarmed at the 'inroads' Afrikaners were making in the schools, started their own private English school. As a result of all these pressures, the education authorities decided to reorganise schooling in Graaff-Reinet, providing the Union High School for the English children and the Hoër Volkskool for the Afrikaans. The establishment of the Volkskool was a personal triumph for Jozua.

During these years of conflict, Jozua managed to maintain an aura of self-control and composure, but his wife took the strain more severely.[17] She was heavily pregnant when the family moved to Graaff-Reinet, and her daughter Reinet was born two weeks after their arrival. Coping with the difficulties of moving house, trying to care for a small baby and keeping up with the demands of six other children were taxing enough, but soon she also had to face hostility from a large section of the community. Shortly after Reinet's birth she became pregnant again. The situation was not made any easier by Ada's own sense of her status as the minister's wife and the impression she conveyed in her daily conduct that her family was slightly superior.[18] On one occasion, a white domestic worker employed by the Naudés brought a charge of ill-treatment against Ada, and while there seems to have been blame on both sides, the case added to her reputation as a difficult woman.[19] Intelligent, emotional and domineering, Ada was also beset with health problems. She hated the fierce heat of Graaff-Reinet, and this added to her nervous state.[20]

Jozua was kept busy with his church work and with his campaign to promote Afrikaans, and so Ada took full control of the children and the home. Beyers later realised that this arrangement had sometimes led to tensions between his parents. He gained the impression that Ada resented Jozua's constant preoccupation with his work; Jozua, in turn, did not always know how to handle his highly volatile wife.[21]

One issue which Ada felt very strongly about was the education of her children. When the family settled in Graaff-Reinet, Jozua thought that it would be convenient and financially sensible for his children to study at the local teachers' training college. But Ada was adamant. No matter how short funds were, she saw to it that each of her eight children went to the University of Stellenbosch.[22] For more than ten years Jozua had to finance at least two children at university, and although some qualified for bursaries, he had to arrange for a larger bank overdraft to meet his commitments. Finally the cost of paying for his children's education and treating Ada's ailments prompted Jozua to sell land that he had bought in Germiston years before. With the passing of years Ada became more set in her ways, and it seems she sometimes used her physical condition to pressurise her husband in allowing her to have her way.[23]

Ada encouraged her daughters to take an interest in church work and three of them eventually married NGK ministers. She also wanted both boys, but particularly her elder son Joos, to follow their father's example and enter the ministry. The Naudé children later developed different opinions about their mother's motives. Beyers's sister Reinet (Netta) said: 'My mother was a perfectionist and she wanted the very, very best for her family. She went to great lengths and made many sacrifices to get the few things she wanted for us. She did not ask much for herself but she absolutely insisted on the best for her children. And she adored those two sons.'[24] Beyers agreed with this to some extent but he felt his mother was very conscious of status. The position of minister was regarded by Afrikaners as the most respected in the community, and he felt that she wanted to bask in the glory of her sons.[25]

Jozua continued to maintain a close interest in politics, and his success at a local level mirrored gains that Afrikaner nationalists were making in South African politics at a national level. National Party support grew steadily at this time and in 1924 General Hertzog won the whites-only general election. The first major issue the new government decided to tackle was the 'poor white problem'. There was a strong feeling in Afrikaner leadership circles that only drastic action could halt the slide of the *volk* towards economic disaster, and joint action by the government, the church and other public bodies was needed.[26] The government immediately initiated legislation to promote the interests of white (mainly Afrikaner) farm and mine workers. Blacks were already barred from owning farms or homes in 'white South Africa', and laws such as the Wage Act of 1925 and the Mines and Works Amendment Act of 1926 were introduced to ensure that skilled jobs would remain the preserve of whites. Hertzog also introduced a programme of legislation to promote the Afrikaans language and culture. South Africa obtained its own flag, to be flown alongside the Union Jack, and Afrikaans was officially recognised in 1925.[27]

Jozua Naudé applauded all these steps. Black–white politics was never an issue in the Naudé household, but the children grew up with the simple knowledge that their parents were on the 'right' side – the side of the white Afrikaner. At that time, blacks were regarded by almost all whites as very backward and primitive and their rights or lack of them were not even considered or discussed. Jozua and Ada were very clear in their minds about what they believed should be the correct relationship between whites and 'non-whites'. In South Africa the former were destined to act as political masters of the country, while 'kaffers' were to be their servants and occupy inferior positions in society. At the same time, Afrikaners had a duty to spread the gospel to the blacks and civilise the country, and to do this they would need to maintain themselves as a separate race. While Afrikaners would fulfil their Christian responsibilities towards non-whites, there would be no social mixing of the races.[28]

In line with this thinking, and because of his own strong evangelical background, Jozua supported mission work among the Coloured people of the town – provided it took place on segregated lines. When Jozua first arrived in Graaff-Reinet, some of the older Coloured families were still members of the white congregation and were permitted to occupy the back pews of the church on Sundays. In the 1930s the NGK accelerated mission work in the Coloured areas of the town and converts were expected to join the Coloureds-only *Sendingkerk*. No new Coloured members were admitted to the white church. When Beyers was a boy a small group of Coloured people still attended his father's church, but by the time he had grown up most of these old members had either died or drifted away.[29]

While on one level Beyers absorbed this racial bias, on another level he displayed that universal quality of children to suspend prejudice while playing with children of other backgrounds. So, when Beyers and his white friends came across Coloured children at the nearby Sundays River, they happily joined in their swimming games, although afterwards they went their own ways to their separate, unequal living areas.[30]

Jozua's campaigns for the rights of Afrikaners made him a controversial figure in the town, and his family was often caught up in this conflict. The tense atmosphere also affected the Naudé children, and they had to endure the scorn of some of their peers who had listened to their parents talking. Beyers with his open, friendly way did not appear to have been unduly affected by any unpleasantness.[31] He possessed some of his mother's sensitive qualities, but like his father he had an optimistic view of life. Being one of the middle children in a large family and with his father away from home a great deal, Beyers became an independent, self-sufficient boy. His mother tried to impose her standards and values on all her children, but Beyers built up a resistance to this. He would sometimes go to great lengths to win this war of wills, as was the case when he finally won the right to play rugby at school.

When Beyers was 16 years old, he underwent one of the most important experiences of his life: he was converted to the Christian faith. It was the practice in the NGK to hold a series of prayer meetings and church services leading up to the day of Pentecost. Beyers was deeply moved by the Pentecostal sermons his father delivered in May and June 1930 and decided to give his life to Christ.[32] His commitment to the faith did not however prevent him from becoming somewhat rebellious as a teenager. Towards the close of his final year at school, Beyers joined with his brother and four other boys in drawing up a letter of protest against the 'authoritarian' attitude of their headmaster, U. J. Cronje. The boys regarded him as extreme and short-tempered. Boldly they had their letter professionally printed and distributed it around the school. In Beyers's words, the letter 'created a hell of a row'. His father, who was chairman of the school committee, was acutely embarrassed by his sons' involvement in the affair, and if it had not been for his intervention, the boys might have been expelled. Beyers said of the incident that 'we were eventually called to order and had to apologise for acting in this spirit of disobedience to the people who were placed in authority over us'.

It is difficult to gauge whether experiences within the family played any role in Beyers's later rejection of the Afrikaner's political values. Already as a youngster, he had developed the capacity to question rather than to accept. If it is asked what made Beyers's rebellion possible, one possible answer is that he was seeking liberation from the 'super-ego' of his father.[33] But if one searches for early influences, it seems his independent nature stemmed more from resentment of his mother. Beyers himself said that his mother was the stronger influence in the home, and he admitted it was from maternal captivity that he sought to escape.[34] Beyers did not speak as readily of his mother as he did of his father, and when he did so, it was sometimes in negative terms.

Of his parents Beyers remarked: 'My mother had very deep and strong feelings against the British as a result of their actions during the Anglo–Boer War against the women in the concentration camps. She never forgot that. I think she was at times deeply prejudiced against them, as well as against the [NGK] ministers like the Murrays and others who were seen to be much more liberal English than Afrikaans, because they were from a Scots background, although they were serving the NGK.'

'My father was always very busy. My mother was always very strong and domineering in personality. She ran the house according to her very strong convictions. She imposed her personality very strongly, especially on the daughters, and she also, I think, wanted to direct our lives, that of my brother and myself, especially with regard to relationships with girls. She held very narrow moral concepts. She very much wanted and insisted that my elder brother should become a minister of religion, whereas he wanted to become a medical doctor. He initially refused, but . . . because there was no way he could find the necessary financial support, he accepted the fact that he would become a minister of religion.

'My father was a person with very deep convictions, strong convictions which he held firmly to, and which he defended. I respected him for that. On the other hand, . . . as a teenager I could not agree with a number of viewpoints which he expressed. I felt very strongly that he should have opposed my mother much more with regard to certain of her views which she wanted to impose on us, especially on her two sons. I came out in strong resistance against that, and I also conveyed that to him in my second or my third year of university when I said that I felt that, in respect, . . . he had allowed her too much, and that she was using her illness very skilfully in order to create the necessary sympathy where she could then impose her thoughts and her ideas, or force him in order to impose those ideas.

'Certainly a measure of my deep concern for the underdog grew out of the conviction that if there was a person whose ideals, wishes were suppressed in this way, and not given the necessary opportunity, that could never be a way in which one could really reach your highest potential. I rebelled against that and felt that was unfair.'

And so Beyers, by the time he left for Stellenbosch University in 1932, had developed an independent, non-conformist streak. According to him, he initially wanted to study law, but because as a minister's son he qualified for a theology bursary, he began his studies with a career in the ministry in mind: 'I always felt that if at the end of my third year or my fourth year at university, I was not prepared to become a minister, I would simply move out and would find my own way if necessary, and that nothing would deter me from that. So in that sense, they [my parents] didn't have that stranglehold on me.'[35]

Stellenbosch, lying in a green, fertile valley about 50 kilometres from Cape Town, boasts a university which has shaped generations of the Afrikaner elite. On campus, white, red-roofed buildings are leisurely dotted between gracious oaks; the beauty is completed by the mountains which surround it – Die Pieke, Stellenbosch, Bothma's Kop and Simonsberg. Beyers revelled in his new-found liberty on the campus. He arrived naïve and impressionable, eager to break out after a protected, claustrophobic upbringing. For the first time in his life he was free to choose – to explore, to socialise, go to dances, meet girls, to read and be challenged by new ideas. Not that Stellenbosch University in 1932 was a liberal institution; it was still steeped in old-fashioned conventions which were often out of step with the new generation of young Afrikaners. It was also the time of the Depression – of grinding poverty for millions of blacks and hundreds of thousands of whites, but the students, though short of money, were removed from this reality of utter deprivation. For Beyers, released from the stifling environment of Graaff-Reinet, Stellenbosch was a breath of fresh air.

Beyers and Joos started university together and, following in their father's footsteps, they entered Wilgenhof, the oldest residence serving students in Stellenbosh and one with proud traditions. Beyers became a well-known figure in the hostel and was later elected its *primarius*, or student chairman. The brothers spent their university days with many Afrikaners who were destined for top positions in church and political life – including future prime minister John Vorster, one of Beyers's adversaries in debating circles.[36]

For his B.A. degree Beyers chose subjects which would give him the necessary qualifications to enter the Theological Seminary, or alternatively equip him for a career in teaching. Showing a preference for languages, he majored in Afrikaans–Nederlands and German. Other minor courses were Sociology, Latin, Greek and History. His ability to learn easily and express himself clearly enabled him to do well in Afrikaans–Nederlands and to enjoy his German studies, but he was not a dedicated student and received average results.[37] Beyers did not regard any of his early lecturers or subjects as particularly crucial to his development; his contact with sociology lecturer Dr Hendrik Verwoerd, who went on to become architect of grand apartheid and prime minister of South Africa, was for example superficial. The impression Beyers formed of Verwoerd was of a brilliant, disciplined perfectionist: he would arrive on time, deliver his lecture without consulting his notes, and leave without encouraging discussion or questions. He displayed an uncompromising logic and expected his students to reproduce his ideas in their examinations. Theologian Charles Villa-Vicencio, who has written a biographical essay on Beyers, asked him whether he was surprised when Verwoerd later advanced his grand apartheid scheme. ' "Yes I was," came Naudé's immediate reply. Then, more thoughtfully he attributed it to what he regarded as Verwoerd's "ruthlessness of logic." It frightened Naudé because it left out important human elements, did not allow for human aggression, irrationality, failure, admission of error, historical irony or grace and forgiveness.'[38]

During the three years he spent reading for his B.A. and just over one year completing his M.A., Beyers immersed himself in numerous student activities. A natural public speaker like his father, he joined the *Universiteitse Debatsvereniging,* one of two debating societies on campus, the other being the *Unie Debatsvereniging,* in which John Vorster was a dominant figure. Every Saturday night the students debated a variety of issues and Beyers became a popular member of his team. Many students flocked to these events – often because it was the only place where young men could take their girlfriends and be back in time for the 10 p.m. curfew at the women's hostel.[39] As a senior Beyers was elected onto the Students Representative Council for two years and served as president in 1937. He was also a regular churchgoer and member of the *Christelike Studentevereniging* (CSV).

Joos Naudé, speaking about his university days with Beyers, remarked: 'Beyers and I were very different in our personalities. I took part in student affairs and enjoyed it, but Beyers was far more active. He was more outgoing and was marked out as a leader.'[40] Joos and Beyers were respectively nicknamed *Oorlog en Vrede*, or War and Peace, by their friends at the Wilgenhof residence. Joos, although quiet-natured, could sometimes become involved in heated arguments; Beyers, on the other hand, was more inclined to hear out the views of other people and use gentle persuasion to try to change their minds.[41]

Beyers also enjoyed walking and outdoor activities, and so he joined the hiking club, the *Berg en Toer Klub* (BTK), on which he served several times as chairman. It was nicknamed the *Bok en Trou Klub* (the Courting and Marriage Club), because it was one of the few acceptable meeting places for young men and women on a campus where strict social codes were enforced. It was through the BTK that Beyers met his future wife.

Ilse Hedwig Weder was born at Genadendal, the oldest mission station in South Africa, to Moravian missionary parents, on 21 August 1913. Founded in 1737, the mission station served the Coloured people in the district. Ilse's maternal grandparents were immigrants from Germany who had sent their daughter 'home' to complete her education. There she had met her future husband and returned with him to Genadendal where they were married and had six children. Ilse's father, who had a business background, ran the mission shop in addition to his work as a preacher. German was their home tongue, but Ilse spoke fluent Afrikaans and later adopted it as her first language.[42]

Although Ilse's parents could not themselves afford to send her to university, she was an exceptionally good scholar and qualified for a bursary at Stellenbosch University where she began her B.Sc. degree in 1931. Ilse excelled at sports, playing tennis and hockey for the university teams, but she was a reserved, serious young woman and did not socialise much in her first year at university. In her second year, a friend persuaded Ilse to join the BTK, which she did in the hopes of 'seeing a bit of the country'.[43] Beyers and Ilse became acquainted on a weekend hike, but it was on an Easter tour to the coastal area of Knysna that Beyers really began to notice the small, brown-haired German girl. The attraction was mutual and by the end of the tour their romance was flourishing.

During the holidays Beyers became a frequent visitor to Ilse's home at Genadendal and was warmly welcomed by the Moravian missionaries. He appreciated the beauty of the mission station, which was set deep in the mountains and near the Sonderend River. What impressed him most was the openness of relations between white and Coloured people, both in Ilse's home and in the congregation. Unlike most Afrikaner missionaries who were very emphatic that there should be no social intercourse with their 'non-white' flock, the German missionaries were less rigidly separatist in their attitudes to race and mission. This broader view of mission work was a result of their close association with Coloured people; it was also helped by the weekly services held at the station, which were addressed by missionaries who had worked in other parts of the world. There was still subtle discrimination, such as in the distance that set apart the houses of the white missionaries and the Coloured families on the station; but, nevertheless, all races worshipped in the same church and Coloured people visited Ilse's parents in their home – quite a revelation for Beyers. For the first time in his adult life he spoke to people of another colour on a basis approaching equality. Deep in his mind he began to question whether the strict segregation advocated and observed by the Afrikaner community was correct. He started to develop an interest in race issues and missionary work, but it would be many years before his feelings and thoughts on these issues would crystallise.[44]

Stellenbosch University represented a microcosm of Afrikaner society and women were naturally required to acknowledge the leading role of men. Female students were not expected to have or voice opinions on political issues, other than to support without question the views of the menfolk.[45] Coming from homes where these standards had also been accepted as the norm, Ilse and Beyers hardly ever discussed current issues. She expressed no interest in politics and Beyers never expected that she should, preferring to debate student and national affairs with his friends.[46]

Beyers himself was not deeply interested in politics, but the subject was hard to ignore altogether, especially since new political ideas had begun to appear on the university campuses in the 1930s. Young Afrikaner nationalists, dissatisfied with the economic and social status of their people, challenged the notion that there should be closer cooperation with English-speaking whites, and aggressively asserted the need to preserve *die eie* – the separate language and culture of the Afrikaner. This mobilisation was encouraged by the Afrikaner Broederbond, which set up various political and cultural organisations to promote the cause of Afrikanerdom in the 1920s and 1930s. The most important achievement of this period was the establishment in 1929 of the FAK, *Federasie van Afrikaanse Kultuurvereniginge* (Federation of Afrikaans Cultural Associations), which enabled the Broederbond to consolidate its hold on Afrikaans culture.[47]

On university campuses the mouthpiece for this assertive nationalism was the *Afrikaanse Nasionale Studentebond (ANS)*. This was established in 1933 after the three Afrikaans universities in the Transvaal and Free State withdrew from the English-dominated National Union of South African Students (Nusas). Stellenbosch was at first not in favour of pulling out of Nusas, and the ANS–Nusas row became a hot issue on the campus. Finally, in 1936, the Stellenbosch SRC seceded from Nusas to throw its full weight behind the ANS.

Although Beyers regarded himself as a nationalist and a loyal Afrikaner, he disliked the all-embracing control which the nationalist movement sought to exert and so shied away from the more exclusive claims of Afrikanerdom. He also began to read widely, in English, Dutch and Afrikaans, and was already something of a 'moderate' in Afrikaner nationalist terms: 'I was questioning all the time. I wanted a justification and an explanation for whatever stand I took. But it was not a very probing, critical questioning, because we were not allowed to do that. In our whole upbringing we had been too much part of an authoritarian structure, which emphasised the authority of the parent, teacher, minister, or party. But there was, at the back of my mind, that constant question: Is this the real truth and the full truth?'

Joos, too, was more open-minded than most of his peers. This was shown in his decision to join Nusas rather than the ANS. His motive for joining Nusas was in fact largely pragmatic – he wished to improve his English – but for many of his nationalist friends it was unthinkable to associate with the *Engelse* when there was an alternative, Afrikaans body.[48]

The two brothers also demonstrated their independence by joining the editorial staff of the clandestine and daring student newspaper, *Pro Libertate*. Launched in 1932 by a small, anonymous group of more liberal-minded senior students, the newspaper challenged some of the less sacred but nevertheless stultifying aspects of Afrikaner culture and politics manifest on the campus.[49] In its second year of operation a slogan was added to the newspaper's masthead encapsulating the spirit of the eager young journalists: 'A University Should Be a Place of Light, of Liberty and of Learning.' Beyers and his brother were keen readers of *Pro Libertate*. Although only mildly provocative, it caused a sensation and critics accused it of practising 'underhand politics', of being negative towards the church and the Theological Seminary, and of usurping the function of the official student newspaper, *Die Stellenbosse Student*. *Pro Libertate* denied the charges and, while affirming its respect for authority and the Christian faith, it declared itself in favour of freedom of thought and expression.[50]

The newspaper's editors had to guard their identities very closely because once exposed they were often subjected to pressure and criticism. For this reason *Pro Libertate* experienced a frequent turnover of staff. But as fast as one group of writers abandoned their task, a new crop would appear to take up the fight. Among these were Beyers and Joos Naudé.[51] Their parents were upset to hear of their involvement with the journal. Ada in particular was angry when she found that her sons were coming home with strange ideas which did not conform with her outlook on life. She also disapproved of her son's relationship with Ilse Weder, whose family were not Afrikaners. Although Ilse's father was a missionary, Ada did not regard him as a real *dominee*, and Ilse was not even a member of the NGK. She tried to get her husband to talk to Beyers, but with Stellenbosch so far away there was little either of them could do to change their son's mind.[52]

Beyers and Joos began to take an interest in the political debates which filtered onto the campus. The Depression had shattered the South African economy and in 1933 the prime minister, General Hertzog, who felt the country's numerous problems could best be addressed by a united government, fused his party with General Smuts's South African Party. But many ardent nationalists still wanted nothing to do with Smuts and accused Hertzog of betraying the Afrikaner by making common cause with the pro-imperialist enemy. When Beyers and his brother returned to Graaff-Reinet during holidays they discussed the fusion controversy with their father. Rather surprisingly, Jozua senior backed the coalition and expressed his full confidence in General Hertzog.[53]

Beyers completed his B.A. at the end of 1934 and, still unsure about a career, he decided to devote the following year to his M.A. The love Beyers felt for his language was evident in the thesis he chose – an examination of the very best in Afrikaans poetry. Entitled 'An Appreciation of Poetry – A Few Aspects of the Problem, Illustrated with Examples out of Afrikaans Poetry', the thesis showed a good understanding of the works of Beyers's favourite poets, many of whom were staunch nationalists, including the beloved C. J. Langenhoven, the formidable Totius and the more modern Uys Krige.[54] The study occupied him during 1935, for Beyers a year of restlessness and indecision. He would soon have to decide whether or not to commit the rest of his life to the church. Beyers was in a dilemma. He believed he would make a good minister: he was a committed Christian, a natural leader and an eloquent speaker. He could enter the Seminary or perhaps become a teacher. But he was also attracted by the idea of a career in business.

The mid-1930s was a time when Afrikaners were not only asserting themselves politically and culturally, but also in commerce and industry. Just as nationalists had set up exclusive Afrikaner organisations in the fields of education and culture, so they were now striving to establish Afrikaner businesses, at a time when English-speaking whites dominated the business world. It was during the launch of these ambitious schemes that Professor D. E. W. Schumann, economics lecturer and later dean of the Faculty of Commerce at Stellenbosch, asked Beyers to consider a business career. He was an ideal candidate for the project Schumann had in mind: setting up bright young men in their own businesses to advance the economic position of Afrikaners as a whole. Beyers, ambitious and eager to be involved in the advancement of his people, was strongly attracted to the idea, but something held him back. In spite of his confused state of mind and his determination not to be forced into anything by his parents, he felt a calling from God; perhaps after all he could best serve the Afrikaner people by entering the church.[55]

And so Beyers Naudé decided to enter the Theological Seminary of the NGK. This launched him into a career of more than 20 years in the ministry of the church, which would come to a sudden halt when he challenged its race policies. To understand the larger social forces which shaped his career, it is necessary to deal briefly with the political and theological contexts which influenced the church's decision to choose the way of apartheid.

During the 1930s, another Stellenbosch alumnus, former *dominee* and newspaper editor, Dr D. F. Malan, emerged as the new leader of Afrikaner nationalism. A prominent Nationalist politician and member of the Broederbond, Malan refused a Cabinet portfolio in the new coalition government of 1934 and broke away to establish the Purified National Party. From then on the fortunes of the National Party and the Broederbond would be deeply intertwined. Leading Nationalists were leading Broeders; together the two powerful organisations, the one operating overtly and the other covertly, would work to achieve Afrikaner hegemony. This became a reality in 1948 when the National Party came to power under the banner of apartheid. While the National Party provided the institutional pillar for apartheid and the Broederbond the ideological pillar, the religious and moral pillar was supplied by the NGK.

It was during the student years of Beyers Naudé that the foundation was laid of apartheid theology in the NGK. New theological ideas from Europe began to influence the church, enabling leaders who propounded a racist theology to win ground. But it was not only the new imported ideas which made apartheid theology possible; the historical traditions of the NGK provided fertile ground for their growth. The Calvinist notion of the 'elect' or chosen people was seized on by Afrikaner ministers who encouraged their followers to identify themselves with Israel of old. As they had been called by God to bring Christianity and civilisation to the African continent, no claim could be made for the equal treatment of Afrikaners and blacks, being against the will of God.[56]

Moreover, for the first 150 years of white settlement the NGK had concerned itself almost exclusively with the souls of white colonists. There were only sporadic efforts to minister to slaves and the indigenous Khoikhoi, and although these 'non-whites' were permitted to join the NGK, the church in no way challenged discrimination in early Cape society. Indeed, as early as 1857 the Cape synod considered the question of segregated worship and holy communion, and while agreeing that it was scriptural for blacks to be admitted to white churches, accepted the principle of racially segregated churches as necessary, because of the 'weakness of some'.[57] In 1881, a separate, 'daughter' church for Coloureds, the *Sendingkerk* or Mission Church, was established; and in time the NGK in Afrika was founded for blacks and the Reformed Church in Africa for Indians. At a later stage, when the NGK had formalised its apartheid policies, its mission work came to be seen as an integral part of the church (and state) strategy to keep the races apart, as a way of ensuring white self-preservation.[58]

In the early decades of the twentieth century, fiercely patriotic Afrikaans students who went abroad were searching for a new brand of Reformed theology which could accommodate their new-found nationalism. They discovered it in the ideas of Abraham Kuyper, the founder of the Free University of Amsterdam. Kuyper was an influential figure in the Gereformeerde Kerken, a splinter church in Holland which had rejected liberalism and rationalism, and he developed a new theology. He declared that human life consisted of separate spheres, such as the church, the state and the family, and that each had sovereignty over its affairs through God. He emphasised the principle of 'diversity', and this was seized on by Afrikaner theologians, who searched and found biblical passages which apparently proved that God willed separate nations.[59]

Throughout the 1920s and the 1930s there was conflict between theologians who adhered to the old evangelical tradition of the NGK and those who favoured the new ideas from Holland. Between them stood a large group of ministers like Jozua Naudé who remained faithful to evangelism and committed to their church's missionary work, but also identified with the idea of the Afrikaners as a 'chosen people' and a separate race.

The final influence which swayed the church into adopting apartheid was the current of romantic nationalism emanating from Nazi Germany.[60] Prominent Afrikaner nationalists, such as Nico Diederichs, Piet Meyer and Geoff Cronje, who studied in Germany, and sympathised with the Nazis because they were the enemies of the hated British, were profoundly influenced by the Nazi idea of racial purity.[61] This group began to work out a racial blueprint for the future. Building on the established pattern of segregation in South Africa, they envisaged a Christian National country where the solution to the racial problem would be found in the final and total separation of the races. They declared that because the Bible supported the diversity of nations, the introduction of apartheid in South Africa could be regarded as the will of God. The NGK, now falling more closely into line with the thinking in the Broederbond and the National Party, started to give attention to race issues. In 1926, for example, the Native Commission of the NGK's Federal Council held a conference with English-speaking churches to consider the 'native question'. At the conference the NGK managed to gain acceptance for a resolution which declared that it was not necessarily unchristian to 'seek the progress of the native people separately from the whites'.[62]

However, a few voices in the NGK began to speak out against the national and political mission the church was taking upon itself. The principal of the NGK's Theological Seminary at Stellenbosch, Professor Johan du Plessis, was a man who adhered to the evangelical, missionary traditions of the church and clashed with nationalists on this issue. In 1928 his opponents seized on a non-political issue, a biblical interpretation in which he held that Christ had completely laid down his divine nature when he had lived on earth, to charge him with heresy. The presbytery commission at first rejected all the charges against him, but his political adversaries continued with a series of appeals, until two years later a special synodal commission found him guilty of heresy and had him removed from his Chair. He took the case to the civil court, which declared his conviction of heresy invalid, and he was technically reinstated. But the church, while it continued to pay his salary and subsidise his house, never allowed him to set foot in the Seminary again.[63]

When Beyers Naudé entered the Theological Seminary in 1936, it was still seething with tension caused by the firing of Professor Du Plessis, and students were divided into two groups – the more liberal 'Du Plessis men' and the conservative 'Oupajane men'. The name Oupajane was derived from Die Ou Paaie journal, edited by Dr Dwight Snyman, which had been founded to counter Professor Du Plessis's journal, Die Soeklig.[64] Beyers read both journals to gain greater understanding of the controversy, and in spite of the fact that his father supported the Oupajane, his natural sympathy for the underdog brought him to side with the Du Plessis faction. He was disgusted by the 'pettiness, the corruption and the closed-minded attitude' of the NGK,[65] and felt that the action taken against one of the church's most eminent and committed academics was 'totally unjust': 'I didn't know Du Plessis, I knew nothing about the theology, but on the human level, what they had done to this man was an absolute shame.' In the aftermath of this sorry episode, the NGK embarked on a purge, and the Seminary came to be staffed by mediocre, anti-Du Plessis academics: Professor D. G. Malan, who was Du Plessis's successor in New Testament studies, E. E. van Rooyen, professor of Old Testament studies and D. Lategan, professor of Church History, who all contributed to Die Ou Paaie journal. Beyers felt his lecturers were proponents of second-rate theology; stifled and frustrated by the lack of meaningful intellectual depth and clarity in the classes he attended, he developed an aversion to his studies. He did very little work and the four years he spent at the Seminary were, academically speaking, wasted. Later in his life, when he achieved greater spiritual maturity and was searching for answers to perplexing questions about his church's race policies, he regretted the poverty of his theological training and tried to correct this by intensive self-study.[66]

Beyers had acquired a miniature chess set, and during many of the lectures given by professors Lategan and Van Rooyen, he would sit at the back of the class and play chess with his future brother-in-law, Frans O'Brien Geldenhuys. He entered the theological library twice, and then only to deliver messages. Taking notes 'was so terribly boring' that Beyers, Frans and other sceptics borrowed the notes of more diligent colleagues when exams drew near.[67] The courses at the Seminary were of such a low standard that many students pursued other degrees at the same time. Beyers wrote his M.A. project during his first year at the Seminary and his friend Frans completed his LL.B. while studying theology.[68]

In the theological desert of the Seminary there was one oasis in the person of Professor B. B. (Bennie) Keet. A brilliant theologian who taught ethics and dogmatics, Keet had a profound impact on Beyers. A Stellenbosch graduate, Professor Keet came from the old evangelical and mission-oriented tradition of the church and, like Du Plessis, was firmly opposed to the racist theology that had been introduced into the NGK.[69] When Beyers first entered the Seminary, Professor Keet was the only 'Du Plessis' man left among the teaching staff and contributed to *Die Soeklig* magazine. The 1930s were a dangerous time for dissidents, and Professor Keet never openly supported all aspects of Du Plessis's theology. Every utterance made by the lecturers would be scrutinised in the theological magazines, and Professor Keet was careful to avoid charges being brought against him. But later, when the NGK began to work out its apartheid charter in detail, Keet spoke openly against it. In 1939 he sounded his first public warning that hostility between the races was increasing as a result of the agitation for racial segregation. In the decades that followed, Professor Keet, writing in the official NGK magazine *Die Kerkbode*, frequently clashed with theologians who claimed apartheid could be justified on biblical grounds.[70]

In his second year at the Seminary, Beyers was again approached by Professor Schumann to consider a business career. But by then he felt it was too late to change course; he was financially and morally committed to the church and 'decided to try to get through with it in the hopes that the ministry would be different'. Beyers made the most of his time at the Seminary by being involved in other activities. During that period he was chairman of the *Berg en Toer Klub*, president of the SRC for one year and *primarius* of the Wilgenhof hostel. Money being desperately short he searched for a part-time job. He had hoped to work as a correspondent for the Afrikaans newspaper *Die Burger* but because its positions were filled, he worked instead for the *Cape Times*, reporting on general student affairs. He also took up photography and sold some of his photographs to earn extra money.

It was as a second-year theological student that Beyers got caught up with a love which he pursued for the rest of his life – his passion for second-hand motor cars. Beyers and Joos began to look around for an old car, justifying the cost by claiming they would save a fortune on train fares between their home in Graaff-Reinet and Stellenbosch. Beyers eventually found an old Dodge in Graaff-Reinet which the brothers took back to the university. Their beloved Dodge gave them excellent service, but it was frequently in need of attention and they learnt to strip and repair the car's engine – the first of many such enterprises.

At the end of 1937 Ilse, who had completed her B.Sc. and M.Sc. with distinction, accepted a teaching post in Pretoria. Beyers still had two years to complete at the Theological Seminary, and they felt they could best endure the separation by becoming engaged. Beyers's mother, still bitterly opposed to the relationship, was upset when he informed his parents that he would be spending Christmas with Ilse at Genadendal, where they planned to announce their engagement. Ada pleaded with Beyers to change his mind, and also begged her husband to reason with her son. But Beyers refused to consider their pleas and he travelled to Genadendal as planned. On Christmas Eve, the night before the couple were to announce their engagement, Ada sent her daughter Hymne to the mission station to try to change Beyers's mind. It was under this cloud that their engagement was announced on Christmas day. The episode created a rift between him and his parents and, although they later accepted his choice of bride, the emotional break would never be healed.[71]

In January 1938 Ilse began teaching mathematics at an Afrikaans girls' school in Pretoria, but after a year she moved to a teaching post at La Rochelle School in Paarl so that she could be closer to Beyers.

During 1938 Ilse and Beyers shared an experience which drew them closer to Afrikanerdom – the centennial commemorating the Great Trek by Dutch-speaking Boers into the interior of South Africa. As part of the celebrations, nine oxwagons left from various historic starting points and moved towards Pretoria. As the wagons travelled through the villages and towns special festivals were held to commemorate the Great Trek, and these aroused a wave of emotional fervour among Afrikaners. In Stellenbosch Beyers enthusiastically participated in the festivals, and followed the progress of the oxwagons with great interest. The celebrations reached their climax in Pretoria in a stirring religious service and political rally on 16 December – the anniversary of the Battle of Blood River, the day the Boers had defeated the Zulu after making a covenant with God, promising to remember victory.[72]

Beyers had travelled to Pretoria to be with Ilse. Dressed in old-fashioned Voortrekker costumes, they joined thousands of Afrikaner families who gathered at the site of the Voortrekker Monument where the foundation stone was laid. Here they heard and applauded a major political speech by the Opposition leader and future prime minister, D. F. Malan, who declared that God had given victory to the Afrikaners over the black heathen a hundred years before, and by His grace, the *volk* had survived. Now Afrikaners were engaged in a new battle in the cities where the black masses were competing with them for jobs. White civilisation was at stake – Afrikaners had to obey the will of God and fight for their freedom in order that the white nation be maintained.[73] The festivities and political speeches reflected a new, more militant mood among Afrikaners, but it was still another ten years before they would achieve power. Earlier, in May 1938, Beyers had voted for the Nationalists in an election which produced a massive victory for Hertzog and Smuts's United Party. But this unity was smashed by the outbreak of war in September 1939. Smuts wanted South Africa to enter the war on the side of the Allies, while Hertzog insisted on a neutral stance. The vote in parliament went against Hertzog and he found himself out in the political cold. A new age was dawning in the history of Afrikanerdom.

It was also the end of a chapter in Beyers Naudé's life. He had completed his studies and received his theological certificate. The open conflict with his parents was over: he would abide by their wishes and enter the church, and they would reluctantly accept his marriage to Ilse. It was also the parting of the ways for Beyers and Joos. Joos would later leave the NGK to work for the British and Foreign Bible Society. Although the brothers remained on good terms, Joos was never to be intimately involved in Beyers's activities.

Beyers's first call was as a trainee minister to Wellington, a small town close to Cape Town. As he set out on his new path, he was determined to serve God and his people to the best of his ability, little dreaming of the tests he would face along the way.

4
Early Ministry: Living with Apartheid, 1939–1954

Beyers and Ilse were married in the quiet rural retreat of the Genadendal mission station on 3 August 1940. The wedding ceremony was conducted by Beyers's father before a congregation of Coloured and white people, and the Coloured church choir sang at the service. Afterwards there was a reception, but only for the white guests. This did not seem strange to the young couple, who had entertained the Coloured guests at a separate function in Ilse's home a few nights before.[1]

They honeymooned at Onrusrivier on the southern Cape coast, in a tiny cottage owned by Ilse's parents. It was a peaceful sanctuary to which they would return many times in their married life. Their first home was in Wellington where Beyers had already begun work. He had arrived in the town in December 1939, an earnest young *hulpprediker*, or assistant preacher, eager to do well in the church, and was installed on 27 July 1940. In keeping with the tradition of the church, the induction service was conducted by his father.

Ilse had by then joined the NGK and she enjoyed her role as a minister's wife.[2] Over the years she would work very hard to create a warm home environment for 'Bey' and their children, and their home assumed a great deal of her character. Ilse's job as a minister's wife was demanding and she devoted much time to many women's groups. She had an energy that belied her tiny frame and a strength and determination which would enable her to cope during very difficult times in their life together.

The couple were to have four children, three boys and a girl. When their first son was born in 1941 a dispute arose with Beyers's mother over his names. Beyers and Ilse had baptised him Johann, after the disciple John, and Friedrich because it was the German word for peace and expressed their longing for an end to the war. Ada Naudé was furious that her grandson had not been given family names. Beyers recalled: 'My mother was terribly angry, exploded. My father didn't like it because it affected him. My mother wrote and seriously criticised us. . . . I said, "Well, I am sorry. You never indicated that you wanted to maintain Afrikaner tradition."' When their second son was born in 1943 they named him Jozua François in an attempt to appease his grandparents. Beyers said: 'They were never satisfied with that. They thought it was second-rate. . . . I never felt bad about it.'

In spite of his earlier misgivings about the ministry Beyers enjoyed his work in Wellington. He was already displaying a great deal of vigour in his work and he was determined to do well. 'I was ambitious to advance in the church . . . I felt a young *dominee* could play a very meaningful role in the life of the Afrikaner people. I accepted the religious, social and political status quo and set out to be a good and successful minister.' Early in his career he identified his main pastoral interests as youth work, evangelism and mission work. In his long and successful ministry within the NGK these three issues always remained pre-eminent in his thinking and activity. As he had held leadership positions in various youth organisations during his student days and being as well the junior minister, it was natural that Beyers would concentrate on building contacts with young people in the college town. The emphasis he placed on evangelism in his ministry was also not unexpected. Both his parents had stressed its importance and his own conversion had been the result of a profound experience at Pentecost. His father had impressed upon him the need to win new converts, and his interest in mission work was heightened as a result of his visits to the Genadendal mission station. He was exposed to the mission policy of his church at the NGK's *Sendingsinstituut*, or training college, in Wellington, where white students were trained for careers as ministers of the Coloured *Sendingkerk*. Beyers did not voice his misgivings, but he was uneasy that the training given to these men was inferior and of a shorter duration than the instruction given at Stellenbosch to ministers for the white church. 'I discovered for the first time the deep feeling of inferiority which a number of these students had, about their status, about their future and therefore also about their commitment. They felt . . . they were regarded as second-class ministers to second-class people, and that imposed an attitude of subservience and a hidden aggressiveness on the part of some of them.'

Beyers struck an impressive figure in the small town. As a young *dominee* he was already marked out as a future leader of the Afrikaner people. With an excellent pedigree and the right education he seemed destined to go far. He had proven himself a natural leader in his numerous student activities, and had an open, confident personality. All he lacked was experience and the qualification of membership of the Afrikaner Broederbond.

In the late 1930s the Broederbond, organised on the basis of small local branches or cells, was expanding throughout the country. The organisation was tightly controlled by the head office in Johannesburg, which set agendas and required regular reports on the monthly meetings of all branches. By the mid-1930s there were 80 cells around the country and almost 1 400 members.[3] Membership of the exclusive society came by invitation only, and was usually only granted when a young Afrikaner had proven his worth to the *volk*.

The senior NGK minister in Wellington, the Reverend Evert J. du Toit, was a member of the Broederbond and considered that Beyers met the requirements necessary for membership. An aspiring member had to believe in the destiny of the Afrikaner as a separate nation; promise to give preference to Afrikaners and Afrikaans firms in public, economic and professional life; speak Afrikaans in his home and outside; be a Protestant of 'firm principles and strong character'; be financially secure and prepared to participate as an active and loyal member of the Broederbond.[4]

In 1940 Beyers was proposed and seconded by members of the Wellington cell. He agreed to join the organisation without hesitation, conscious that he was following in the footsteps of his father.[5] His application was promptly approved by the Broederbond's executive committee, and he was then invited to the important initiation ceremony. 'It is a solemn, serious, religious affair which usually takes place at the home of a Broeder, in a room darkened by dim lights or candles. The ceremony involves a prayer, hymn singing, Bible reading, and a series of questions put to the aspirant member as he finally takes the oath to keep Broederbond secrets until his death, whether [or not] he resigns.'[6] It was an oath Beyers Naudé would not keep.

With his enthusiasm and natural abilities, Beyers's work as assistant preacher prospered. But he soon outgrew this position and in April 1943 he accepted a call to be minister in the tiny Karoo town of Loxton, not far from Graaff-Reinet. Nothing seemed to have changed in the country of his youth. The sun blazed hot on the Karoo plains and koppies, and the farmers, though fewer in numbers because of the disappearance of many *bywoners*, still talked about their new lambs and the low price of wool. 'We enjoyed life there. I had a very intimate relationship with the congregation because there were only about 450 adult members, including all the farmers and a small number of people in the town. Practically everybody in the town, except for a few English-speakers, belonged to the NGK.' Beyers had by that stage bought another car which served him well on the many overnight visits he made to farmers on the dusty, bumpy Karoo roads. He said: 'I visited every family on every farm twice a year, usually accompanied by an *ouderling* [elder]. We would enquire about the family, about personal conflicts and tensions between people, try to resolve these, and at the end, read a part of the Bible and say a prayer. Normally we visited four or five or six families a day.'

His years in Loxton coincided with the Second World War, which once again created bitter divisions in South Africa. Beyers was opposed to his country's participation in the war, and like many Afrikaners was sympathetic to the German cause because they were the enemies of the British. His wife's German parents were also initially supportive of Hitler, but as the war dragged on they came increasingly to question Nazism.[7]

During these war years, a major new actor marched onto the stage of Afrikaner politics. This was a paramilitary organisation that identified strongly with the Nazis, known as the *Ossewabrandwag* (OB), or Oxwagon Guard. Formed in 1939, its goal was a one-party republic on the model of German National Socialism. Some of its members committed acts of sabotage in defiance of the Smuts government, which retaliated by detaining many suspects. But the *Ossewabrandwag* was not only a threat to the government, it became a serious rival to the National Party. The leader of the movement, Dr J. F. J. van

Rensburg, initially a prominent member of the Broederbond, was soon engaged in a power struggle with the National Party.

In Loxton several of Beyers's congregation were active members of this pro-Nazi organisation. 'The emergence of the *Ossewabrandwag* was seen as a very serious internal conflict in the Afrikaner community and we were asked in the Broederbond to try to reconcile these two conflicting viewpoints.' Beyers was invited to join the *Ossewabrandwag*, but his loyalty to the Broederbond and his aversion to authoritarianism made him refuse. 'I felt no need to become involved because Dr Malan, the Nationalist leader, was in my view doing a good job. I was never actively involved or interested in the *Ossewabrandwag*. I got their literature and read through that, but it sounded too radical and emotionally unbalanced to have any real meaning or significance.'

Although Beyers regarded himself as a loyal Afrikaner nationalist, some questions began to disturb him. As a result of his contact with the impoverished Coloured people of Loxton he started to wonder whether whites really treated others with justice. The Coloured people lived in a separate, squalid township not far from the white town. A white lay-preacher served the small mission church in the township and occasionally Beyers was asked to officiate. 'Once a quarter, or when there was communion and baptism, I conducted services in the little mission church in Loxton. Looking at the terrible poverty, the lack of any real or proper education, I began to ask, "How can we justify this?" Whites were always justifying why the people got the wages they did, and that there was very little they could do about it. I started to question this. . . . This was also linked to my very strong sense of mission. . . . I said to myself, "Part of your mission, certainly, is to uplift the people." And in that sense the knowledge and experience I gained in Genadendal, where at least you had a community of Coloureds who were living on a higher standard and who were able to sustain themselves to a certain degree, raised the question why it was not possible to have this in other parts of the country.'

Beyers left Loxton in 1945 and moved to the Transvaal to minister to the congregation in Pretoria South. The church had been established to serve members who lived in an extensive rural area on the southern border of the country's capital city. The move coincided with a change in the balance of political forces in the country. The National Party, under the skilful leadership of Dr Malan and with the help of the Broederbond, had gained the upper hand in the power struggle with the *Ossewabrandwag*. But these two groupings did not have the sympathy of all Afrikaners; many still supported Smuts's United Party and when the NGK took a decidedly anti-war stance many Afrikaans families whose sons were in the forces left the church. There were some ugly scenes at this time. Young men who came to church in uniform were shunned by many members of the congregation, and some hard-line nationalist ministers would ask them to leave. Beyers disapproved of this: 'There were very severe tensions in our congregation, but I said, "These people are members of the NGK and as members they have to be treated and ministered to in exactly the same way as anybody else." I went out of my way to see to it that no discrimination took place. I know some of the Nationalists and the *Ossewabrandwag* people were very angry and dissatisfied with me. . . . But we discussed this in the church council, and I said, "As long as they are members of the church and accept the service of the church, we have a responsibility, a spiritual responsibility towards them."'

A year after their arrival in Pretoria South, the Naudés' third son was born, and they named him Emil Hermann Karl after Ilse's father. At that time the family was living in a small house in Irene, about 20 kilometres from Pretoria. From this base Beyers and Ilse laid the foundations for a rapidly expanding church. The morning church service was initially held in Irene, but was later transferred to the developing area of Lyttelton. Afternoon services were held in at least one of the other settlements of Olifantsfontein, Bapsfontein and Elandsfontein. Beyers had his hands full conducting services, visiting members of his congregation, and supervising the church-building programme.

Beyers persuaded the church council that the first church hall should be built at Lyttelton instead of Irene, a site upon which an influential member of the NGK and wife of a future Governor-General of South Africa, Mrs E.G. Jansen, had set her heart. His instincts about Lyttelton proved correct; it expanded rapidly after the war, eventually being declared a separate town and renamed Verwoerdburg after the architect of apartheid.

By 1948 it had become clear that the Pretoria South region was far too large to manage. When it was decided to split the congregation Beyers accepted the call to Olifantsfontein, knowing that it would be easier for the church to find a minister to fill the Lyttelton position which was closer to the city of Pretoria.[8]

In 1948 the National Party came to power on the platform of apartheid. At the same time as the political programme of apartheid had been developed by nationalist ideologues in the 1940s, the NGK had also elaborated its theology of apartheid. In 1942, members of the NGK formed a Federal Mission Council and assigned a special commission to refine the policy of segregated churches for the various so-called race groups.[9] The Federal Mission Council also promoted segregation in other spheres. Its commission on education, for example, proposed that the education of black children be organised under the Department of Native Affairs rather than under the Department of Education, so that the school programme for blacks 'could be made more suitable for their special character and circumstances'. The Council also pleaded for the prohibition of sex and marriage across the colour line.[10] In the 1940s, too, NGK theologians extended their search for biblical texts to substantiate their call for church apartheid. Busy with his church work, Beyers did not concern himself too much about these political and theological developments. 'It never really worried me. I didn't get involved, I didn't look at apartheid theology critically, compare it to real, meaningful theology. I did not look at the specific texts of the Bible and try to get the correct interpretation. . . . I was not enough of a theology student. That was the tragedy – my lack of theological training and my unwillingness to be really involved.'

This 'unwillingness to be involved' is probably the key to understanding why Beyers kept silent about apartheid, because there is evidence that as early as 1948 he felt unhappy about this policy. In that year, the Transvaal synod of the NGK gave its sanction to apartheid. Dr Ben Marais stood virtually alone at the synod in opposing a church report which set out a biblical justification of apartheid. In spite of his protestations, the report was accepted by an overwhelming majority. But at the close of the synod Beyers and twelve other ministers asked that the records reflect that they did not support the report. Ben Marais said of Beyers's behaviour: 'He did not say a word, but had his name taken afterwards. My point of view was that if you were against something, you had to stand up and say it in the circle where it was appropriate.'[11]

Beyers met enough Afrikaners in his work to know the Nationalists were going to do well in the election. Shortly before polling day he met Smuts for the first time and they discussed the Nationalists' chances. 'I told him my feeling was that his party was going to lose. I said to him that I believed a change was taking place within the country and . . . that he would not gain the support. . . . He didn't accept that.'

On 26 May 1948, white South Africans, along with a minority of Coloured people in the Cape still entitled to vote, went to the polls. Beyers, although harbouring some misgivings about the National Party's apartheid programme, followed the Broederbond line in voting Nationalist. All over the country there was a swing away from Smuts and the United Party. In the aftermath of war, when many South Africans had tired of war shortages, the Nationalists, with their promise of not only white bread but a whites-only future, narrowly won the day. In Graaff-Reinet Beyers's father was jubilant. On 31 May 1948, the anniversary of the Treaty of Vereeniging, he wrote a joyful letter, addressed to his sons: 'It is now 6 in the morning. We have drunk coffee and read the old chapter, Lamentations 5, which I have been reading for the last 46 years on this day. . . . Thank you very much for your lovely telegram. It meant so much to me because it showed that you have also found that the Word . . . has become real. . . . The sun of freedom which went down at Vereeniging, has after 46 years risen more magnificently and more wonderfully than when it disappeared. My vision at the Tugela waterfall has been fulfilled.'[12] Not long afterwards, Jozua died of a heart attack.

Beyers continued to make steady progress in his work and in 1949 was appointed student pastor in Pretoria East, where he worked with Dr Ben Marais and Dr Johann Luckhoff. His special responsibility was the welfare of the students at the University of Pretoria, and in the six years he spent there he worked hard to promote youth work. One of the theology students at Pretoria at the time was Dr Nico Smith, a man who would like Beyers, but by a different route, come to reject apartheid. The two men's paths were destined to cross several times in their careers, and Dr Smith remembered his student pastor with affection. 'I had very close contact with him when he was student chaplain. He had come out of the Stellenbosch Seminary and it was unbelievable how little he knew about theology. At the time I thought, "What this chap knows about theology is dangerous." But he had the gift to make you enthusiastic, and you didn't know why because there was no theology behind it. I was very fond of him.' [13]

Beyers and Ilse's fourth child and only daughter, Liesel, was born in 1950. Ilse had her hands full running the home and helping with church work, and the family usually employed one or two servants to help in the home. Of this period Ilse said: 'His programme was fully laden and I had the children. Sometimes students came to babysit so that I could go out. I had small Bible study groups and I tried to do house visiting. It was always a very full programme, but I could share in his work, and I enjoyed it. The students were very nice. On Sunday night we had groups of 20 or 30 at our house. I had to bake, because you always had to feed the students. Our eldest son was a bit older by then and he could also help.'[14]

During this time steps were taken to unite the four provincial synods of the white NGK, and Beyers helped found the *Kerk Jeugvereniging* (KJV) – a national youth group for young, working Afrikaners. 'I wanted the KJV to be a channel for young people to become involved in meaningful work of mission, in evangelism and service, in welfare work, and in a ministry of compassion.'[15] He assumed his first executive position when he was elected chairman of the KJV in 1951, and by then was also *skriba*, or secretary, of the Synodal Youth and the Federal Youth Council.[16] Young people would seek him out at youth camps and conferences, and he thoroughly enjoyed this attention. He was becoming increasingly well known and popular.

While Beyers was going from strength to strength in his church work, the government was pressing ahead with its new race programme. A whole battery of apartheid laws was enacted in the late 1940s and early 1950s: the Prohibition of Mixed Marriages Act (1949), Group Areas Act and Population Registration Act (1950), the euphemistically named Abolition of Passes and Coordination of Documents Act (1952), Reservation of Separate Amenities Act (1953) and Bantu Education Act (1953). Moreover, in 1950 the government gave itself wide powers to suppress radical political activity by enacting the Suppression of Communism Act. The term 'communist' was interpreted so broadly that it could cover almost any activity the government wished to restrict or suppress. It provided for periods of detention without trial, and was the forerunner of numerous other draconian security laws and proclamations.

In the same year the NGK's Federal Mission Council held a conference to discuss the 'native question' and called for the total separation of the races. The two most important figures in the NGK who opposed their church's race policies at this time were both well known to Beyers. They were his former lecturer in ethics, Professor Bennie Keet, and his senior in Pretoria, Dr Ben Marais.

In 1952 Marais published an important book, *Die Kleur Krisis en die Weste* (*Colour, the Unsolved Problem of the West*), in which he examined racism in North America and Brazil. According to Marais, segregated churches were a very late development in the history of Christianity and were a fruit of slavery. He firmly rejected any biblical defence of segregated churches but said it could be justified on practical grounds – provided it did not break down Christian brotherhood. Marais put the arguments of apartheid theology to the test by asking thirteen of the world's leading theologians to reply to a series of questions dealing with nationalism and segregation in the Christian church. The theologians, who included the 'giant' Karl Barth, and the influential Emil Brunner, J.H. Bavinck, H. Berkhof and Franz Leenhardt, were unanimous in their rejection of racial segregation.[17]

The book sent shockwaves through the NGK, and Marais encountered a great deal of hostility from many of his colleagues and members of his congregation. A review in the official church journal *Die Kerkbode* was equally critical, and rejected Marais's claim that apartheid in the church was destroying Christian fellowship.[18] Professor Bennie Keet sprang to Marais's defence and the debate raged for months before *Die Kerkbode* settled it in favour of apartheid.

Marais's work had a great impact on Beyers Naudé. 'The book was a very clear and disturbing challenge to the traditional theological concepts which I held up till then. . . . Reading the book brought home to me a number of crucial questions about the biblical understanding of church, of race, of human dignity, of the unity of the church, of the whole pattern and structure of the NGK. Pronouncements were made by theologians of great repute . . . men like Karl Barth, Brillenburg, Wurth and Bavinck, and they all challenged the basic theological presumptions on which we based and justified our whole policy here.'

While new questions were beginning to surface in Beyers's mind, he held back, fearful of being disloyal to the Broederbond. 'On the one hand I was a member of the Broederbond, looking at all these issues from primarily the interest of the Afrikaner people, and on the other hand, Ben Marais was a colleague, a friend. . . . He was criticised and partially ostracised, but I never discussed it with him – I was cautious because of my allegiance to the Broederbond.'

Although Marais had not said so in his book, he was highly critical of the Broederbond because it operated in secrecy. Commented Beyers: 'This led to tremendous tension within the church council and within the congregation. Johann Luckhoff and I were both members of the Broederbond. I was in the invidious position where my loyalty to a secret organisation made it very difficult for me to feel free to study and evaluate certain basic theological views which were in conflict with the traditional views of the NGK. . . . I had this increasing feeling of doubt and unhappiness about the position in which I found myself. It was virtually impossible for me to be open to a fellow theologian, to differ with him, to debate and to discover the truth.'

Marais's book made Beyers even more determined to improve his knowledge of theology, and from 1953 he began an intensive programme of reading and self-study. He concentrated on interpretations of the Bible, on church history in South Africa and other countries, and on the role of race in the Christian church. For the first time he seriously studied the works of Karl Barth and the modern Dutch theologians and realised there was something fundamentally wrong with the NGK's race policies.

It was during this crucial period, in July 1953, that Beyers, as chairman of the *Kerk Jeugvereniging*, embarked on a six-month study tour overseas. His motivation for going abroad was to investigate church youth work in other countries, but also to find answers to new questions which students at the University of Pretoria had raised with him. 'With independent African states beginning to emerge, I began to think about the future role of the church on the continent and in South Africa. I thought about the old concept of mission, and wondered whether the church would be ready for the challenges it would have to meet.' He was accompanied by the KJV's general secretary, the Reverend Willem de Wet Strauss, and they toured the United States, Canada, Great Britain, Holland, France, Italy, Germany, Sweden and Switzerland. The South Africans received a polite reception from the various overseas Reformed churches which had helped draw up their itinerary, and they were also assisted by the youth department of the World Council of Churches to which the NGK then belonged. The two men naïvely thought they would be able to avoid political issues merely by declining to talk about them, but everywhere they went – at youth camps, conferences and seminars – people would question them about South Africa.

'We were asked very penetrating and painful questions. . . . In two or three cases people who had left the country confronted us about the situation of the black and Coloured community of which I had no clue. I had to go abroad in order to be confronted by situations of injustices in my own country.' At first, Beyers tried to defend his church's race policies. 'I used all the arguments, all the references in the Old Testament, I knew them by heart, the whole lot of them. But I realised very soon that I was up against theologians who could shoot down the one straw doll after the other. I became increasingly cautious about using these arguments, realising that something was wrong.'

Strauss did not involve himself too closely in these debates, preferring to concentrate on gathering information on youth programmes. On their return the two men published a long and tedious book giving details of their tour. It dealt with the various types of youth work they had encountered, but made no attempt to analyse their experiences. It also made no mention of the issue with which they had been confronted day after day – apartheid.[19]

The book contained not the slightest indication of the real impact the overseas tour had on Beyers. The tour broadened his vision and understanding of church and society. Now convinced that the NGK was wrong to support apartheid, he still refused, however, to speak out: 'I felt I was theologically inadequate . . . and I was still a member of the Broederbond. . . . I felt that I first had to prepare myself, find the necessary theological insight and knowledge and justification for my stand. . . . I began to see if I could find allies within the NGK, ministers who could be convinced, because I knew I was up against an ideological barrier that would be very difficult to break.'

Beyers continued his private theological study, and the more he read the more uneasy he became. 'I was led to the conclusion that there was no way in which the policy of apartheid could be justified on scriptural grounds. In this process I had to overcome all the accepted views, traditional outlooks, deep feelings of loyalty, and to see that this was essential if I wanted to remain obedient to the call of Christ and to the truth of the gospel. But it was a very painful process, and I think fear certainly played a very large part at that stage in my life. I began to realise something of the price that would have to be paid.'

Beyers purposely did not discuss these feelings with Ilse, and his Broederbond colleagues refused to be drawn on the issue. In spite of this inner turmoil he considered himself still a loyal Afrikaner. When he accepted a call to Potchefstroom in the western Transvaal in 1954, Beyers still supported his church, the Broederbond and government. But during the next ten years his Christian commitment and conscience would draw him into open confrontation with all of them.

5
Awakening and Sharpeville, 1955–1960

It was quite an achievement for the NGK congregation in Potchefstroom to have attracted Beyers and Ilse Naudé to their church in 1955. The popular couple had received numerous other calls over the years, and some of Beyers's colleagues believed that by accepting the Potchefstroom invitation, he was moving sideways.[1] Beyers felt he needed the experience and exposure in a large congregation, and indeed during the five years he spent in the town he came to be recognised as an up-and-coming church leader. His years in Potchefstroom were to prove decisive in his theological and political development.

A two-hour drive from Johannesburg, Potchefstroom is situated in the heart of the maizelands of the western Transvaal and is not far from the western Witwatersrand gold mines. The small town is symbolic of the conservative, independent spirit of Afrikanerdom. An early Voortrekker foundation, it later became the base for the smaller Afrikaans Reformed church, the Gereformeerde (or Dopper) Kerk. Deeply committed to the neo-Calvinism of Kuyper, the Doppers were staunch advocates of Afrikaner isolationism and apartheid. The Doppers founded the Potchefstroom University for Christian Higher Education and were a driving force behind the government's apartheid policy in education.[2]

The NGK in Potchefstroom was responsible for a very large farming district and the Naudés battled to reorganise the church after years of neglect by the previous minister. Beyers always placed great importance on visiting in his ministry, and he was appalled to find that some families had not been contacted for many years.

As Beyers's ministry unfolded, so he came increasingly to be driven by a tremendous energy. According to Ilse, her husband 'worked himself to pieces' in Potchefstroom. 'He discovered entire families that had never been baptised, and so he had to devote much of his time in visits to farming families.' Ilse also worked hard to revitalise the women's organisations and accepted as well all the responsibilities in the home. 'Bey was of the old stock who thought the wife was there for the children, to run the house and to see to all the work of the minister's wife.' The two oldest Naudé boys often accompanied their father on his visits to farms and enjoyed the attention which members of the congregation lavished on the *klein predikantjies* (little ministers).[3]

The hard work in Potchefstroom left little time for one of Beyers's favourite interests – youth work – and he was forced to bow out of the church's youth organisation, the KJV. His concern centred almost exclusively on the white congregation and he took little interest in mission work among people of other colour in Potchefstroom, apart from preaching occasionally in the local *Sendingkerk*.

The conservative Dopper influence also permeated the NGK in Potchefstroom and Beyers was conscious that his awakening political views were far removed from those of his congregation. 'My ministry in the congregation confirmed once more my awareness of the deeply conservative political views that our Afrikaner people of the *platteland* held. In Pretoria I had dealt with younger people, students who were more open. In Potchefstroom I had to deal with the ordinary rank and file members, including miners from Klerksdorp. In thinking through the implications of proclaiming a message of a totally different approach with regard to apartheid, I constantly asked myself: "How are these people going to react? They will never be able to understand." I realised that this would come as such a terrible shock. I constantly thought about it and asked: "Now how and where and when do I start portraying this aspect of the gospel which has been totally neglected?"'

Beyers deliberately avoided raising such issues with his congregation, and most of his close friends on the church council knew only the side of Beyers that he presented to the world. He was ambitious and wanted to achieve recognition and position within the church. He enjoyed being elected to various synodical commissions and willingly accepted the positions of leadership which the church was beginning to grant him.

Beyers's great drive – so reminiscent of his father's – partly explains his ambition. Yet this aspect of Beyers's personality does not account for his later actions, when he challenged his church at tremendous personal cost. According to Beyers, the central force in his life was 'obedience to Christ and His message'. 'That should be seen as basic to my whole life and actions, and my father, in one aspect of his preaching, inculcated this very strongly. . . . The other aspect of his preaching was strongly nationalist, in which he unwittingly compared and linked the Afrikaner people to the Israelites. But this first aspect, obedience to Christ, played a very significant role. I would ask myself: "What is the primary truth to which I must adhere in order to be loyal and committed to the gospel as I proclaim it?" That was the guiding light, which forced me from step to step, from one position to another one, sometimes against my will, sometimes with trepidation and fear in my own heart. More and more, either through theological study, intuition, or through the experience later on of being confronted by Christians from the Coloured, African and Indian community, I was forced to draw certain conclusions – that the truth was elsewhere than in the pronouncements of the NGK.'

And so while outwardly Beyers remained a loyal Afrikaner, inwardly he was uncertain and confused as he struggled to make sense of the government's race policies. Each Sunday Beyers urged his congregation to follow the way of Christ. He preached many times on the greatest command in the New Testament – 'love thy neighbour'. In his heart he now believed that apartheid was incompatible with this command, but he never once pointed it out, for fear of estranging his conservative congregation.

While Beyers's thinking was moving away from acceptance of the prevailing racial order, the National Party government continued to extend apartheid. In 1954, Native Affairs Minister Hendrik Verwoerd spelled out his ideal for the future: total separation of the races in every single sphere of life, social, political, economic and religious.[4] Soon the term apartheid gave way to 'separate development' in government parlance, and Verwoerd's policy began to be applied systematically across a broad social front. The key goal was to reverse the movement of black people to the 'white' cities by forcing them to live on 13 per cent of the country's land in ethnically divided black reserves, later known as 'homelands'. In the next decade more than two million black South Africans were forcibly uprooted and dumped in these barren, underdeveloped areas.[5]

The leadership in the NGK firmly backed government policy during this time, but concern about apartheid was growing in the English-speaking multi-racial churches. While the majority of ministers in the NGK sided with the government, Ben Marais alone continued to oppose the biblical justification of apartheid. Privately Beyers agreed with his friend, but a hurdle remained: he was still a member of the Broederbond.[6] Beyers continued to serve it loyally throughout the 1950s, and faithfully attended monthly meetings. 'We would discuss the circular from head-office which dealt with cultural, religious, political or economic issues. . . . Specific assignments would be given where the Broederbond felt a dangerous situation was developing, when the dominant position of the Afrikaner community was being threatened. We would discuss what could be done, by way of approaching individuals and lobbying them to change the thinking in favour of the whole Afrikaner community. . . . Where it became clear that there was a threat to the Afrikaner people, the Broederbond would not hesitate to apply very strong measures to prevent any serious harm to the dominant position of the Afrikaner people. If necessary the Broederbond would call upon the government or others, to say more serious measures would have to be taken to achieve a specific goal or to prevent something from happening.'

At meetings, Broederbond members would also discuss forthcoming elections to school, church or political committees and would decide who should be selected. Beyers observed: 'If there was a choice between two people who were regarded as equally good Afrikaners, the one who was a member of the Broederbond would definitely have been preferred.'

Beyers's uneasiness about belonging to the Broederbond is evident from an incident that occurred at the NGK's Transvaal synod of 1955. The synod had been discussing the *bête noire* of the Afrikaner establishment – the Freemason organisation – when Ben Marais stood up and criticised the Broederbond. Marais recalled: 'I was not a member of either organisation, and I had no intention of taking part in the debate. But when I saw that the loudest critics of

Freemasonry were all Broederbond members, I stood up and proposed that we accept that no minister of the NG Kerk should belong to any organisation which had an oath of secrecy. It was an hour before the normal adjournment of the afternoon session, and so the moderator called for an early break to consider whether my motion was in order. The next morning when the synod reopened, the moderator stood up and said he had decided that my motion was not in order and could not be discussed. He put his decision to synod and by about a three-to-two majority, they supported the moderator's stand. That night Beyers Naudé came to me and he told me what had happened the previous night after the synod had adjourned. He said to me: "You know, Ben, I can't look you in the eye." And I said: "Why, Beyers?" Then he told me that after the adjournment, by word of mouth and by telephone, the Broederbond had called a special meeting of members. . . . They had discussed a strategy should my motion be accepted for debate. Then Beyers told me that at that meeting, one speaker after another got up and said: "Now, Ben Marais must be broken in the church." Beyers told me he felt ashamed, he felt he did not belong at that meeting.'[7]

Other non-Broederbond colleagues also noticed ambiguities in Beyers's thinking at the time. Nico Smith, who worked for a while with Beyers in Potchefstroom as assistant minister and who was not yet a member of the Broederbond,[8] said: 'We often had long, involved theological discussions. I knew that Beyers was in the Broederbond but I didn't know how it functioned. What always puzzled me was that we would have discussions and decide what we believed was theologically the way, but then at a church meeting Beyers would take another stand. I realised that Beyers had changed his mind. That was the influence of the Broederbond. They forced you to conform to a certain way of thinking.'[9]

Beyers agreed with this assessment of the Broederbond. 'At Broederbond meetings I began to feed in my ideas and concerns and asked what we were going to do about them. I told them we can't close our eyes. But they would come up with counter-arguments, and so I would say to myself, "Perhaps I am wrong, perhaps I should take more seriously what these people are saying."' The prospect of advancing his career also caused Beyers to temper his criticism of apartheid. 'I was told by my colleagues that if I handled my career wisely I would become the moderator of, first, the regional synod and then of the national synod. I think it is important to realise that at that stage, the moderator of the NGK was the second most powerful position in the country [after the prime minister]. So I kept silent.'[10] A position on the NGK moderature was the carrot that was dangled before him. Beyers did not want to sacrifice everything he had worked for, by challenging apartheid. He may have known the price to be paid, but was not yet prepared to pay it.

On a personal level the Naudé family was happy in Potchefstroom. Ilse often felt though that Beyers's heavy commitments impinged on his personal responsibilities and that he did not not always have enough time for his children.[11] Their daughter Liesel had a different view. 'I have never looked at my parents as being separate because they were always together in my mind. When I grew older I knew what the problem areas were in their relationship, but they always had such a respect for each other, a deep love for each other. As parents they always tried to do things together. . . . I can never remember a time when my mother would say yes and my father no. . . .

'My mother is a home bird . . . she has always felt that he has not given enough time to his family. But if I look at my childhood, whatever time he gave us was quality time. I certainly have no feeling or memory that my father was not there when I needed him or that I did not know him. . . . My parents stimulated us, always encouraged us to think about things in an analytical way and ask questions. What they gave us, or me, was invaluable.'[12]

Their youngest son, Hermann, remarked: 'My father was not there and yet he was always there. Not there because he was always very busy doing his work as a *predikant*, yet whenever I needed him he would always stop what he was doing or even hold up a visitor and make time to listen. My mother was also very busy with all her committees and responsibilities as a minister's wife. But as children we were never neglected. We always had time to talk. People marrying into the family found it difficult to sit in on a Naudé discussion because we all talked simultaneously and there was usually more than one conversation taking place. There has always been very open discussion in our home, on the personal level initially, and then later on, on the political level as my father started questioning things. He always asked for our feelings relating to his decisions. Not that it would have made any difference to his decisions, but it was his way of getting it across to us.'[13]

Beyers's mother Ada, although aging rapidly, was still a powerful, dominant figure in the Naudé family. After her husband's death she moved around the country, living for fairly lengthy periods with her various children. *Ouma* Naudé would arrive, complete with her own sets of pots and pans, on her younger son's doorstep and move in with the family for a few months.

Liesel Naudé vividly remembered her grandmother. 'My father never spoke about her. Whenever we started moaning and groaning about her, he would not allow it, and he would say: "She is my mother." She was a real formidable character. As a child I hated her at times because she made my mother so miserable. She knew exactly what she wanted and would get it regardless of whether it hurt somebody or not. She would come and visit, and then if something happened in the house that she didn't like, she would phone one of the other daughters and say they must please come and fetch her, she didn't want to stay with us anymore. None of them would ask to speak to my mother first. They would just arrive at the door and say they had come to fetch *Ouma*. So there was a lot of friction and as children we reacted very strongly. . . . As a grandmother she was also warm and loving, but she had a very strong will.'[14]

During his ministry at Potchefstroom, Beyers's political and theological views came to be shaped in a number of decisive ways. In spite of their ultra-conservatism on race issues, Beyers found more depth in the theology of the Doppers than in his own church. Gereformeerde Kerk members who attended his church services and Bible studies gave him a new understanding of the demands of the Scriptures. 'For the first time I really got to know some leading members of the Gereformeerde Kerk. I had the opportunity to discuss and debate issues with them, specifically from the theological and biblical viewpoint, which is something that had not happened in the NGK. The Doppers showed more concern for evaluating their actions and political and social issues in the light of Scripture. In that sense, it strengthened my approach to assessing and evaluating what was happening in the country in terms of one's Christian faith.'

Charles Villa-Vicencio has summed up the influence of the Dopper theology on Beyers: 'Today, when he is asked to explain theologically what the Word of God is, his response is rather precise. "It is . . . one's understanding of the declared will of God made known in the Scriptures." This must be tested within a community of people of goodwill, including both Christians and those who care not to be known as such. It must be concretised in relation to ongoing political and economic analysis, and ultimately verified in a deeply personal inner conviction. He is today at once a deeply spiritual and a profoundly secular person. Potchefstroom was an important point of transition in this regard.' [15]

The period was also significant in the general sense that the 1950s was the last decade until very recently that major criticisms of apartheid were allowed to be heard within the NGK. Three years after the appearance of Ben Marais's controversial book on apartheid, Professor Keet published a short work, *Whither South Africa?*, in which he challenged the biblical validity of apartheid. In just 96 pages Keet demolished the arguments from Scripture in defence of apartheid, pointing out that it was only because segregation and discrimination existed in the first place in South Africa that NGK theologians had searched for passages in the Bible to support the policy. Moreover, he contended: 'When we speak of apartheid we do not mean merely distinctions, but divisions that are at variance with God's ordinance and the unity of the human race.' He warned Afrikaners who dreamt of complete racial separation that they were living in a make-believe world.[16] The response of the NGK was summed up in a review of the book in *Die Kerkbode*. It criticised Keet for being negative and defended the church and government's apartheid policy as having had a 'positive' impact on all the country's races and on the church's mission work.[17] Keet's book reinforced Beyers's own doubts about apartheid and he continued to expand his theological knowledge.

Ministers like Beyers who disagreed with the policy of apartheid but who were still loyal to the church often took ambiguous and contradictory positions on controversial issues. One telling example of this was the debacle over the government's attempt to prevent racial association in the churches by introducing in 1957 the so-called 'church clause' to the Native Laws Amendment Act. The publication of a draft bill prompted an immediate protest from the English-speaking churches, and the Church of the Province of South Africa (CPSA) warned the government that it would be forced to disobey the law.[18] The Federal Council of the NGK was also opposed to the amendment and in an unusually critical statement outlined its reasons for rejecting it. The eight-point statement stressed the complete freedom the church should enjoy and warned the government against exceeding its power and impinging on the sovereignty of the church. Initially the Council released only the first part of the statement and the points more critical of the government were excluded. In keeping with the close cooperation between the NGK and the state, a delegation from the church met with Bantu Affairs Minister Hendrik Verwoerd to discuss the issue. After listening to their views, Verwoerd explained how English churches were provoking the government by deliberately arranging multi-racial church services. After he assured them that the new law would be applied circumspectly, the NGK decided not to release the full statement.[19]

The decision to back down caused division within the church. Beyers Naudé was one of those who tried, not very successfully, to reach a compromise at the Transvaal synod in 1957. He proposed that the Federal Council's original statement be approved as 'an explanation of the church's standpoint as it is grounded in God's Word'. But his motion also thanked the government for granting the church an audience and called on the synod to accept 'officially' the church's less critical statement. Theologian R. Lombard has summed up the NGK's contradictory behaviour: 'the anomalies in the decision of the Transvaal synod were evidence of the conflict of conscience the church clause caused the NGK. The church was aware that the government, with the clause, was infringing on the terrain of the church, but at the same time did not want to withdraw their support for the government and apartheid.'[20] The controversial church clause did become law but was never strictly enforced.

Another important event in Beyers's development during this time was the World Reformed Ecumenical Synod which met in Potchefstroom in August 1958. Hosted by the Gereformeerde Kerk, the conference brought together representatives from the smaller, conservative Reformed churches worldwide. It was attended by delegates from South Africa, Holland, England, the United States, France and Australia, and included a large group from the NGK. Although not an official representative, Beyers attended all the public sessions of the synod. It dealt with a variety of social and church issues, but placed particular emphasis on the crisis facing Africa and the problem of race relations. The synod devoted four days to the latter, during which time strong critiques of apartheid in the church were launched by various overseas delegates.

NGK theologians also contributed a great deal to discussion at the synod, and the South African influence on the proceedings was reflected in the cautious statement issued by delegates on the race issue.[21] Despite the failure of the synod to condemn apartheid, the contribution of the overseas delegates made a profound impression on Beyers, and he became aware of the gulf which already separated the thinking of his church and the world Reformed community. 'The synod, combined with my own studies, confirmed my conviction that there was no way the NGK could ever justify on the basis of the gospel and in the light of the Christian confession of the Reformed tradition, its attitude to apartheid.'[22] According to Beyers, he also saw for the first time 'how ministers of the NGK searched desperately for the right words to answer the questions and criticisms which were spoken out with love by the representatives of the overseas Reformed Church members.'[23]

During 1958 Beyers was elected to the moderature of the Transvaal synod as *assessor* or vice-chairman. One important consequence was that younger ministers, who had encountered him as students in Pretoria, began to seek him out to discuss their dilemmas about apartheid. Most of them served as missionaries in the separate African, Coloured or Indian churches, and they were disturbed by the implementation of residential apartheid which deeply affected their members.

Charl le Roux, one of those who approached him for help, recalled: 'I had known Beyers as a child when I was growing up in Wellington. He was an open, friendly, communicating minister. In those days many ministers were quite stuffy, but he was relaxed and approachable. In the 1950s I had been involved with mission work in the Indian community and they had many problems and frustrations. We took Beyers to the heart of all this. At that stage many people were living in slums, they were pushed into a corner. He saw all this and it changed his whole outlook.'[24]

In many parts of South Africa, the authorities had begun uprooting 'non-white' families from their homes to comply with the government's idea of racially 'pure' residential areas. For the most part, the removals which took place under the Group Areas and Natives Resettlement Acts had the support of the white local authorities and white residents. In Johannesburg, the vibrant black township of Sophiatown was rezoned for whites and its inhabitants were forcibly removed 20 kilometres south of the city to the undeveloped area of Meadowlands, now part of Soweto.[25] Coloured and Indian people living in areas close to Johannesburg were also affected by the law and their sufferings stirred the conscience of their white NGK ministers. Beyers recalled that ministers like Chris Greyling, François Malan, Charl le Roux and Gert Swart came to seek him out for his advice. 'They told me about the problems they were experiencing and of the growing resistance of African, Coloured and Indian Christians to the stand the white NGK was taking on apartheid. These people were challenging the white ministers by saying, "How do you justify what is happening to us on the basis of Scripture?" The ministers invited me to come and share their experiences with them. And when they told me what they were experiencing, I said to them: "I have to accept that you are telling me the truth, but I cannot believe it." And so they invited me to come and look for myself. And I did. And what I found was a shattering experience.'

Beyers went on four or five visits to the Indian communities of Pageview and Fordsburg in Johannesburg, to the newly created Indian 'group area' of Lenasia, to the African migrant compounds and to Coloured slums. 'For the first time I was confronted with the terrible effects which the apartheid system had on human lives: the Group Areas Act, job reservation, prohibition of mixed marriages. I was confronted by a family where the father and the mother were classified so-called Coloureds, but their one child was classified white and the other Coloured. The mother said to me: "Do you realise what has happened to us? In the daytime they may be together, but they dare not go to the same school.

This white child dare not live with us, neither can we live where this white child is living. Our family is split from top to bottom." '

Visiting a mine compound in Johannesburg that housed migrant labourers, Beyers was shocked by the cold, the greyness of the hostels, the concrete bunks, the rudimentary toilets, the lack of privacy in sharing a room with ten or twelve other men. He was struck by the monotony of their lives and by the realisation that these men were denied a normal family life, only allowed to see their wives and children once a year on holiday. 'I will never forget that experience as long as I live. I said to myself, "If this is what apartheid is all about, it is evil, it is inhuman, it is something which can never be supported. . . . I asked one of the ministers who accompanied me: "What happens to these men and their normal human and also sexual needs?" And he said: "It is inevitable that they go out and find satisfaction with women around or they bring them into these compounds if they can." For all practical purposes they developed a second relationship with another wife or woman in addition to their rural family. The break-up of family life as a result of all this was terrible.'[26]

Beyers was horrified by his ignorance of his own country. 'I realised I had been living in a wonderful "white world." And right next to me was a black world and a brown world and an Indian world that I knew nothing about. . . . I went to the South African Institute of Race Relations and bought their annual surveys on race relations. I bought copies of all the laws, and for the first time in my life I began to study the race laws of the country. . . . It brought me to the conclusion, not only on theological grounds, but also on practical grounds, on the grounds of justice, these laws were even less acceptable.'[27]

Beyers knew it would be futile for him and the small group of like-minded ministers to try to change the policies of their church. But from then on, a new idea began to take root in his mind. He knew that the only effective way of changing the church's race policy was to convince enough of its ministers that it was wrong. Yet because of their shallow theological and political education especially in respect of racial issues, they were unable to do so. He realised that his ability to face up to the issues in his country had been made possible by his intensive study, and so he urged them to do the same. 'I made the point time and again that it was of vital importance to prove to the church that its theological insight and judgement and understanding was wrong. I said that if we don't base our convictions on clear biblical and theological grounds, then there was no point in doing anything. I sent them back to rethink and restudy. Then I said that if it was possible for them to gather around them any others who were interested in these issues, to do so, because it was the only way that we would be able to bring about meaningful change in the NGK.'[28]

Speaking of Beyers's concern about race issues, David Bosch, a leading Afrikaner theologian and an old friend, remarked: 'I would say Beyers's early interest in race issues stemmed from his deep commitment to mission, and this was the tradition out of which he had come. In the late 1950s the NGK experienced a missionary revival, and it was because of his interest in spreading the gospel to black South Africans that he was willing to make contact with NGK missionaries. They then introduced him to their black congregations, and he was able to witness their suffering under apartheid. His typical evangelical approach created the opportunities for him to be exposed to what was happening in South Africa.'[29]

Beyers also had to face up to the effects of the Group Areas Act in his capacity as a member of the Transvaal moderature. Although his church firmly supported residential apartheid, it had some qualms about how the law affected Indian traders, who were being forced to uproot successful, established businesses. When representatives from the Indian community appealed to the NGK in the Transvaal for help, a meeting was arranged with Beyers's brother-in-law and moderator of the synod, Frans O'Brien Geldenhuys. Geldenhuys expressed sympathy for these people, but after arranging a meeting with the relevant minister to discuss the issue, the moderature issued a statement accepting government assurances that the law would be applied as 'reasonably' as possible. As assessor Beyers was instructed to monitor the situation of the Indian traders, but in reality he did nothing. He said: 'I knew that if I started to get involved I would have to give a report that was in total conflict with the viewpoint of the NGK. I thought it would create such a serious situation that it was better to do nothing.' Beyers tried to discuss these problems with ministers who were fellow Broederbond members. He recalls long conversations with colleagues like Bertie Brink, Willem Landman, A. P. Smit and A. J. van der Merwe. Of his behaviour at this time, Beyers observed: 'It is interesting that my first loyalty in sharing Christian concerns was with fellow members of a secret society because my bond with them was closer than the bond to the wider Christian community.' The response of his colleagues was to warn Beyers not to 'play with fire'. 'They said to me, "Do you realise if you start proclaiming these convictions that your whole future will be destroyed? There will be no acceptance in the Afrikaner community. You will be totally ostracised, pushed out and left in the cold." That's why I remained silent. I didn't even share my doubts with my wife and with my children. I was afraid of the effect it would have on them. It was wrong because I think in later years I discovered that this made it very difficult for Ilse to be able to accompany me in all the different steps which we were to take. I think it was a very serious disservice I did to her.'[30]

In late 1959 Beyers Naudé received a call to the new Aasvoëlkop church in the wealthy suburb of Northcliff north-west of Johannesburg. The church was an offshoot of the Linden congregation, served by arch-conservative minister and close confidant of Verwoerd, Gideon Boshoff. The Aasvoëlkop church was originally responsible for about 600 adult members spread out over a very large area, including the affluent suburbs of Northcliff, Emmarentia, Blackheath and Roosevelt Park, as well as the poorer area of Greymont. Its members numbered very influential and powerful Afrikaners, such as the chairman of the Board of the South African Broadcasting Corporation, Dr Piet Meyer, and the former editor of *Die Transvaler*, Jannie Kruger. This elite position was Beyers's reward for faithful service to his people – he himself realised that he was being brought into the heart of the cultural and political life of Afrikanerdom to fill a leading role.

Not all Beyers's friends were in favour of his move to Aasvoëlkop. Dr Willie Jonker, a close family friend and minister in the Johannesburg area at the time, said: 'Beyers was very popular and was being brought to Johannesburg, not only as a church leader, but as a leader of the Afrikaner community. The Broederbond had advised him strongly to accept the position. I had never joined the Broederbond and had strong reservations about the way it operated. They did not only want a minister, but a strong Afrikaans cultural leader in Johannesburg, and Beyers was invited there for that purpose.'[31]

The family lived in Roosevelt Park in a house bought by the church, and the congregation met in a school hall while funds were being collected for the building of a church. The Naudé children were beginning to scatter by the time the family moved to Aasvoëlkop. The eldest son Johann was studying at Pretoria University while François had remained at boarding school in Potchefstroom to complete his final year at school.

Beyers and Ilse worked hard to build up the Aasvoëlkop church. A monthly newsletter was established, a women's group and a youth group were set up, as were Sunday school and catechism classes. Beyers continued to place emphasis on pastoral work, and with the help of his church council divided the congregation into nineteen wards and arranged visits to every family.[32] It took two years to collect funds and purchase the necessary land for the church building and manse, but when finally the long-awaited church began to take shape Beyers showed his practical flair. The church was designed by an architect and an elder in the congregation, Hannes de Bruin, and Beyers enthusiastically involved himself in the building programme.

Maintaining his interest in South Africa's political problems, Beyers became part of a small group of ministers in the NGK which hoped to lead their church away from apartheid. In consultation with other moderate voices in the Afrikaans churches, he helped establish Bible study groups to consider apartheid. Study groups were formed in Johannesburg and Pretoria, and these eventually expanded to include some African and Coloured churchmen as well as ministers from other denominations. At first the meetings were held on a very informal basis, but early in 1960 the Johannesburg circle became more formalised when Gert Swart was appointed secretary of the Rand Ecumenical Study Circle. The study circle was strongly supported by the ministers in Beyers's circuit, and at one stage all but one of the thirteen ministers took part in the meetings. Another important figure who lent weight to the group was Beyers's friend Willie Jonker.[33] As the groups expanded the organisers battled to find suitable places where black and white could meet. The Methodist Church in Johannesburg was sympathetic and offered a venue, but throughout their existence, the groups struggled to find venues. The study groups kept as low a profile as possible but they were always viewed with suspicion by the conservative majority in the NGK.

The Bible study movement showed a new and very important development in Beyers's thinking. He began to take an interest in ecumenical matters. Explaining this development, Beyers remarked: 'Through my private theological study I developed a totally new concept about the nature of the church. I realised that the church in the New Testament sense was the one body of Christ and that all the historical divisions which had grown up since the Reformation, between the different confessional groups, and the divisions which had grown in South Africa, were no longer valid, they could not be maintained and that therefore one of the major tasks would be to help Christian people realise what the concept of church and Christian unity was. I realised that to begin to talk about church unity to the people concerned would be futile. It was better to start with the concept of Christian unity, the need for Christians to be one in order to fulfil the mission of the church. Without the united church or the united standing of the Christian community, there was no possibility of making any impact on the world with regard to our message or mission. I had read many articles issued by the World Council of Churches on this subject and they were very helpful in shaping my vision and understanding. The demand for Christian unity was a biblical demand. It was a new mission and evangelism, and it was totally different from what had been presented by the NGK. It was the mission of the whole church to the whole world, not of one church to a small number of people around them. The church had to look at the needs of the world and say: "If we are truly the people of God, proclaiming the gospel of salvation and liberation, the transforming of human beings and society, then the church has to be one; we must be united, otherwise we are going to create tremendous problems and divisions."'

While Beyers's theological and political thinking had come a long way since the mid-1950s, he was still far removed from appreciating the full depth of black anger and resistance to apartheid laws. Although he had seen for himself the suffering these policies caused he was still cautious in his political outlook, believing that it would be from whites – and from Afrikaners in particular – that the impetus for change would come. Events would rudely prove him wrong.

Beyers knew very little about the black political movements which had been formed to oppose white rule. The chief black political group was the African National Congress (ANC), formed in 1912 to campaign for equal political rights for blacks. Its protests against mounting discrimination were ignored and, by the 1950s, the ANC, along with other pressure groups, stepped up the non-violent struggle against apartheid. In December 1956, 156 people were arrested and charged with treason as the result of the adoption of a 'Freedom Charter' at a national conference in Kliptown, Johannesburg, the year before. During the five-year trial, charges were dropped against many of the accused and finally in March 1961 all those remaining on trial were acquitted.[34]

The greatest opposition to apartheid in the rural areas was to the new Bantu Authorities system, whereby African chiefs were arbitrarily appointed by government officials to rule areas.[35] In the urban areas opposition centred on the pass laws, which forced all Africans to carry identification on their person stating whether or not they were permitted to work in a designated white urban area. By 1958, almost 400 000 people had been convicted of pass law infringements.[36] The standard treatment for violators was arrest, fines and jail for those who could not pay. Organised opposition to the pass laws was complicated by the divisions which had appeared in the ranks of the ANC. The breach culminated in March 1959 with the establishment of the breakaway Pan-Africanist Congress, which objected to the 'non-Africanist' element in the ANC.[37]

In 1960 the ANC and PAC simultaneously launched campaigns to protest against the pass laws. The PAC called on members to leave their 'passes' at home on 21 March 1960 and present themselves for arrest at their nearest police station. On this day police fired on a crowd of protesters at Sharpeville township in the Transvaal, killing 69 people. The massacre sparked waves of anger and defiance throughout South Africa. The ANC and PAC called for a day of mourning on 28 March and there was a huge work stayaway. In response the government outlawed both the PAC and the ANC and declared a state of emergency. Thousands of people were detained in dawn raids. Cape Town was brought to a standstill for more than a week as the black labour force stayed away from work. Political unrest flared in most of the other major centres and the government used an iron fist to restore order.[38]

The Sharpeville massacre and the 1960 unrest created a grave crisis for many sectors of society, including the churches. Although Beyers was only half aware of it, the shockwaves would also touch his life.

6
Cottesloe, December 1960

The blood that was spilt at Sharpeville may have shocked the country but it did nothing to shake the government's self-confidence. Prime Minister Verwoerd made that clear when he announced: 'The government sees no reason to depart from the policy of separate development because of the disturbances.'[1] Beyers, although he was clearly disturbed by the events of March 1960, was still reluctant to challenge the government's policies openly. Indeed in the months to come, he would even agree with his church when it placed the major responsibility for the township unrest on 'communist agitators'. For Beyers was still preoccupied with the interests of his white congregation and in advancing as a leader in the NGK. After serving for three years on the Transvaal moderature he had become a familiar figure at important church meetings, and in the course of 1960, while still serving as assessor on the Transvaal moderature, he was also nominated as acting moderator of the newly formed Southern Transvaal synod.

Outwardly, he was still a very typical *dominee* – conservative in his dress and confirmed in his old habits. Although not considered a 'great theologian', he was well liked by most of his fellow ministers. His relaxed style, his warmth and his concern for people's personal problems made him very popular with his congregation. Klippies Kritzinger, a NGK minister who later served in the 'Indian' Reformed Church, commented: 'Beyers was a very friendly person and had a great pastoral heart. We were living in a neighbouring congregation, but my parents no longer attended church. I went to a service at Aasvoëlkop and liked it, so I joined the church. It had nothing to do with political considerations, I was attracted to him as a person.'[2]

Beyers, in his public utterances on Sharpeville at the time, did not show an appreciation for the real issues at stake, and merely looked at black unrest as a threat to the mission of his church. Writing about the Sharpeville massacre in the church newsletter in May 1960, he said: 'The NG Kerk stands condemned before the whole world as a church which has neglected its Christian calling with regard to the non-whites, which has not done enough to plead for their legitimate needs. It is clear that the NGK has a great responsibility to correct the outside world's twisted image and to convince overseas churches of the sincerity of our intentions and the scriptural basis of our standpoint.

'If we are not careful . . . these events could be exploited and misused with the result that our mission could be set back. It is through such events that we as Christians are tested, in our motives and in our mission work. However strongly the true Christian condemns any form of incitement and violence, he will continue to search for ways to extend the Kingdom of God to unbelievers. The past events should make us realise that the church must continue, with even greater speed and seriousness, in its missionary activities so that more people can find the light that exists in Jesus Christ.'[3]

Sharpeville brought many sectors of South African society to a crossroad. After nearly half a century of non-violent opposition to white rule, the ANC had been declared unlawful. The ANC went underground and changed its policy, concluding that armed struggle was the only way to win equal political rights for blacks. Nelson Mandela took charge of the organisation's military wing, *Umkhonto we Sizwe* (Spear of the Nation), with a view to sabotaging government installations. The PAC, also banned, went underground too and established its military wing, *Poqo* (We Go It Alone). In August 1962 Mandela was detained and a few months later a number of other ANC leaders were arrested in Rivonia, Johannesburg. In 1964 they were convicted of sabotage and sentenced to life imprisonment.[4]

Sharpeville also created a serious rift between the NGK and the English-speaking churches. Although the NGK in the Transvaal and the Cape were still members of the World Council of Churches, the disagreement over Sharpeville threatened to destroy the last remaining bonds between the churches.[5] In their statements, most of the country's English churches blamed the violence on apartheid. In March 1960, nine leading members of the Transvaal, Free State and Cape moderatures of the NGK issued a statement deploring the 'shocking' declarations against the government which had been made by churches at home and abroad and called on these churches' leaders to behave more responsibly. The NGK acknowledged 'shortcomings' on the part of the church and government, but reaffirmed its support for apartheid, or 'independent, distinctive development', providing it was 'carried out in a just and honourable way'.[6] The Anglican Archbishop of Cape Town, Joost de Blank, responded to this by delivering a scathing attack on the NGK. He described the Sharpeville massacre and its consequences as the gravest crisis in the history of South Africa's churches, and declared black protests were directed not only against the government but at churches which supported its race policies. In a letter to the World Council of Churches he demanded that the NGK be expelled from the world body.[7]

The Archbishop's remarks caused serious tension between the Anglican church, officially the Church of the Province of South Africa (CPSA), and some of the other English-speaking churches on the one hand, and the NGK and the government on the other. The executive committee of the World Council of Churches felt De Blank's reaction was extremely unhelpful.[8] In response to appeals from the Archbishop, the WCC decided to send a representative on a 'mission of fellowship' to try to heal the rift among member churches and guide them to a just stand on race issues.

The man chosen for the mission was one of the associate general secretaries of the WCC, American-born Dr Robert Bilheimer. Coming from a Reformed church – the Presbyterian denomination – Bilheimer could identify and sympathise with the group of NGK ministers who were trying to lead their church away from support for apartheid. Beyers met Bilheimer for the first time in April 1960 at a special meeting Bilheimer had requested with leaders of the NGK to gauge their views on the crisis in South Africa. The NGK representatives informed him that the ANC accounted for less than one per cent of the views of black South Africans and that 'communist agitators' were largely responsible for the violence. Beyers's political views, in public at least, were still extremely conservative. He told Bilheimer that the majority of blacks were satisfied with the situation in South Africa, but because of lack of organisation, their voices had not been heard. He also claimed that black people actually approved of the pass laws, but conceded that there was room for improvement in policing them.[9]

At the meeting Bilheimer stressed the need for inter-church dialogue and proposed a meeting to discuss the churches' responsibility in the time of crisis. This proposal was to lead to the historic Cottesloe consultation of December 1960. As the tension between the NGK and Archbishop De Blank formed the biggest stumbling block to dialogue, Bilheimer during his first two-week visit to South Africa held many meetings with both sides to try to resolve the problems. By the time he flew back to Geneva he had a tentative undertaking from both the NGK and the CPSA to participate in a church meeting. The only other Afrikaans church which belonged to the WCC, the conservative Hervormde Kerk, also appeared willing to take part. The churches agreed that the consultation should be multi-racial and that it should include representatives of the WCC. The meeting would focus on trying to establish the facts of the South African situation and determine the church's role in seeking racial justice in a rapidly changing world.[10]

Beyers was drawn into the arrangements for Cottesloe when he was nominated by the Transvaal NGK as one of its two representatives on the planning committee. The other NGK representatives were the Transvaal moderator, A. M. Meiring, and two members of the Cape moderature, A. J. van der Merwe and Willem Landman. Bob Bilheimer flew back to South Africa for the first meeting of the committee in July 1960. Bilheimer was elected chairman of the planning committee, and a small executive took charge of the administrative arrangements. This consisted of Beyers Naudé, J. B. Webb of the Methodist Church, G. Sidebotham of the CPSA, and as secretary Fred van Wyk, an associate director of the South African Institute of Race Relations.

Beyers's work with the committee enabled him to build up enduring relationships with people who would later support him when he established the Christian Institute. The most important of these contacts was Fred van Wyk, an Afrikaner and member of the NGK, who became a close and supportive friend. He played a very important part in the organisation behind the Cottesloe conference, and would exhibit the same organisational flair when he helped Beyers launch the Christian Institute three years later.

At that first Cottesloe planning meeting, agreement was reached on the topics for discussion: the factual situation in South Africa; the Christian understanding of the gospel for relationships among races; an understanding of contemporary history from a Christian viewpoint, particularly with regard to rapid social change; the meaning of the state of emergency in South Africa; and the witness of the church in respect of justice, mission and cooperation. Each church agreed to compile memoranda on these topics.[11]

It was agreed too that a multi-racial conference would take place in Johannesburg from 7 to 14 December 1960 and that the delegates should all meet and stay in one place for the duration of the proceedings. In the months preceding the conference Beyers found himself deeply involved in these arrangements. It was a new experience for him to be working closely with churchmen outside his own denomination. While initially suspicious of the liberal CPSA and Methodist representatives, Beyers gradually came to the realisation that these churchmen's strong views on apartheid and the Sharpeville shootings, although in conflict with his own views, were not without foundation. 'For the first time I began to realise what in fact the Anglican Church and others had been doing. They had been studying these race issues and had come to conclusions so different from what I had read and heard about in the Afrikaans community.'

While churchmen on the planning committee were developing a rapport, tension between the CPSA and the NGK on an official level was threatening to scuttle the whole conference. Archbishop De Blank warned he would withdraw his church from the conference after he was attacked in an editorial in *Die Kerkbode*.[12] Eventually this row was smoothed over but matters came to a head once again in August 1960 with the deportation of the CPSA's Bishop of Johannesburg, Ambrose Reeves. Reeves, who had been nominated as a delegate to the church conference, was an outspoken critic of the government. He had left the country shortly after the declaration of the state of emergency, taking with him documentary evidence of police brutality at Sharpeville and elsewhere. On his return in September 1960, he was deported by the government. De Blank again threatened to withdraw his church from the conference unless it was held outside the country or unless the government agreed to allow Ambrose Reeves to attend in South Africa. At the request of the planning committee, the World Council of Churches nominated Beyers Naudé and Frans Geldenhuys to seek a meeting with the authorities.

When they met Minister of the Interior Tom Naudé in September 1960 they asked him whether the government would be prepared to give reasons for Reeves's deportation and to allow him into the country to attend the consultation.[13] The Minister declined on both points. Although the meeting failed to move the government, it demonstrated to the CPSA that the NGK leadership was at least willing to raise the issue officially.

The controversy over the bishop's deportation attracted a great deal of media attention. It brought Beyers into close and direct contact with journalists who would in the future focus so frequently on his own activities. His handling of the issue showed a certain naïvety. 'Although our meeting with the Minister was supposed to be very confidential, somebody leaked it to the *Sunday Times*. Margaret Smith, who was then a senior reporter at the *Sunday Times*, phoned me on the Saturday after our meeting. She said she had information that we had seen the Minister, and asked whether I was willing to make any comment. I said I preferred not to make any comment. Then she said: "Well, if that's the case, then I will have to publish what I have without any comment on your part." I replied that if that is what she had to do, then there was very little I could do about it. Then I thought about it and realised that such a report would create more confusion and that it would be better to give the facts, which I then did. The next day, the report was the front-page headline in the *Sunday Times*. When I entered the church vestry where the church council had gathered, the atmosphere was icy. I could immediately sense the anger, especially from the *ware* [real] Afrikaners, for speaking to the *Sunday Times* . . . in those days you didn't dare speak to the enemy English press. It was seen as an act of serious betrayal to the Afrikaner cause and it was very difficult for me to overcome that.'

The diplomacy of Bilheimer and Fred van Wyk, combined with the pressure exerted by the other churches, finally persuaded the CPSA that the conference should go ahead in Johannesburg as planned, without the attendance of Reeves.[14]

The planning committee then faced another major problem – finding suitable accommodation for the delegates at a time when no suitable multi-racial establishments existed at all. After months of searching, they finally secured a hostel run by the University of the Witwatersrand in Cottesloe, a small suburb of Johannesburg close to the city centre.

Although by no means the first multi-racial conference to be held in South Africa, and what is more only a quarter of the delegates were 'non-white', the organisers were very conscious of the fact that whites and blacks would be living together. This self-consciousness is evident in a letter written by Beyers to one of the Cape NGK representatives, Willem Landman. He described the hostel as 'old military buildings comprising separate wings, each with twenty single rooms, linked by covered passages'. Beyers explained that Fred van Wyk was responsible for placing delegates in the various blocks. He said that some blocks would house whites only while the 'non-white' delegates would be spread out over two blocks, together with some white delegates from South Africa and overseas. 'Now my question: is there any representative from the Cape who would like us to arrange it so that he can be housed in the wings (where the non-whites will be) for the witness that it will represent? If you feel we should place one of your men there, could you please indicate which of your ten is prepared to do it?

'It is surely not necessary (and perhaps also not wise) to discuss this formally with delegates: this is the reason for my personal, confidential inquiry. If you wish your entire group to be placed with the white group, please let me know. In any case, we will all eat together and other refreshments will be served together.'[15]

Not all quarters in the Afrikaans churches looked forward to the coming conference. The Hervormde Kerk began to express serious reservations about the meeting, as did some leading figures in the NGK in both the Cape and Transvaal. They felt the ultimatums and criticisms delivered by the CPSA had not created the right atmosphere for dialogue. They also expressed a fear that the Afrikaans churches would find themselves placed before an inquisition at the conference.[16] In spite of these misgivings, they were persuaded by Bob Bilheimer to continue with the meeting.

By October 1960 Bilheimer had made three trips to South Africa and had built up a sound relationship with the South African members of the planning committee. Writing about Beyers in one of his reports, he described him as 'a very quiet, but very genuine liberal. Speaking of criticism of himself in the DRC [NGK], he said that he knew that some time the storm would break over him, and that when it did he would simply continue and carry on from there. Naudé is one of those who so eloquently disprove the idea that the DRC is monolithic.'[17]

While all the participating churches were well prepared for the consultation, the NGK probably invested the most energy in getting ready for the meeting. More than forty theologians in the Cape and Transvaal were asked to contribute to the conference memoranda, ranging from Ben Marais to the right-wing Andries Treurnicht. The views expressed in the documents were essentially conservative, but in some aspects broke with traditional NGK thinking. The document prepared by the Cape NGK was particularly significant. In general, the NGK theologians blamed the Sharpeville violence on agitators and legitimated the apartheid policy of the church and government by declaring it was the most just under the circumstances. But they also recognised that black South Africans had some fundamental rights which were denied them, and views like these were out of step with official government policy.

The memoranda prepared by the English-speaking churches placed the blame for the township violence squarely on the government's pass laws, as well as on low wages and a general denial of the rights of black South Africans.[18] In its paper, on the other hand, the Hervormde Kerk rejected any racial mixing and staunchly defended apartheid as a fair and just system.

Beyers was convener of the Transvaal NGK paper on the prophetic calling of the church. The document produced by his five-man study group employed the ambiguous language favoured by many NGK theologians. It acknowledged that if legislation prohibited membership of the church on grounds of race, colour or culture, it was negating the prophetic calling of the church. However, the paper defended the establishment of separate mission churches in the NGK on the grounds that 'language and culture, race and people are not done away with as distinguishing elements, but have, inter alia, led to the establishment of independent indigenous churches'. On the issue of justice, the memorandum declared the church should express itself against 'every form of injustice irrespective of by whom or to whom it is perpetrated'. It also criticised the selective morality of the CPSA and other English-speaking churches: 'Good examples of such different criteria are to be found in the immediate reactions of church leaders and organisations to the disturbances in South Africa, compared with their silence or mild protests with regard to the shocking events in the Congo.' In reference to the Sharpeville crisis it stated that 'uncritical acceptance or approval of the historical situation by some members of the Afrikaans churches, as well as the negative and unscriptural actions of certain Anglican bishops during the recent crisis, must be deplored'.

On the issue of black political rights the tone of the memorandum was paternalistic and even racist. 'The church is also called upon to warn both its members and the community against rash concessions to communities who are not yet ripe for acceptance of the responsibility of government. Present events in Africa must serve as a serious warning to all persons and groups who so easily advocate conferring full rights and privileges on communities who are not yet ripe for democratic responsibilities.'[19]

The Cottesloe consultation has been described as 'a compromise that failed'.[20] For a whole week, eighty South African delegates, one observer from the Christian Council and six representatives of the World Council of Churches gathered to discuss the pressing problems facing South Africa and the churches. The prepared memoranda, which were to remain confidential, were intended to form the basis of discussion but not limit it.

Each day started with morning worship, whereafter the representatives broke into their four groups for an hour of Bible study and discussion of the agenda questions. Discussions were also held in joint plenary session when report-backs were given. No provision had been made in advance for the consultation to produce a statement, and the consultation was strictly closed to the press and public. Many participants later testified to the feeling of fellowship which developed among the majority of the delegates. This mood was summed up in the World Council of Churches report on the consultation: 'The unity which arose among the members of the Consultation was noteworthy. In part, this was owing to the fact that all present had a full opportunity – even repeatedly – to express themselves, whether in the discussion groups or in plenary session or both. . . . There was no sense that people were holding back. But the growth of unity cannot be explained wholly or even mainly in these terms. The unity within the Consultation was too profound to be described other than as the gift of God by His Spirit.'[21]

Beyers, although he kept a low profile at the conference, was also excited by the spirit of brotherhood that developed at Cottesloe, and by the positive effect this had on the leading NGK delegates. For Beyers and many other white churchmen it was the first time they had ever lived with people of other races. They were moved by the sincerity and earnestness of black churchmen who spoke not of lofty theological principles, but of the pain and suffering which racial discrimination caused. They were impressed, too, by the theological incisiveness demonstrated by the overseas delegates. According to Beyers, no thinking NGK minister would have been able to justify his views on the basis of Scripture when faced by a man like Visser 't Hooft, general secretary of the World Council of Churches, who conducted daily worship.[22]

The most important outcome of the growing spirit of unity was the 'spontaneous and widespread demand on the part of the delegates for a statement'. A drafting committee was appointed by the conference, and it began to draw up a statement based on points which the majority of delegates supported. The draft statement was discussed and amendments were proposed. Finally, the amended document was voted on, paragraph by paragraph, with an 80 per cent majority being required for acceptance of any point.

As the statement took shape, the conservative Hervormde Kerk delegates became increasingly disapproving of and opposed to what was emerging. All along they had been out of step with the mood and direction of Cottesloe. Finally the entire delegation withdrew from the proceedings and in a separate statement reaffirmed their commitment to the policy of 'separate development'. The delegation added that the statement which had been drawn up 'contains such far-reaching declarations' that it could not be supported.[23]

In its introduction, the Cottesloe statement as finally approved rejected all forms of racial discrimination, but admitted that 'divergent convictions have been expressed on the basic issues of apartheid. They range on the one hand from the judgment that it is unacceptable in principle, contrary to the Christian calling and unworkable in practice, to the conviction on the other hand that a policy of differentiation can be defended from the Christian point of view, that it provides the only realistic solution to the problems of race relations and is therefore in the best interests of the various population groups.'

Among the more important proclamations of the statement were that all races had equal rights to share in the privileges and responsibilities of their country, that no Christian could be excluded from any church on the basis of race, that there were no scriptural grounds for prohibiting mixed marriages but that 'due consideration should be given to certain factors which may make such marriages inadvisable', that the migrant labour policy was unacceptable, that the policy of job reservation for whites should be replaced with a more equitable system, that South Africans of all races had the right to own land wherever they were 'domiciled', that a policy which permanently denied such people the right to partake in government was not justifiable, and that there was no objection to direct representation of Coloured people in parliament.[24]

For the English-speaking churches, the statement was very moderate, and in fact they were accused of compromising to the extent that they had joined the 'architects of apartheid in asserting unity and equality in terms compatible with separate development'.[25] Far more significant, however, was the fact that the NGK delegates, for the first time, had come to express marked differences from government policy. The NGK delegates were aware of the risks they were taking, and much discussion took place among them on how they should proceed. Finally, it was decided that they should issue an additional, separate statement, motivating their reasons for signing the document.

This statement, written in Beyers Naudé's steady, neat handwriting, made it clear that in supporting the Cottesloe statement, the NGK was not giving up support for the government's policy of apartheid. 'We wish to confirm that . . . a policy of differentiation can be defended from the Christian point of view, that it provides the only realistic solution to the problems of race relations and is therefore in the best interests of the various population groups. We do not consider the resolutions adopted by the consultation as in principle incompatible with the above statement.'[26]

Beyers recalled the soul-searching that took place the night the NGK delegates met to decide on their final stand. 'I did not really agree with the statement which the NGK delegation drew up. My thinking went much further than that. But men like Willem Landman argued that if we did not set out our justification for accepting the Cottesloe statement we would never get it passed by our synods. They pleaded that we should not become divided amongst ourselves. When they mentioned the policy of differentiation I said, "What do you mean by differentiation?", but they said, "Don't let's go into that now." So I said I would go along with it, I would support it, just for the sake of getting it through the synods.'

Beyers also remembered the warning that was sounded by another leading Cape delegate, Dr A. J. van der Merwe, at that meeting. 'I remember he warned us . . . "You must realise that the path you are choosing will bring tremendous tension to the whole NGK; those of you who stand by it are choosing a path of suffering." '[27]

The last day of the Cottesloe consultation ended on a high and hopeful note. The spirit of Christian brotherhood which had developed was encapsulated in the reconciliation won between the NGK and the CPSA, an aspect that was largely overlooked in spite of the massive newspaper publicity which the conference attracted. For months Archbishop De Blank had kept the Cottesloe organisers in a state of alarm with his threats to pull out of the meeting, but at the end of the conference he offered a hand of friendship to the church he had so often condemned. He said: 'in the light of what we have learnt here and the information now put at our disposal, we confess with regret that in the heat of the moment we have at times spoken heatedly and, through ignorance . . . have cast doubt on the sincerity of those who did not accept the wisdom of such action. . . . Where, in the past, we have at any time unnecessarily wounded our brethren, we now ask their forgiveness in Christ.'[28] His apology was accepted by A. J. van der Merwe on behalf of the NGK.

Many commentators have pointed to Cottesloe as the Damascus in Beyers Naudé's life, when, for the first time, he saw the light. But at the end of Cottesloe, Beyers did what he had done so often before – he backed down for the sake of Afrikaner unity. In supporting the NGK's qualifying statement, including approval for a policy of 'differentiation' or apartheid, he agreed to something he knew in his heart was wrong.

The significance of Cottesloe for Beyers was that it was the last time he would allow himself to be so compromised. He committed himself to defending what had been decided by the church consultation and stood by his commitment. When the storm broke after Cottesloe, when the government, Afrikaans newspapers, the Broederbond and the rank and file of his church rejected the compromise, when the church swung against them and they were called to order, Beyers Naudé and his colleagues had to choose whether to fall in line or not.

It was the reaction to Cottesloe, far more than the event itself, that proved decisive in Beyers Naudé's life. As A. J. van der Merwe correctly had predicted, the next few months would be very hard for those who wished to remain true to Cottesloe. Beyers tried to describe that crisis. 'I felt I had been struggling for such a long time. I asked myself: "How long are you going to remain silent and fearful?" Eventually I came to the point where I said I can't continue to live this way. It is not possible. How will I live? What will I preach? . . . How do I justify this kind of duplicity? I realised I would have to live a life of hypocrisy and deviousness. I felt it was not possible. But I realised on the other hand the price one would have to pay.'

7
The Storm after Cottesloe, 1961–1962

The reaction to Cottesloe was swift and brutal. Suspicion and opposition to the conference had begun to emerge even while the deliberations were still in progress, as the result of an unfavourable report which appeared in the conservative Johannesburg newspaper, *Die Transvaler*. Much of the blame for the Cottesloe debacle has been placed on the Hervormde Kerk.[1] It was the first to break an undertaking made by all the churches not to issue further press statements. Shortly after the conference had ended, it made public a statement condemning the proceedings. This left the Afrikaner community bewildered. How was it possible that the smaller Dutch Reformed church had rejected the Cottesloe findings, while the powerful and 'loyal' NGK had sided with the English-speaking churches? The nuances of the conference, and the NGK delegation's own qualifying statement, were largely ignored in the outcry that followed Cottesloe.

Afrikaans newspapers, with the exception of the Cape Town-based *Die Burger*, took an extremely negative view of proceedings, while the enthusiastic support for Cottesloe among the English newspapers only served to confirm Afrikaners' fears that the NGK delegates had been infected by the 'liberalism' of the World Council of Churches and the English-language churches.[2] The issue dominated the Afrikaans media for weeks, with politicians, newspaper editors and churchmen all questioning or condemning the conference. Moreover, a statement issued by the Transvaal moderature defending their delegation's position and reiterating support for the policy of 'differentiation' failed to calm NGK adherents. They had reason to doubt the moderature since three out of its four members had been present at Cottesloe.[3]

Beyers entered the debate in an article he wrote for the Sunday newspaper, *Dagbreek en Sondagnuus*. Although he worded it cautiously and stressed that the findings were not the official view of the NGK a clear message came across: he was calling on Afrikaans Christians to take the message of Cottesloe very seriously and to rethink their attitude to race issues. He wrote: 'If the report of the study contains or implies criticism of the policy of the government, it stemmed from the formulation of scriptural principle, and is in no way meant as an attack or as uncharitable criticism.' But he warned: 'The discussion and the findings place every one of our Afrikaans churches at the crossroads: either to accept or reject the principles of the Bible which have been formulated. Every church now feels the urgent need to state its standpoint clearly and unequivocally and to motivate it on the basis of God's Word.'

Anticipating that the Afrikaans churches could come to a different conclusion than that reached at Cottesloe, he said: 'It is not enough to talk of traditional concepts and historical viewpoints: the truth of the Bible holds sway as the highest norm and as the last word for the Church of Christ because we believe that only in the truth can the life and the welfare of our nation and of every other nation be found. For this reason the church may not remain silent.'[4]

If Beyers had hoped to head off the backlash against the Cottesloe findings he was mistaken. Writing in the same newspaper a month later, a leading Afrikaner nationalist attacked Beyers and repeated the accusation that the Archbishop of Cape Town and the World Council of Churches had manipulated the NGK delegates.[5]

The fate of Cottesloe was finally sealed by two powerful forces acting in concert, Prime Minister Hendrik Verwoerd and the Afrikaner Broederbond. Verwoerd was well aware that the NGK delegates to Cottesloe had represented the cream of the church leadership and that they had the potential to sway many Afrikaners. It was necessary to cut them down to size and this is what he achieved in his New Year's message delivered in 1961. Cottesloe, he declared, had been an attempt by outsiders to interfere in South Africa's internal affairs. The Cottesloe statement had not yet received the support of the NGK, but only of a few individuals in the church who had attended the consultation. The NGK synods would have the final say on the matter. Verwoerd's message was clear: the NGK should reject Cottesloe and support the policies of the National Party.[6]

The Broederbond paid heed. It sent out a special circular informing members that the executive council of the organisation had rejected the Cottesloe decisions at a special meeting held in Pretoria. The circular reminded members of Verwoerd's warning and said it wished to 'prevent any serious detrimental effects on our nation as a result of this conference'.[7]

Beyers, who was chairman of the Broederbond cell in his area, was deeply upset by this interference. 'It created a very serious crisis of conscience on the whole question of ultimate loyalty and ultimate disobedience. The authority of Scripture and the demands of the gospel were in conflict with my own nation and their political aspirations. . . . Although not the final straw, unconsciously I was at the point where I said, "If this is what the Broederbond can do, then it has become a very dangerous influence in my life."'

As preparations were being made for the four provincial synods to be held later in the year, opposition to Cottesloe mounted. Letters flooded in to the secular and theological newspapers, protesting against the findings. Beyers and his colleagues were shocked to hear that protest meetings were being called in various towns. On 24 January 1961, a crowd of about 1 500 angry Afrikaners packed into the Silverton town hall, close to Pretoria, to attend a meeting organised by a cultural organisation, the *Afrikanerkring*. Speakers representing the three Afrikaans Reformed churches strongly condemned the Cottesloe statement and those present unanimously supported a motion to that effect.[8] A similar meeting was held in Brits, addressed by a former Cottesloe delegate, A.B. du Preez, who had 'seen the light', and Koot Vorster, future moderator and brother of B. J. Vorster.[9]

The mass meetings were followed by numerous church council meetings, where leading members called on their church to withdraw from the WCC. Beyers's own congregation took a stand against the consultation. In February 1961 the Aasvoëlkop church adopted a resolution stating that the issue had caused tremendous division in the NGK generally and in the community in particular, and recommended that at the coming synod the NGK in the Transvaal withdraw from the World Council of Churches. The concluding statement revealed the confusion of members, who were still very fond of their minister even though they disagreed with his views. It said: 'We express our deep thanks to our minister for his example of Christianity, integrity and sincerity.'

The church council's decision, and Beyers's own cautious comments on the issue, were published in the church's monthly newsletter in March 1961. He wrote: 'Judgment of the findings of the church conference can only be based on . . . the Word of God. Theological pronouncements demand theological reflection, and if this is considered from any other angle, the truth becomes blurred. For that reason we are convinced that the [Cottesloe] findings can only be assessed in terms of the Bible – and as such deserve serious reflection.'[10]

The leadership of the NGK in the Free State and Natal churches, neither of which were members of the World Council, had also come out against the Cottesloe statement, and in March the Federal Council of the NGK likewise rejected the findings. Conservative influences in the Transvaal and the Cape were clearly holding sway in the build-up to the synods, and the 'Cottesloe men' realised it was inevitable the Cape and Transvaal synods would vote to leave the World Council. Cape delegate A. J. van Wijk voiced his concerns in a letter to Bilheimer: 'The possibility that the Transvaal church may decide to leave the World Council, that they may repudiate the decisions of Cottesloe, and that some of the leaders who attended the Consultation – men like Bey Naudé – may lose their position of leadership, must be regarded as fairly strong.'[11]

Predictably, the Hervormde Kerk had voted at a synod in March to leave the WCC – a decision which received widespread publicity.

A month before the Transvaal synod met, the General Synodical Commission of the Transvaal NGK appointed an '*ad hoc* committee' to study the merits of the Cottesloe statement and to determine whether the church should stay part of the World Council. The committee was dominated by men opposed to Cottesloe and it became clear that the findings would not receive a fair hearing at the synod. When the synod met, it first considered the recommendations and findings of the committee; a report compiled by the Cottesloe delegates and submitted to the committee was merely available for information. The committee found that in some respects the Cottesloe findings intruded into areas on which only the synod was empowered to speak. Among its many objections, the *ad hoc* committee remarked that at the start of Cottesloe the intention had not been to issue and vote on a statement: as a result of the change in procedures, black church delegates had actually represented and voted on behalf of the NGK. The committee also found that while the Cottesloe delegates might have believed the policy of 'differentiation' was not incompatible with its findings, some of the Cottesloe statement did indeed conflict with the policy of apartheid.[12]

When the Transvaal synod met on 5 April 1961 the tone of the synod was set immediately by elections to the moderature. Moderator and Cottesloe delegate A. M. Meiring clung to his position by a narrow margin of only nine votes, while Beyers and his brother-in-law Frans O' Brien Geldenhuys were both, in Beyers's own words, 'kicked out'. Using the *ad hoc* committee report as a basis, the synod discussed the Cottesloe deliberations for two and a half days, with speaker after speaker condemning the findings.

When discussions ended on 10 April 1961 the Cottesloe delegates were asked to sit like accused men in the front of the hall, and were given an opportunity to speak. While most still supported the spirit of the findings, some began to retreat. Beyers thought long and hard about what he should say. 'For me it was a turning point in my life, because the night before the final decision was made at the synod, I had to decide – would I because of pressure, political pressure and other pressures which were being exercised, give in and accept, or would I stand by my convictions which over a period of years had become rooted in me as firm and holy Christian convictions? I decided on the latter course . . . I could not see my way clear to giving way on a single one of those resolutions, because I was convinced that they were in accordance with the truth of the gospel.'[13]

The first Cottesloe delegate to renege on the findings was A. B. du Preez, who had been active in whipping up opposition in the weeks prior to the synod. When it was his turn to speak, he implied that the Cottesloe findings were the responsibility of the Cape and not the Transvaal NGK, and told the synod he did not believe it could support any of the Cottesloe decisions. Altogether six Cottesloe delegates addressed the synod and were heard in 'dead silence'.[14] Most defended the findings in apologetic tones. In his address to the synod, Beyers said he was prepared to admit the possibility that the Cottesloe delegates had made errors with regard to procedure, but added that he would accept changes to Cottesloe only if these were based on the Scriptures. In an attempt to appease the conservatives he argued that the delegates had never agreed to voting and land-ownership rights for all 'non-whites', but submitted that if complete segregation was impractical they were entitled to something. 'I will admit if I am wrong, but what is the alternative?' he asked.[15]

Finally the synod voted to reject all the Cottesloe findings, claiming that these should first have been debated by the church. The synod also reaffirmed its support for what it called the policy of 'differentiation'. It resolved further, without allowing any debate, to withdraw the Transvaal NGK from the WCC.[16] Six months later, the Cape synod considered the Cottesloe findings and was, on the whole, less hostile to them. Some of the findings were accepted, some were rejected, and a study commission was appointed to investigate the issue further. But the synod followed the Transvaal NGK by voting to leave the WCC.

Beyers was dismayed but not really surprised by the outcome of the Transvaal synod: 'The debate at the synod was not really a theological debate . . . the theological and biblical aspects receded far into the background and the political issues clearly decided the stand of the church.'[17] He went back to his church in Aasvoëlkop uncertain of the future, although he realised he was headed for conflict with the conservative majority in the NGK, the National Party and the Broederbond. At that stage Beyers had still not considered leaving the church. He was deeply involved in his pastoral work; the church-building programme was progressing well and the new parsonage in Northcliff had just been completed.

Beyers sensed a deep confusion among many members of his congregation. 'There was a seed of doubt about whether they could really trust my leadership. I considered very carefully what kind of ministry I should present and I deliberately refrained from raising any controversial theological issues which could be seen to be "too political", not because I didn't want to preach about it, but because I felt it was important to play a pastoral role of trying to help our people to realise the deep implications of the gospel. In my private discussions with members of the congregation, I tried to promote this in the form of Bible studies and discussions.'[18]

Before Cottesloe, the inter-church Bible study sessions had been progressing steadily. Groups were meeting at several places on the Witwatersrand and in Pretoria. After the synod, when a notice was sent out to all participating churchmen to attend the next study session, the response was devastating. Two-thirds of the NGK ministers, referring to the decision taken at synod, answered they were no longer prepared to consider an alternative race policy based on a study of the Bible. Beyers noted: 'I had to simply accept that the power of the synod, the political pressure, the newspapers, the radio and the Broederbond were so overwhelming that it would be impossible to bring the church to another view for the next five or eight or ten years. But the one-third that remained did meet to discuss this and to ask: Where do we go from here? We decided to go quietly on. We realised we were a small group, that we could create problems, but we felt we had a responsibility to help the church. . . . And so we went on, but in a very quiet way, with the study groups that survived.'[19]

The Afrikaner establishment's furious response to Cottesloe shocked the WCC and particularly Bob Bilheimer who had invested so much time and energy in the project. In September 1961 he returned to South Africa for a three-week visit, much to the disgust of leading members of both the Hervormde Kerk and the NGK. He had been invited by A. J. van Wijk, minister of the NGK 'mother church' in Stellenbosch, to address theological students at the Seminary, but because of the negative reaction from the NGK establishment and a critical editorial in *Die Kerkbode*, the meeting had to be cancelled. In his report on the visit, Bilheimer remarked on the fear in church circles about being associated with the 'Cottesloe men'. 'Rev Attie van Wijk had me stay in his home, invited faculty and DRC ministers of Stellenbosch, but only a few came, and no ministers because they were afraid to be in association with me.' Bilheimer also met with some NGK ministers in Durban, 'but only on condition that no one, especially the press, would know of it'.

Referring to the 'Cottesloe men', Bilheimer wrote: 'The DRC group are magnificent. Of the 20 delegates . . . some have defected, some are hesitant, and about a dozen are fighting hard. These are men who show forth the joy of a new obedience. Their faces are alight, their spirits are buoyant. I have no hesitation in saying that this little group of DRC men is engaged in one of the most decisive struggles of the Spirit and the Church that we are privileged to witness. Their verdict is: We shall lose a battle or two, but we shall not lose the war.'[20]

Bilheimer also made contact with Beyers Naudé and Fred van Wyk, and the media came out in force when Beyers arranged for Bilheimer to address the Rand Ecumenical Study Circle in Johannesburg, the surviving Bible study group in Johannesburg. Afterwards Bilheimer met privately with some of the Cottesloe men, including some from the English-speaking churches. Among those present were Beyers and Frans O'Brien Geldenhuys, for whom such a meeting meant considerable risk. Bilheimer told the ministers that he was convinced it was necessary for people in the churches to make contact with one another because they were trapped in isolation. 'It is also of crucial importance for people across the colour line to get to know and trust each other, as happened at Cottesloe, because without that trust there is no hope.'[21]

The ideas outlined by Bilheimer corresponded with the thinking of Beyers and some of his colleagues. By 1962 the small group who still supported the Bible study sessions felt the time was ripe to launch an independent Afrikaans theological journal to stimulate theological debate about racial and political issues in South Africa, and to promote the ideal of Christian unity. Beyers explained the origins of the journal: 'After Cottesloe I was deeply concerned about the violation of the gospel by the church. . . . I saw clearly that the only hope, if there was any hope to change the NGK, was to confront it with the truth of the gospel. I discussed this with some of the ministers who had participated in the Bible study groups and also with Albert Geyser, Willie Jonker, Gert Swart and some lay members of the NGK and Gereformeerde Kerk. Out of that grew the general conviction that we needed to have a theological journal of some kind.'

They decided to name the new monthly journal *Pro Veritate*, 'For the Truth'. Beyers did not want to become editor because he felt his theological education was not up to scratch. 'But none of the others were willing to undertake the task. Perhaps they were afraid of the risk involved. I was stupid enough to take that risk, perhaps knowing better than most of them the possible implications and consequences. Perhaps there was also some form of bravado in it, or personal ego, one never knows fully. But I decided to take it on. . . .

'One of our biggest problems was how we would finance *Pro Veritate*. We didn't want to use any money from overseas, because this would make it suspect, so eventually a number of us simply decided to make our own contributions. Fred van Wyk also played a significant role in assisting us in finding us the finance for the first year. When we started the paper, we had enough money for four issues, and nothing more.' And so, working from Beyers Naudé's parsonage in Aasvoëlkop, they prepared the first edition of *Pro Veritate*. None of them had any professional writing or editing skills, but they relied on their faith and determination to get the first few issues out.

The initial issue appeared on 15 May 1962 and was sent to NGK ministers countrywide free of charge, with appeals to them to subscribe to the new journal. The front-page lead story set the tone for the coming years. Written in Afrikaans from a Reformed viewpoint, it demolished biblical justification of apartheid by citing biblical texts which emphasised the unity of the Christian church.

In his first editorial Beyers highlighted the need for cooperation between Christians and churches in South Africa and for a more serious and intensive study of the Bible to find answers to troubling questions. Recalling the spirit of Cottesloe and referring implicitly to the Afrikaner churches, he wrote: 'Churches can no longer operate in isolation . . . and hope to challenge worldwide movements like communism, Islam and secularism. Churches which do not want to work with others in areas where a united witness is essential are weakening their own witness and are inadvertently strengthening the forces of evil.'[22]

Reaction to *Pro Veritate* in Afrikaner church circles was not unexpected. Members of the Aasvoëlkop church council asked Beyers to withdraw from the journal. In neighbouring Linden, the Reverend D. Beukes introduced a motion to that effect in the local church circuit. Beyers was also approached by individual members of the Broederbond who expressed serious reservations about *Pro Veritate*'s 'onslaught' on apartheid. Beyers would not hear of withdrawing however, and *Pro Veritate*, despite its precarious financial position, continued to appear once a month. The promoters had hoped to draw in about 400 NGK ministers throughout the country – the number they believed were sympathetic to the ideas of Cottesloe. The ability of the Broederbond and the Afrikaner establishment to force members of the *volk* into line was clearly demonstrated in the smear campaign that came to be waged against *Pro Veritate*. Critical items began appearing in *Die Kerkbode*. The secular Afrikaans press also showed extreme hostility to the initiative.

In a report to Bob Bilheimer about developments in the church, Beyers's friend Fred van Wyk wrote: 'Our ecumenical newspaper, *Pro Veritate*, is doing amazingly well with Beyers as final editor, and pressure is being exerted on Beyers by many of his DRC friends not to risk forfeiting his status as DRC minister by undertaking any other ecumenical work.'[23]

Confusion and unhappiness over Beyers's role in the ecumenical movement grew steadily in the Aasvoëlkop parish. At one level his congregation were very happy with their minister. His sermons were in the best evangelical tradition of the NGK and he had been the driving force in raising funds for the new church and hall, the foundation stone of which had been laid in February 1962. Beyers still undertook a great deal of pastoral visiting and counselling and lent a sympathetic ear to the problems of his flock. However, he would not abandon the 'extra-curricular' work which was causing such a stir. The allegations that *Pro Veritate* was an enemy of the NGK soon stuck to the person of Beyers Naudé.

In an attempt to clear the confusion Beyers decided to depart from his non-political approach in the pulpit and to state his views plainly. Preaching in the Emmarentia school hall on Sunday morning, 27 May 1962, Beyers told his congregation: 'For quite a while the claim has been doing the rounds in church circles that certain of us ministers, including myself, are half-secretly proclaiming ideas with regard to race relations, but that we are too frightened to speak of these issues in our own congregations. . . . You would have noticed that since last year's synod I have deliberately not referred to these issues in my sermons. This silence has been incorrectly interpreted by some people to indicate that I do not have the courage to speak of these convictions openly because I could not justify these ideas in the Scriptures. . . .

'Because I don't want a single one of you to be unsure of what I believe, I want to now spell out the following. . . . I believe that the Bible is the only true Word of God. . . . Every believer must accept and be obedient to the authority of the Word, as the authority which is higher than any human authority. . . .

'Nobody can be excluded from the Church of Christ on grounds of race or colour. . . . I am not saying for a moment that the church only exists when people of all races worship together . . . history has shown time and time again that God wills rich diversity . . . But to try to forbid mixed worship is against the Word of God. . . .

'All people are called to love one another . . . the outcome of this love is that I should allow other people to have the same rights and opportunities as my group demand. . . .

'Truth and justice is renewed in the church, and a nation is strengthened . . . only when people search for the truth and justice which is the will of God. Therefore, all laws which hinder love and justice between people are against the will of God. . . .

'I do not regard these issues that I've raised as being political ones, but I speak of them as deep Christian convictions which have grown in me over a long period and which are the basis of a serious study of the Word of God. I am not saying these things to bring the government into disrepute, to intimidate any group or to indoctrinate you. . . . I am also not saying this to give support to the enemies of our church. No! There is just one motive, one goal in me: to proclaim nothing other than Jesus Christ, Jesus Christ who was crucified."[24]

The address served to antagonise and anger the conservative element in Beyers's church further. At the June council meeting a formal complaint was lodged against the sermon. One of the leading voices against Beyers at that meeting was Jannie Kruger, former editor of *Die Transvaler*. Beyers was not without support, however, and some of his friends spoke up on his behalf. After a long debate, the motion was put to the vote and defeated by a two-thirds majority.[25]

Though relieved at the outcome, Beyers was shocked by the strong feelings that had been shown. 'I realised I was up against unconscious and conscious ideological imprisonment on the part of the Afrikaner people which made it impossible for them to discern and understand the truth. As this awareness grew it created tremendous agony within me. I knew it would be absolutely impossible to bring about the fundamental change to the NGK, unless a number of individuals were prepared to go out on their own, to be the voice of prophecy and to challenge the church and prepare the way for the renewal.'

As the events in Beyers's church were being repeated in NGK circles everywhere, the small group of anti-apartheid Afrikaner ministers began to give serious thought to the establishment of an independent ecumenical organisation. The aim was to present Afrikaners with alternatives to apartheid theology and to unite Christian witness, especially on race issues, in South Africa. Prominent figures in those early days included Beyers Naudé, Hervormde Kerk theologian Albert Geyser, Fred van Wyk and Dr Jan Schutte, a leading minister from the Gereformeerde Kerk.

Members of the Broederbond continued trying to dissuade Beyers from his course of action. On several occasions he had received hints that he was destined for high office in the church if he kept out of controversial issues. He had also been warned that he would be placing his career in jeopardy if he persisted in challenging the status quo. His loss of position on the Transvaal moderature was proof of this. In the closing months of 1962 Beyers cast around for support from prominent NGK theologians. He knew many people were sympathetic to his stand and that the bulk of the 'Cottesloe men' still privately supported his views. However, they were not prepared to take the drastic step of entering into open confrontation with the government and Afrikaner establishment. The memory of the Cottesloe furore was still fresh and many felt it was preferable to work for change quietly, from the inside, and not to jeopardise their positions.

In the search for support for the proposed ecumenical body Beyers wrote a carefully worded letter in August 1962 to two former 'Cottesloe men' in the Cape, Willem Landman and A. J. van Wijk. He said: 'you will remember that the possibility of full-time ecumenical work was raised for the first time in August 1961 when Bob Bilheimer visited South Africa. . . . You will also remember that the reason for creating such a mobile Christian institute (preferably with the head office in Johannesburg) was among others, to organise and initiate courses, conferences, Bible study weeks and discussions . . . for different church groups and Christians on issues which affect the church in Southern Africa. A further goal would be the creation and building of ecumenical study groups in various centres, the distribution of factual information on the ecumenical movement, and to help Fred van Wyk with his ecumenical activities. . . .

'As for my own position, I want to make it clear that I am not looking for any other work than what I am presently doing. It is going well in the congregation. . . . The point is simply that I can't go on for much longer with all my congregational work and carry out all the other activities as I am doing at present – in any case not for longer than the end of this year. If we are convinced that the work of Christ can be done from within but also from outside the NGK, then I am prepared to make myself available for such work. Preferably, I would like to retain my status [as minister], but if that is not possible, then I would be prepared to lose that status after all possible channels to retain it are exhausted.'[26]

Many of the people Beyers approached at that time backed down and later kept their distance from the Christian Institute. Beyers said: 'I was deeply disappointed but I did not condemn them. I realised then that we were up against a situation of such intransigence that it would take many, many years before we would be able to move this massive body called the NG Kerk.'

One event which helped Beyers make up his mind about his future was the first national synod of the NGK in Cape Town in October 1962, which united the four white provincial churches. He had been told by some of his Broederbond friends to be patient and await the outcome of the synod. They assured him that the Cottesloe findings might get a more positive hearing from this body. Beyers, who was not elected as a delegate to the synod, doubted this assurance and he was proved correct – the synod avoided any reference to Cottesloe.

Even before the national synod was held, Beyers, Fred van Wyk, Albert Geyser and some other colleagues began making preparations for the launch of the Christian Institute. In the closing months of 1962 several meetings were held among ministers and laypersons in Johannesburg to discuss the Institute's formation. On 1 November 1962 about 200 people met at the Central Methodist Church in Johannesburg, where Beyers hoped the Institute would be launched. But the meeting, chaired by the Reverend J. B. Webb of the Methodist Church, did not go according to plan. The views of mainly Afrikaner laymen and clergy, who were afraid of an open clash with the NGK and who claimed that the time was not right for the launch of the CI, prevailed. They warned that the Afrikaans churches, through their synods, could make it impossible for their members to participate. One of the strongest arguments against formation of the Institute was that the Southern and Northern Transvaal synods of the NGK were due to meet in April 1963, and it was suggested that the CI's establishment be delayed until after this date to escape condemnation at the synods. [27]

Beyers was disappointed with the outcome of the meeting. A provisional committee including both Fred van Wyk and Beyers was appointed by the meeting to consider the objections, and it finally decided to go ahead with the establishment of the CI. Even before the CI was formally constituted, however, the provisional committee had opened an office in Dunwell House, Braamfontein, and employed a secretary to assist with this work.[28] As 1962 drew to a close Beyers felt determined not to allow further objections and opposition to hold up the creation of the new organisation which he felt was vital to the churches in South Africa.

8

Leaving the Fold:
The Christian Institute Established,
1963

In the heyday of apartheid, the Afrikaner nation was often described as monolithic and unchangeable – fanatically committed to maintaining power through racial separation. Perhaps this was an exaggeration, but Beyers knew of no other people who were so closely knit and so rigidly controlled. 'An ordinary Afrikaans child is born in a very conservative, deeply religious Afrikaner home. His parents have their set of religious, political, moral and social values. The child attends an Afrikaans school where the vast majority of the teachers are *verkramp* or very, very conservative.

'Even before he goes to school, the child moves into an Afrikaner church, normally a conservative, Afrikaans-speaking community where the minister preaches the gospel according to Hendrik Verwoerd or John Vorster or whoever is there at the time. So his thinking, up to the time he leaves school, is indoctrinated in every respect. . . . If the child is privileged enough to go to university, there is a 95 per cent chance he will go to an Afrikaans university. There, at least, there is a little stretching of the mind, but the majority would not be influenced to such a degree that they would be prepared to make that break.

'After the person's return from university, he moves directly into a privileged Afrikaans community, as teacher or a businessman. A few may deviate, fall in love with an English-speaker perhaps, but that is the exception. The others who don't go to university, the vast majority, find their employment in some form of Afrikaner community or government institution. So where is the opportunity to break through this whole thinking? It is such a close-knit community. The bond is strengthened by the father, the Broederbond, the church, the teachers.'

It was all the more remarkable therefore that in 1963 Beyers Naudé sought to lead a group of Afrikaners out of the laager to join other Christians in challenging apartheid. In doing so Beyers betrayed the Broederbond – an unforgivable crime for many Afrikaners and one which would forever damn the Christian Institute in their eyes.

Although he had rarely discussed church and Broederbond concerns with his wife, Beyers began sharing his growing anxiety about the secret organisation. Ilse remarked: 'Often we would go for walks and Bey would say, "I can't stay in the Broederbond any longer." And I would say, "Well then, why don't you resign?" And he would tell me that I did not know the Afrikaner, that they would never forgive him. And I would say, "Well, it's up to you, if you want to go on living like this." Of course, from the day he resigned, he did have problems.'[1]

Beyers finally took the step of resigning from the secret organisation in 1963 – at about the same time that damaging exposés about the Broederbond began appearing in the *Sunday Times*. The reports, based on information leaked from the Broederbond, revealed that the organisation had launched a campaign against 'liberal' tendencies in the Afrikaner churches.

Shortly after this the NGK began preparing for its Southern Transvaal synod in Pretoria. Beyers knew that his editorship of *Pro Veritate* would be raised at the gathering but, with his letter of resignation in the hands of the Broederbond executive, he felt he could face his colleagues without fear. However, what followed on the first day of that synod, on 26 March 1963, came as one of the biggest shocks of his life – he was elected to the very highest office, as moderator of the synod. Another surprise was the election of his friend Dr Willie Jonker as actuary. Beyers was a little taken aback when, at the start of the synod, his name was proposed as one of the three candidates for moderator. He thought he stood no chance in the secret ballot but the results of the first round of the election showed that A. J. V. Burger received 63 votes, H. J. C. Snijders 64 and C. F. B. Naudé obtained 163 votes. A second round of voting for the candidates with the two highest scores took place and the result was: H. J. C. Snijders 167 votes and C. F. B. Naudé 209 votes.[2]

Beyers Naudé was declared the new moderator of the synod and asked to take the chair. 'I was totally dumbstruck. . . . I never expected it. I hadn't prepared myself. The chairman of the synod naturally has to do far more preparation than the ordinary delegates. And so at the end of that first day, I went home and had to go through all the reports. I worked until about 4 in the morning preparing myself for the proceedings, and that happened practically every night. . . .

'I remember that synod so well. I knew that I would be watched with hawk's eyes by people waiting for me to put a foot wrong. . . . I knew that my only safeguard was to be straight down the line so that nobody could point a finger and say that I was manipulating the meeting. . . . I think that created, perhaps, a sense of trust on the part of the people, even among those who were initially very suspicious. They felt that regardless of what my opinions were, in this regard they could trust my impartiality.'

Many people who attended the synod were impressed with the neutrality and calmness that Beyers had displayed and the smooth way that it had been run.[3] Beyers was nevertheless uncertain of himself as the synod unfolded over the next fourteen days. He still could not understand how, in the light of his involvement with *Pro Veritate*, he had been chosen as moderator. He had to proceed particularly carefully with regard to two motions on the agenda, from two separate church councils, calling for an investigation into membership of the Broederbond. It was a reflection of a rather surprising development: a certain resentment had surfaced among some Afrikaners towards the Broederbond because of the feeling that special positions in church and society were often reserved for Broederbond members.

The synod decided to appoint a special committee under the chairmanship of Dr A. C. Barnard to study the two controversial resolutions. The unexpected recommendation of this commission was that the Broederbond should be investigated. When the issue came up for debate at the synod the recommendation was strongly opposed by the Reverend D. Beukes, the minister in Linden. Beukes, who later went on to become moderator of the general synod of the NGK, was a leading Broeder and member of the executive committee. He declared that such an investigation would only divide Afrikaners. In a highly unusual move Beukes issued an official Broederbond statement at the synod which defended the organisation and claimed it was working in the interests of the Afrikaner and his church. Beukes insisted that any new investigation into the Broederbond would only cause friction and he defended its code of secrecy as a 'practical' method of operation. When the issue was put to the vote, the Broederbond's strong influence became clearly evident – the motion to launch an investigation was defeated and the synod reaffirmed a previous finding that the organisation was 'wholesome and healthy, merely seeking the progress and best interests of the Afrikaner nation.'

The debate on the Broederbond had taken place on the second last day of the synod, 9 April. On the same day, a report was tabled which dealt in hostile terms with *Pro Veritate*. It was the moment Beyers had been expecting and dreading. Proposed by the minister from the Farrarmere congregation, the motion accepted the principle of free-thinking theological magazines but called on ministers of the NGK not to participate in the 'dangerous' business of *Pro Veritate* because it could lead to 'turmoil and a split in the church'. Beyers stepped down from the chair during the debate and had to listen as numerous speakers voiced their opposition to criticism from outside the church. Finally the synod passed a motion which stated: 'Owing to the tension and divisions which this newspaper has caused, and because of the dangers it poses to the unity of the church, the synod calls on members and officebearers not to participate in the *Pro Veritate* efforts and asks them to support our own church newspaper.' In another reference to *Pro Veritate*, a motion was accepted exhorting members to abide by decisions of the synod and not to criticise these publicly.[4] It was clear that the Broederbond's campaign to put a stop to public criticism in church circles of the policy of apartheid was gaining ground.

Beyers believed that the motion on *Pro Veritate* was the Afrikaner establishment's way of telling him that he still had a big future – provided he abandoned his challenge to apartheid. It was his moment of truth. 'It was tempting, but for me the decision was clearly taken. I remembered how many people had withdrawn from the issue after Cottesloe and I knew there was not the least possibility that there would be enough ministers willing to take a stand in public. I knew that – I had no doubt in my mind. I was open to conviction if there was any real, valid indication that this would not be the case. I remained open to it, but I think, rationally and emotionally, knowing the Afrikaner people, and especially realising what had happened since Cottesloe, I realised it simply would not happen.' On the last day of the synod Beyers was called on to state whether he would resign from *Pro Veritate*. He asked the synod for time to consider the request and promised to supply the answer within a few weeks.

In addition to all these pressures, Beyers was still having to manage his usual church work. The congregation was expanding rapidly and for a few months in 1963 he was assisted by a temporary minister. It was clear that a second, permanent post would soon have to be created. In his monthly church newsletters Beyers avoided all reference to the controversies surrounding him. To read those newsletters, with their talk of the building fund, deaths, marriages and births, church fêtes and youth camps, and poor Sunday school attendance, it is hard to believe that this was the same minister who in the powerful position of moderator of the Southern Transvaal synod, was moving into open confrontation with the church leadership and the government.[5]

Beyers's election as moderator had surprised most of his close friends, including Fred van Wyk, who had been spending a great deal of time on arranging the launch of the Christian Institute. A few days after the election he wrote to Beyers to inform him of the latest developments with regard to the CI: 'The fact that both you and Dr Jonker are . . . on the moderature is not only a miracle, but one that demands that we rethink our position. . . . I am hoping to write a short letter to Bob Bilheimer to tell him that he must accept that we will do the best we can given the changed circumstances.'[6]

Fred van Wyk may have been having second thoughts but Beyers was determined to push ahead with *Pro Veritate* and the establishment of the Christian Institute. It seemed inevitable that he might lose his position as a minister in the church. In a letter to Fred van Wyk written in April 1963, Beyers discussed the various tactics that were being employed by the small group of ministers opposed to the decision of the Southern Transvaal synod. The aim was to voice their opposition to the clamp on external criticism of the NGK in as many newspapers as possible, and also to promote *Pro Veritate*. He wrote: 'Don't be afraid that I might resign – we must go forward! Can you arrange . . . for small advertisements to be placed in the *Transvaler, Vaderland, Dagbreek, Burger, Mail, Star* and *Times*: "Subscribe to *Pro Veritate* – the Christian monthly newspaper on actuality affairs. Africa R2. Overseas R2,50. P.O. Box 487, Johannesburg." '[7]

Beyers's first major obligation as the new moderator was to attend the All Africa Conference of Churches in Kampala, Uganda, in April 1963, in which about 350 representatives from forty African countries participated. This was Beyers's first exposure to a church conference in Africa beyond the borders of the white republic. It was still the age of innocence as far as South Africa was concerned; the marked hostility to the race policies of the South African government and the churches which supported it, that would dominate so many church meetings around the world in the years to come, was absent from this meeting. Rather, it was this unknown Afrikaner churchman who took some people by surprise – there was some disbelief when the conservative-looking *dominee* spoke sympathetically about the spirit of *uhuru* that was sweeping over post-colonial Africa.[8]

On his return to South Africa early in May 1963 pressure continued to mount on him to make his decision known on the editorship of *Pro Veritate*. He was by now a well-known media figure, and numerous reports speculating about the matter appeared in the English and Afrikaans press. In an editorial in *Pro Veritate*, on 15 May 1963, Beyers announced that he would not resign as editor. To resign, he said, would create the impression that 'here is a minister who is willing to sacrifice or give up his deep convictions for the sake of an important position of trust which his synod has conferred on him'. *Pro Veritate* would be willing to cease publication only if the NGK joined hands with the other Protestant churches in South Africa and created a broad, ecumenical journal.[9]

Moves to launch the CI were gaining momentum at this time. Several meetings of the provisional committee to establish the Christian Institute were arranged by Fred van Wyk and Beyers, and it was agreed that the two men would be entrusted with writing the first draft constitution. Finally, at a meeting on 13 June 1963, the formal decision was taken to establish the Christian Institute.

An inter-denominational sub-committee was appointed to consider the draft constitution and a sixteen-member provisional board of management was elected, made up of leading figures in the English-speaking churches, as well as several prominent Afrikaners, including Albert Geyser, Fred van Wyk, A. J. van Wijk from Stellenbosch and Beyers Naudé. There were only two black members of the board. In July, invitations were sent out to all interested parties to attend the launch of the Christian Institute at the Methodist church in Johannesburg the following month.[10]

On 15 August, about 180 people gathered at the church under the chairmanship of Dr J. B. Webb to launch the Christian Institute of Southern Africa. According to the constitution which was adopted, the aim of the Institute was to serve the church of Christ in every possible way. It was to be based on the Word of God and on the conviction that it was desirable and necessary to foster Christian unity. Membership was open to any Christian and was not intended to 'detract from the loyalty of any member to his own Church or creed'. The functions of the Christian Institute were to search for a deeper insight into the will of Christ for his church through study circles and discussion groups and to strengthen the witness of the church by holding courses and conferences. Other functions were to distribute publications, serve bodies which complemented the CI, and 'render any other services which the Institute may be called to perform in the name of Christ'.

The CI was to be controlled by a board of management and a chairman would be elected annually. The CI also set up an executive committee, and a board of trustees to oversee finances. Annual subscription fees for the first year were set at 50c a member.[11]

Pro Veritate was to remain a separate entity, not formally connected to the CI. But for all practical purposes the newspaper did become the mouthpiece of the Institute, reflecting the changes which occurred within it over the years.

Once the board of management was formally constituted, its members were asked to find a suitable director but it was a foregone conclusion that Beyers Naudé would be offered the job. When the offer was made, the controversy around him began to erupt in earnest. A reporter from *Die Transvaler* had surreptitiously attended the founding meeting of the CI and the next day the newspaper carried a lengthy report about the CI.[12] *Die Transvaler's* article created a furore and soon conservatives in the NGK were lobbying for action to be taken against Beyers Naudé.

Afrikaners who supported the Christian Institute, NGK ministers like Ben Engelbrecht, Bennie Keet and Ben Marais, supported Beyers Naudé as the best candidate for director. In their opinion the CI would have no hope of swaying the Afrikaans churches and their members away from apartheid unless it was led by a respected Afrikaner minister. There were a few significant figures who could not go along with the formation of the Institute. One of them was Beyers's friend, Dr Willie Jonker. He agreed with Beyers's principles but felt that the ecumenical study circle, and not a formal organisation like the CI, was the most effective way of challenging the NGK.[13] Dr Jan van Rooyen from the Parkhurst NGK, for his part, did not believe the CI was being launched in the right way. Van Rooyen was not happy that Dr Webb, a Methodist and a liberal opponent of the government, was playing such a leading role in the CI. He felt this would discourage Afrikaners from joining and he favoured the launch of an ecumenical movement for Afrikaans Reformed Christians only.[14]

Beyers was convinced that his friends were wrong to hope for change from within the NGK and he also rejected the proposal of creating an exclusive Afrikaans organisation. 'It would have defeated the whole object of creating an ecumenical body. They wanted change but they did not want to take the whole step and face the full implications of it. I said, Either you take the matter to its logical conclusion or you do nothing.'

Beyers Naudé's opponents in the church and the Broederbond realised that he held the potential for drawing a significant group of Afrikaners onto his side. In consequence, they began to lobby among Afrikaners to oppose him as much as possible and to discourage support for the Christian Institute. Several church councils passed resolutions calling on Beyers to rethink his attitude towards the CI and *Pro Veritate*. Shortly after the launch of the Institute, his own church council issued a statement appealing to their minister to reconsider his editorship of *Pro Veritate* and his relationship with the CI. The anger and strength of the opposition was reminiscent of the Cottesloe controversy, and Beyers realised he was up against the same intransigent spirit. The CI in fact tried to deflect some of the criticism by issuing a statement saying that membership was open to people as individuals and not as representatives of any church.[15]

A few days after the Aasvoëlkop church council appealed to Beyers, the Paardekraal Monument church council in the Krugersdorp area convened a special meeting to discuss the formation of the CI. It resolved to send a letter to the synodical commission of the NGK in the Southern Transvaal, requesting that a special session of the synod be convened. The letter declared: 'We have discussed the present situation in our church with great frankness, particularly in the light of *Pro Veritate* and the recently established Christian Institute. With concern and alarm we have noted clear group formation in the church.' The council said it regarded the Christian Institute's job offer to Beyers 'in a very serious light' and called on him to withdraw from both the journal and the CI.[16]

Pressure was steadily mounting on Beyers from the Afrikaner community to indicate whether or not he would become director of the CI. Finally Beyers announced that he would accept the position as director and that he intended to apply for permission from his church to retain his status as minister. He made his application to the examining committee of the NGK, which scheduled a meeting in Pretoria early in September to consider the request.

In the meantime, a group of NGK ministers, distressed by the possibility of open conflict between Beyers and the church, called for 'brotherly discussion' to avert the crisis. They approached Beyers to reconsider his position,[17] but while he was sympathetic, he held out little hope that his church would be prepared to hold a frank meeting on the issue.

At its September meeting, the examining committee members decided that Beyers could not retain his status as a minister if he accepted the appointment with the Christian Institute. Beyers received a short letter to this effect. Without giving any reasons for its decision, the committee refused his request. Beyers decided to delay making a final decision, pending the outcome of the call for a 'brotherly discussion'. In a statement to the press he said: 'I will decide after a ruling has been given by the moderature . . . on a request for a brotherly discussion of all the ministers of the church in Southern Transvaal to be held to discuss tensions and group formations in the church.'[18]

The moderature, perhaps fearful of the support Beyers might receive at such a 'brotherly discussion', decided against holding the meeting, and the ball was back in Beyers Naudé's court. By mid-September 1963 it was clear that Beyers could not put off his decision for much longer, and he announced that he would make it known in a sermon to his congregation on 22 September.

A few weeks before this, six NGK ministers came to see him to plead with him not to leave the church. They were men who had supported the Cottesloe findings but who believed change should come from within the church. Beyers described that meeting: 'Six of them came to see me in the parsonage, including Frans, my brother-in-law. They pleaded with me to change my mind and to stay on in the church. Then I asked them: "If I were to decline the CI job, what guarantee do I have that there would be enough ministers who would be prepared to stand with me, not by me, but with me, in order to challenge the NGK on our biblical understanding of its prophetic task at this point in history?" I said that if there was an adequate number, say ten, I would be prepared to stand down. They said they would go home and think about it.

'A week before I had to make my decision, I phoned Frans and asked him: "Do you remember that discussion we had?" He said, "Yes." I said, "Could you give me any indication of where you and the others stand? Is there any indication of any commitment?" And then he said to me, "But, Bey, you should know the answer. Do you really believe that you will find ten people to stand by you?" I said, "Frans, if that is what you feel, then, in a certain sense, you have made my decision for me." '

But in reality it was not as simple as that. Relinquishing his position represented a crucial step for Beyers. 'I had to decide whether I would remain within the . . . church [leadership] and therefore within the confines and restraints which were clearly set for myself and for my future ministry, or otherwise to risk the step into the unknown, into what to me had become a decision of obedience to my faith. It was a very difficult decision. It was very painful. But it became clear to me that I had no option. If I wanted to remain obedient to my Christian calling, if I wanted to also help my own people in a wider sphere, I had to accept this directorship.'[19]

Beyers did not consult with his wife about what he should do, claiming later that he was motivated by a desire to protect his family. In this respect he was still the patriarchal *dominee* who made the decisions for the family and expected his wife to follow him. 'I conveyed my decision to her and said these were my convictions. And she said if that was the case she accepted it. But I think she realised something of the price she and the children would have to pay.'

The night before he made his decision known, Beyers spoke to Ilse about the road that lay ahead. 'I said to her, "With this decision, we will in all probability be moving into the wilderness for ten to fifteen years. . . . It's going to be very painful, it's going to be lonely, it's going to be difficult but I hope that I will be able to support you in the sacrifice which I know that you and the children will have to make." '[20]

Beyers and Ilse rose early that Sunday morning as was their custom. Their children Liesel and Hermann, who were aware of what was to come, prepared for the morning service as normally as possible. When they arrived at the church, the family moved into the pews and Beyers went into the vestry to greet his church council. The atmosphere was tense. The congregation began arriving at the church and soon all the pews were filled. More people streamed in and extra chairs were placed in the aisles, as if this was some special Christmas or Easter service. When Beyers stepped into the pulpit he saw that the beautiful church he had helped build was overflowing with people. He glanced around at the familiar faces, filled with anxiety. And then the church service began with a prayer and the singing of a hymn.

Beyers read Acts 5: 17–42, which tells the story of Peter and the apostles who had refused to stop preaching the gospel in spite of being arrested and punished by the Jewish authorities. The apostles had been brought before the High Priest and the Council of Elders in Jerusalem to explain why they had defied orders by preaching the message of Jesus Christ. In the words of Acts 5: 29: 'Peter and the other apostles replied, "We must obey God, rather than men." '

Beyers then told his congregation: 'I know some will say, Is it not sheer audacity to draw an analogy from this story to the situation in which we find ourselves today? Only the Holy Spirit, my brethren, can persuade each of you to what extent Acts 5 applies to our situation. As for myself, I have tried to find guidance for my own decision in other passages of Scripture, and I have tried to find reasons which would enable me to sever my connection with *Pro Veritate* and the Christian Institute and continue peacefully and happily with my pastoral work. But time and again – sometimes with great conflict, fear and resistance in my heart – the Lord brought me back to this passage of Scripture. . . .

'The decisions of synods, presbyteries and sessions, and the consequent reactions, have clearly indicated to me that although the synod has not in so many words prohibited pronouncements which are not in accordance with church policy and the traditions of the past, in spirit and in practice these decisions come to this: that the God-given right and freedom of the minister and member to witness to the truth of God's Word in the spirit of the prophets and the Reformers is so restricted that the minister of the gospel in principle no longer enjoys the freedom to declare his deepest Christian convictions in the way or at the place and time given by God to speak through his Word and Spirit.

'Consequently the choice facing me is not primarily a choice between pastoral work and other Christian work or between the church and *Pro Veritate*, or between the church and the Christian Institute. No, the choice goes much deeper: it is a choice between obedience in faith and subjection to the authority of the church. And by unconditional obedience to the latter, I would save face but lose my soul.'

Beyers said he also had a message for his congregation and his church. 'If our church continues with its tragic withdrawal from the Holy Catholic Church in South Africa and Africa, we shall, spiritually, wilt and die. O my church, I call today with all the earnestness that is in me: awake before it is too late, stand up and stretch out the hand of Christian brotherhood to all who reach out to you in sincerity. There is still time, but time is becoming short, very short.'[21]

His congregation had listened to his sermon in unhappy silence and many were weeping. An elder of the church stood up to thank Beyers. He was Danie du Plessis, member of the Broederbond, at whose house the Broederbond had been launched in 1918. A shaken Du Plessis remarked: 'We had prayed and hoped that the decision would be different. There was so much which . . . he could have done for his *volk*. But God willed it differently.'[22]

The following night Beyers met with his church council to tender his resignation formally. He had to serve six weeks' notice before he could leave his church, and those weeks were hard and difficult for the whole family. Beyers's announcement had received widespread attention in the media – a fact which angered many conservative churchmen. A few days after the sermon the Vereeniging church council approved a resolution in which it objected to the fact that some newspapers were putting a 'martyr's cloak' on him.[23]

Not surprisingly, Beyers's sermon was attacked in an editorial in *Die Kerkbode*: 'We are prepared to accept the sermon as a struggle between a brother and his church . . . but as a church we also struggle with our brother in all love, and especially on points where we believe that his stand is without foundation.' The editorial added that the church could not accept that the choice Beyers faced was simply one between 'faith' and 'authority. . . . The fact that we did not officially attend a few church conferences in the most recent past does not justify the reproach that we were engaged in a planned and frightened process of isolation. . . . We believe that it is clear from the most recent past why we do not welcome any discussion simply for the sake of discussion. A discussion must be a good discussion, or it will ruin good morals. A dangerous discussion must not be praised unconditionally.'[24]

Afrikaans newspapers carried a flood of letters, mostly from outraged readers who condemned Beyers's decision. The letters came not only from members of the NGK, but from the two other Afrikaans Reformed churches. One such attack was delivered by the chairman of the general council of the Hervormde Kerk, the Reverend A. Oosthuizen. His analysis of what the Christian Institute intended to do seems in retrospect to have been remarkably accurate. Describing the CI as 'nothing else than a church front against apartheid', he warned that it was the CI's object to 'persuade the churches to establish a Christian community where there will be no racial separation. . . . In reality, the Institute tends to use the churches to wreck the policy of separate development.'[25]

While the Aasvoëlkop congregation was deeply opposed to Beyers's decision, there was still a great deal of love and affection for him. Nowhere was this better reflected than in the farewell the church gave to Beyers and Ilse. They held a special function to bid them goodbye and the church editorial committee issued a farewell newsletter with glowing tributes to both. One of the contributions was written by Beyers's friend and the actuary of the Southern Transvaal synod, Dr Willie Jonker. He wrote: 'In the course of years . . . we often spoke together about many things. . . . I can say one thing about him, and that is he is a man who goes his own way. He asked my opinion about many things . . . but in his haste he never followed my advice. The worst was I could never be angry with him for not listening to me, because I knew that he was always trying to be honest with himself and with others. . . . I had to believe he had good reasons for ignoring my well-intentioned advice.'[26]

Beyers's farewell sermon on 3 November was also a moving occasion. He told the congregation: 'It is of the greatest importance that the church of Christ should see just where God is busy and what he expects from every professing Christian: to take the Word seriously again, to wrestle with the Word so that once more it becomes the infallible rule for all our thinking and living, for our very being. . . . With this message I bring to an end my ministry to you – so different from what any of us ever dreamed or expected. What lies ahead, no one knows – but that is not really important. . . . Even if you forget everything else, if you remember only that for the first four years of the life of this congregation, God sent you somebody who in the midst of many human failings continually tried to summon you and bind you to obedience to God's Word, then my ministry here has not been in vain.

'And if you are uncertain, if you have doubts, do not turn away. Wrestle with Him, the living Word, just as Jacob wrestled with God. . . . Whoever does that will discover what every man and every community must discover: the answer to our question, the light for our life, the hope for our future, lies in total obedience to Him who is the living Word – and to Him alone.'[27]

At the end of the service, the chairman of the Linden circuit called Beyers to come down from the pulpit. He handed him a document of dismissal, whereupon in symbolic and dramatic gesture, Beyers drew off his black minister's robe.

One member of the congregation described what happened that morning. 'He delivered a magnificent sermon and the people were very touched, even those who were against him. When he pulled off his gown, a man sitting in front of me who was a big shot in the Railways, and one of the men who blamed Beyers, he sat there and wept like a baby. Beyers was loved and so well liked that even his enemies couldn't take it.'[28]

Then Beyers and Ilse walked down the aisle and stood at the door as the people streamed out in silence. Beyers said: 'It was like a funeral procession. Some people's eyes were filled with tears. Some people were looking the other way. Other people were simply passing by without greeting us. My own emotions were those of deep sadness, I was torn in my heart. Again and again I asked myself: "Did I do the right thing? Was this God's will? Will this ever lead to anything worthwhile for the sake of the church and the Afrikaner people?" But there was also a feeling of deep conviction in me that what I was doing was right. . . . I felt very deeply for my wife, because for her it was a severance of a very deep bond between her and the women of the church. She had been very active in the different women's organisations and it meant a tremendous amount to her.

'When we went home after that, we had our lunch meal in practically total silence. None of us felt like speaking. We were too overwhelmed. And it was only towards the evening, when Ilse and I walked outside, that for the first time we were able to begin to talk about this. And it was possible for us to say to one another that whatever happens, we will be together and God will be with us.'[29]

Dr Frederik van Zyl Slabbert, former leader of the Progressive Federal Party and co-founder of the Institute for a Democratic Alternative for South Africa (Idasa), was a young member of the Aasvoëlkop church. He recalled the emotions evoked by Beyers's decision: 'Beyers was highly respected. There was something verging on adoration of him among establishment Afrikaners. He had been mixing with the who's who of Afrikanerdom, and he was their unquestioned spiritual and moral leader. It took enormous courage for him to leave. It's the kind of courage people don't normally respect or understand.'[30]

For Ilse the move out of the church was to prove traumatic, and it was a testimony to her love for Beyers that she always stood with him. Beyers's decision also brought with it financial uncertainty. After 23 years' service Beyers had to forfeit the church's contribution to the pension fund and the widow's fund. The family had no savings but with the help of two gifts from friends and with a loan from the Christian Institute, Beyers and Ilse scraped together enough money to put down a deposit on a house in Greenside, close to the Northcliff area where they had lived for the past four years. It cost R12 000. The house had a spacious lounge which Beyers felt would be ideal for multi-racial meetings, since finding venues for such gatherings was still extremely difficult. The house was large but extremely run-down and the family had to spend much of their spare time renovating and improving it.[31]

Meanwhile Fred van Wyk had been energetically working out a budget for the first year of the Christian Institute's operation. At an executive meeting of the board of trustees attended by Van Wyk and two other members, it was decided that the CI's new director should receive approximately the same remuneration that he had previously received from the NGK. With all his allowances it would be possible for him to pay back the loan from the Christian Institute for the deposit on his house and also to meet his monthly repayment for the bond he had taken with a building society.

Even in the early years the Christian Institute depended largely on grants from overseas church organisations. It was a fact which was often criticised by opponents and was one of the weaknesses in the structure of the organisation. The reality was that there was simply not enough financial support within South Africa for such organisations. Beyers never believed there was anything wrong in accepting money from overseas donors. In his view, the Christian church was a united worldwide body, and if a member in South Africa needed assistance, then it was the Christian duty of wealthier overseas churches to help.[32]

Beyers received many invitations to speak on public platforms, but these were mostly confined to English-speaking audiences. In October he addressed a large meeting in Cape Town and this was followed by several other speeches in various parts of the country. The continual demands on his time often became a burden to Beyers and especially to Ilse. In the years to come his exhausting programme would give him little time for quiet reflection.

Another issue which attracted public attention at the time was the dispute about whether or not Beyers should be allowed to retain his status as minister. Beyers was not without support, and Bennie Keet stepped into the fray by writing to *Die Kerkbode*. In his letter, Professor Keet pointed out that other ministers were working in other spheres without a loss of status. He argued: 'Now that membership of an inter-church institute has become a matter for disciplinary action, the time has come to call a halt.'[33]

Beyers had in the meantime decided to appeal against the synodical commission's decision to defrock him. A 'legal commission' was appointed to investigate the case. It came as no surprise to Beyers when, in November, the commission reaffirmed its earlier decision to deprive him of his status as minister. The commission also adopted a resolution disapproving of the formation of the Christian Institute, claiming it would create opposition to the racial and ecumenical views of the NGK. A more important indication of the hostility towards the Institute came a few days later when the powerful *breë moderatuur* of the NGK issued a statement likewise disapproving of the formation of the Christian Institute – a step which Beyers regarded as the start of the long battle between the NGK and the prophetic movement.[34]

Speaking about his early hopes and aspirations for the Christian Institute, Beyers said: 'Although I was still not fully aware what awaited me at the CI, I at least had enough awareness of the Afrikaner people and especially the NGK to realise that it would be a long and lonely road. Another feeling was that of sorrow that a number of ministers, missionaries of the NGK who had proved their sympathy and support up to the establishment of the CI, started to either withdraw or compromise or become silent the moment that there was a strong criticism or opposition on the part of the NGK.'[35]

But even before Beyers and his supporters could begin their daunting task of trying to reach out to all Christians, the 'Broederbond scandal' erupted. In a dramatic announcement, the Broederbond declared that it had traced the source of leaked secret documents to former cell chairman Beyers Naudé. Beyers and his family had lived through a very difficult year – but the last three months of 1963 were to be among the most difficult of his life.

9
Broederbond Exposés, 1963

The 'Broederbond affair' was one of the most anguished episodes in Beyers Naudé's life. He later apologised to the Broederbond for having broken his promise of secrecy but the Brothers never forgave him. Yet was there need for an apology? Many people praised Beyers for revealing the true nature of the organisation; others, however, including some of his former Afrikaner friends, were disappointed by the underhand manner in which he and Albert Geyser had gone about their task.[1]

Beyers Naudé's clash with the Broederbond represented, moreover, one of the most significant events in his life. The reaction of the Broederbond, strongly negative in kind, was to be a major reason for Beyers's inability to sway more than a handful of Afrikaners to his beliefs and views in the years to come. The relentless campaign which the Broederbond was to wage against him also influenced his future direction and strengthened his determination to oppose the conservative policies of Afrikaner nationalism.

From 1962 there was growing concern among a number of non-Broederbond Afrikaans churchmen that the organisation's control over the church was advancing too far. Its role in the post-Cottesloe ferment and other actions sparked debate and controversy within the church. At about the same time, *Pro Veritate* was officially launched, and it seemed as if the kind of opposition the journal represented to the Broederbond was likely to grow. The Broederbond became concerned about this dangerous drift towards independent thinking and decided to strike back.

In August 1962, the executive council of the Broederbond issued a special three-page memorandum on the tendency within the church to question apartheid. Equating these views with 'communism and liberalism', the Broederbond warned: 'Even within our own circles it is sometimes argued with a great measure of fanaticism that our policy of apartheid is not biblical. The executive council solemnly calls on our Church leaders to combat this liberalistic attack on our Christian spiritual convictions and on the Christian-National philosophy on which our national struggle on the cultural, social, economic and educational front is founded, and to expose it firmly and clearly.'[2]

Another document issued by the Broederbond in October 1962 voiced similar sentiments. In an obvious reference to Beyers Naudé and his ecumenical group, the circular from the executive council declared: 'The Afrikaans churches cannot allow the formation of groups outside or within the church to continue.' And in a swipe at *Pro Veritate*, it called on churchmen to stop criticising their church in public. 'Everyone is surely aware of the fact that in each of the churches there exist groups who are not only acting disloyally to the church but are also busy with the formation of groups alongside or against the church.' This should not be permitted, and these 'elements' should be forced to work through the 'official channels', said the document.[3]

Beyers had long discussions about the Broederbond with theologian Albert Geyser, who had become an outspoken critic of apartheid theology. Geyser, a member of the Hervormde Kerk, had begun his academic career as a loyal Nationalist, and was a professor of theology at the University of Pretoria. He became involved in the apartheid debate in the mid-1950s after the Hervormde Kerk was challenged by the WCC to provide biblical justification for its race policy. Geyser, a New Testament expert and an excellent linguist, was appointed to the Hervormde Kerk's two-man commission to find such justification. The commissioners began their study confident that they would find confirmation for their church's Article Three which confined membership to whites only. But contrary to their expectations, both theologians came to the conclusion that the Scriptures did not provide justification for apartheid. The church leadership was infuriated by what they regarded as betrayal. Geyser's attacks on apartheid theology steadily increased until he moved into open confrontation with the church leadership.[4]

In October 1961 Geyser was charged with heresy on a dubious technical offence – he had been accused of teaching an heretical tenet of Arianism – but this had nothing to do with the real objection against him. The 'trial' was held at the Hervormde Kerk's headquarters in Pretoria, but the commissioners closed it to the press and general public and refused to allow Geyser to record events independently. The press soon got wind of the 'shabby trial', and it created a furore both in South Africa and in Holland, where the Hervormde Kerk still had strong ties with its Dutch 'mother church'. According to observers who were permitted at the hearing, Geyser acquitted himself brilliantly of the charges, and blamed the Broederbond for orchestrating the campaign against him. During the long trial, Geyser's family was ostracised by the Afrikaner community and the Broederbond forced his father to resign from the organisation. On 8 May 1962, the church commission, which was dominated by Broeders, found by a 13–2 majority that he was guilty of heresy. Geyser was defrocked as a minister of his church.[5] He was determined to fight back and took his case to the Supreme Court in Pretoria.

Geyser remained convinced that the Broederbond had engineered the charges against him, a view he shared with Beyers. Beyers also discussed his concerns about the Broederbond with Geyser's loyal supporter in the Hervormde Kerk, Professor A. van Selms, who served on the editorial board of *Pro Veritate*. Van Selms was to rock the Afrikaner establishment in June 1963 with a fifteen-page booklet attacking the Broederbond and describing Christians who were members as hypocrites.[6]

According to Beyers, it was Geyser who raised the subject of the Broederbond documents with him. 'Geyser said to me, "I cannot judge your concern about the Broederbond, except if I am able to read what the Broederbond has been saying all these years." ... He also wanted the documents because of the fight with his own church, to fight the injustice which they did to him. ... His was a desperate stand, on his own, against his whole church leadership. They were more militant and much worse than the NG Kerk. I can understand why he felt he was standing with his back against the wall, that he needed every possible form of evidence. ... But I knew, that with the promise that you make, you dare not make available any documents outside the membership of the Broederbond. But I felt for me there was so much at stake, that I had to simply take that step, knowing that it was totally inadmissible to share them with him. I was chairman of my circle, so I got all the documents and gave them to him to read.'

'I gave him some, and said: "See if this gives you the necessary information." Then he asked for other documents. ... So whatever I was able to get, I gave to him. ... Initially we did not discuss the documents because I was so involved with work in the congregation.'

Geyser later said he realised the documents were invaluable. Never before had the Broederbond's secrecy been breached. He took the documents to his offices at the university and painstakingly photographed every page with his Leica camera and then returned them to Beyers. A little later Geyser contacted a friend, Charles Bloomberg, who was political reporter on the *Sunday Times*, and gave him the negatives of the Broederbond documents. The *Sunday Times* had already run several stories on the Broederbond's grip on the churches, civil service and Afrikaner business; other reports had dealt with the activities of its junior arm, the *Ruiterwag*.[7]

The first major exposé featuring the Naudé documents appeared in the *Sunday Times* on 21 April 1963. Beyers was immediately caught up in the controversy. The headline across page three of the newpaper shouted: 'SECRET BROEDER PLAN TO OUST NEW DEALERS', and the report dealt with a Broederbond plot to silence 'New Deal' advocate within the NGK, Beyers Naudé. The newspaper also published copies of the Broederbond notices issued in August and October 1962 which called on Afrikaner churchmen to stop criticising apartheid. Other secret documents showed how the *Federasie van Afrikaanse Kultuurvereniginge* (FAK) worked as a front and how the Broederbond circulated the names of prospective new members before they could be admitted to the organisation.[8]

The exposé shook the Broederbond and the government. The next week in parliament the prime minister, Hendrik Verwoerd, sharply attacked the *Sunday Times*, describing it as the newspaper which printed the most 'untruths'. Verwoerd's attack was widely reported on the state-controlled South African Broadcasting Corporation, whose chairman, Dr Piet Meyer, was also chairman of the Broederbond.

Alarmed by the breach in security, the Broederbond called in the help of 'expert friends' in the security police.[9] The man appointed to head the investigation was the chief of the Security Branch and a member of the Broederbond, Colonel Hendrik van den Bergh. Beyers Naudé must have been a prime suspect already, but the Broederbond hierarchy was determined to know for certain who the 'culprit' was. That the leak would eventually be identified was evident from the start. In that first exposé, the *Sunday Times* gave the investigators a major clue. Describing the origins of one of the secret documents it reproduced, it explained that it had been sent by registered post to the secretary or chairman of each cell.[10]

The exposés created a wave of hysteria and concern among Afrikaner nationalists. In an attempt to justify security police involvement in the case, the Sunday newspaper *Dagbreek en Sondagnuus* said: 'This attack on the Broederbond by the underground forces clearly carries the Communist pattern of sowing suspicion and of undermining the Church and religion in South Africa.'[11] In the months that followed, the *Sunday Times* published other damning reports. One dealt with Broederbond opposition to service organisations like Rotary, Lions and Round Table for being 'un-Afrikaans', while another revealed how the Broederbond, through its special *Helpmekaar* (Help One Another) service, ensured 'jobs for pals' and advancements for its members in business and the public service. The disclosures shook the country.[12]

At the same time, in May 1963, Albert Geyser's appeal against his defrocking had reached the Supreme Court. Geyser appeared in the witness box and publicly accused the fifteen-man church commission which had tried him of being hostile and biased towards him. The trial attracted a great deal of publicity and was becoming a major embarrassment to the Hermvormde Kerk. On the eighth day of the trial, the counsel for the church asked for an adjournment during which they reached an agreement with Geyser and offered to pay all costs, amounting to about R100 000. The out-of-court settlement was a vindication of Geyser's stand against the Broederbond and his church. But, as details of the settlement were kept quiet, it did nothing to restore his standing in the Afrikaner community. He had no chance of ever gaining a teaching post at an Afrikaans university and remained for the rest of his working life at the University of the Witwatersrand. He finally left the Hervormde Kerk when the church's general synod refused to review his case.[13]

In the meantime, the security police investigation into the leaked Broederbond documents was continuing and they decided to carry out a raid on the *Sunday Times* offices in Johannesburg on the pretext that they were investigating a 'theft' of Broederbond documents. On 1 October 1963, four policemen marched into the acting editor's office, produced a search warrant and demanded the photocopies of the Broederbond documents. After a two-hour search, and armed with the documents, they left to continue the witchhunt. Once in possession of the photocopies, the Broederbond began to recall documents, and by a process of elimination finally identified the leak.

On Monday 11 November, a security police delegation, led by Colonel Van den Bergh, called on Beyers Naudé. Colonel Van den Bergh told Beyers that he had been identified as the source of the leak and demanded a full explanation. Beyers told him that he had only lent the documents to Geyser and he denied giving the documents to the *Sunday Times*. From there, the security police called on Geyser, who verified Beyers Naudé's story. Beyers realised it was only a matter of time before the whole matter became public, and he agonised over what he should do. 'It was a terrible, absolutely terrible time. That was the period where I went through hell. I deeply regretted it. I understood why Albert Geyser, with his terrible experience at the hands of the Broederbond, did what he did. I conveyed to him my deep regret and said that it had damaged the whole witness we were going to give.'

Even before the Broederbond could meet to consider the issue, word spread that Beyers Naudé was the 'traitor'. He received angry calls and visits from friends and Broederbond members. He realised he had to speak out. More than a week after the visit by the security police, Beyers issued a lengthy statement and copies of letters to the media in Johannesburg. The press described his statement as 'sensational', and the issue dominated the front pages of both the Afrikaans and English newspapers for days afterwards.

In his statement released on the night of Tuesday 20 November and published the next day, Beyers declared: 'As a result of malicious rumours reaching me yesterday and today, indicating that I was responsible for certain Broederbond documents falling into the hands of the press – rumours which apparently arose when Security Branch policemen visited me on Monday . . . I am forced to make public the contents of two letters which I wrote to the chairman of the Executive Council of the Broederbond. The first of these letters, which reflects briefly the true facts of the case, is dated 12 November [1963] and reads as follows:

Dear Sir,

After an interview I had yesterday with Colonel Van den Bergh of the Security Branch, about a charge of theft concerning Broederbond documents, I consider it my duty to inform you, as well as the division to which I belonged before my resignation . . . about what I told Colonel Van den Bergh. In addition I shall tell you what gave rise to this affair. (Something I did not tell Colonel Van den Bergh because it concerns very closely my relation to the Broederbond.)

During March this year, I submitted certain Broederbond documents to a fellow theologian who is not a member of the organisation. The documents, in my opinion, confirmed my personal deep concern that the Broederbond, contrary to the Scriptures, wants to use the Church of Christ to further its own interests. I showed the documents to my colleague because I wanted his advice in choosing between two loyalties and about which I could not think clearly at the time. To enable him to form his own judgment on the issue at stake, I entrusted the documents to him for a certain period. They were returned to me.

From my interview with Colonel Van den Bergh I gathered that photostats were made of the documents and that copies came into the possession of the press. It goes without saying that this happened without my knowledge.

Because you have the right to know why I broke my [Broederbond] oath by discussing the documents with a non-member, I now give my reasons: My division [of the

Broederbond] was for a time aware of the misgivings that I, as a Christian and clergyman, had about the principles and methods of the organisation where the Christian Church was concerned. I failed to find a satisfactory assurance that my objections were unfounded when I discussed my misgivings with fellow clergymen who are members of the Broederbond. And my concern increased after further circulars and study documents were issued by the Executive Council from August 1962 onwards, but I always hoped that other views would be forthcoming.

When this did not happen and it was becoming clear that the Broederbond question would be discussed at the Southern Transvaal Synod . . . I realised . . . that if I delayed my decision any longer it would impair any clearness of conscience and the Christian convictions before the Synod. As I only had a short time at my disposal I decided to call on the advice of the fellow clergyman I mentioned before.

I do not think it is necessary for me to state how I feel about the matter. I therefore hope and pray in all sincerity that you will understand and accept my explanation in the spirit in which it is offered.

Respectfully yours, C.F.B. Naudé

Beyers also released a copy of his letter of resignation to the Broederbond, which was dated 14 March 1963. Here are extracts from the letter:

Dear chairman and members,

Since August last year, there have been a number of events which have caused me to reconsider my membership of the Broederbond. After long and serious deliberation I have decided that for me, as Christian and clergyman, there is only one honourable way open, to relinquish my membership of the Broederbond. I owe it to you and to myself to illustrate briefly the reasons. . . .

1. Attitude of the Executive Council towards the onslaughts against our continued existence as an independent, Christian-National, Western community in South Africa. Here I wish to refer to the Circular Letter Extraordinary dated August 1 1962, and to certain phrases in the document entitled: 'A positive relationship between the three Afrikaans churches for effective joint action.' These phrases refer . . . to the ministers of the . . . churches who voiced opinions about race relations in Church and State affairs which differed in some aspects from the traditional views of the Church and the Broederbond.

The manner in which this matter is stated implies that these views are either liberal or that they foster liberal-mindedness. Further statements are made concerning Biblical views and interpretations over which there have been differences of opinion among the three Afrikaans churches for many years. . . .

[Beyers continued:] My objection . . . is that the basic doctrines of the Broederbond, on grounds of which sweeping conclusions are drawn, are based on an interpretation of the Scriptures to which I decidedly do not subscribe and which I was not ashamed to say either in my preaching or at meetings of my church. By imposing itself on the field of religion and making categorical theological judgments, the Broederbond is unlawfully influencing the Church in a dangerous manner that is preventing the Church from drawing independent and sober conclusions from the Scriptures. . . .

. . . The documents taken as a whole leave the unambiguous impression on members of the organisation that any other view is not permissible, that it is treasonable towards the Afrikaner people and the manifesto of the Broederbond, equating dissension with liberalism and humanism. The manner of leading Broeders towards me, and other clergymen in the organisation, left the indelible impression that my conclusions are correct.

It is no secret, and you are all aware of the fact, that I have very serious misgivings about some of the legislation, views and practices of the State and the Church which concern our relations with other population groups. From the political stand I wish to mention the Immorality Act, the Race Classification Act, the Group Areas Act and the new Bantu Laws Amendment bill, all of which contain stipulations that violate the demands of the Bible for neighbourly love, justice and mercy.

I also wish to mention the impossibility of implementing total apartheid without seriously endangering the existence of the Afrikaner people and the injustice perpetrated on millions of non-whites. As far as the Church is concerned I want to mention the refusal to allow non-whites to attend services in our Church, the fear of making closer religious contact with these people and the irreparable harm it inflicts on our efforts to Christianise the heathen.

These objections do not arise in me from political considerations or out of personal interest, even less from a false liberalism or worldly humanism. They are the fruit of my Christian convictions and my observations of the Bible. . . .

[A little later, Beyers declared:] I want to assert that the road which the Broederbond prescribes, no matter how sincere and honest its intentions, will eventually break the Afrikaner people, not preserve it. It is exactly this self-vindication that leads to self-destruction. . . .

When I joined the movement I satisfied my conscience with the justification that secrecy was necessary because of the plight of the Afrikaner people at the time. The past year has, however, convinced me that I can no longer accept this argument as valid. I came to the view that personal secrecy did not leave me free to practise my pastoral work unhampered because it affects and can even destroy the highest form of Brotherhood – the bond of religion between Christians . . . . The Broederbond creates a rift between minister and minister, church member and church member, and Afrikaner and Afrikaner, on matters where there should not be a rift between us. . . .

I would be disloyal to my sense of justice if I did not give thanks for all the beautiful things the Broederbond gave me: my love for the Afrikaner people, our language, our country, our land; the readiness to serve at all times without seeking reward; the joy of sacrificing for the sacred convictions of righteousness and justice. Without abandoning any of these treasures I wish to continue as a Christian and Afrikaner to give my best in the service of God and my country.

Sincerely yours, C.F.B. Naudé

Concluding his statement to the press, Beyers noted: 'This which I have now been forced to disclose, after an interview with the Security Branch, is part of what I wanted to tell my fellow clergymen in brotherly conclave – an opportunity repeatedly sought but turned down as a result of the decision of the Southern Transvaal Synodical Commission on 5 November. For this reason, and against my wishes, I am compelled to make this disclosure because I also wish to preserve the good name of the Christian Institute with which I am connected. I want to wipe out any false impression that the Security Branch visit had anything to do with the Christian Institute.'[14]

The Broederbond reacted by issuing the following day its own statement in which it accused Beyers of dishonesty and broken promises. For Afrikaners the affair had taken on the proportions of a national crisis. This was evident from the fact that the SABC saw fit to interrupt its regular radio programmes to broadcast a 15-minute statement from Beyers Naudé and a 15-minute reply from the Broederbond.

The Broederbond quoted from another letter that Beyers had written to the organisation in June 1963 in which he had promised not to break his undertakings to the organisation. The Broederbond also accused Beyers of removing documents from the home of the area secretary who was out of town at the time. The Broederbond statement declared: 'In his letter of resignation to the secretary of his area, Mr Naudé says that he felt convinced that further discussion with him would make no difference to his decision and would therefore be useless. After Mr Naudé's resignation had been accepted and he had been congratulated on behalf of the Bond with his election as Moderator of the Southern Transvaal Synod . . . he assured the executive council in a letter dated 3 June 1963, that he would not break his undertaking to the Bond, while at the same time he had already broken his undertakings . . . as he now admits in his letter of 13 November 1963. . . .

'The Bond does not apologise for the fact that it has, since its founding, wholeheartedly supported and actively propagated the apartheid policy of our country and is still doing so. If this has now become a bone of contention to Mr Naudé, the executive council is sorry that he waited 22 years to fight in the way he is doing now.'[15]

That night Albert Geyser admitted to the press that he was the unnamed theologian who had handed the documents to the *Sunday Times*. In his statement he posed searching questions about the security police involvement in the case. In many minds, it was not only Albert Geyser and Beyers Naudé who were on trial but the Broederbond itself.

In his statement Geyser said that Beyers had visited him seven months previously to discuss his crisis of conscience over the Broederbond. 'He gave me a number of documents issued by the organisation so that I could draw my judgment from them and assist him in his struggle. At that time I was very busy preparing for my court action against the General Commission of the Nederduitsch Hervormde Kerk and I asked for time to read the documents at my leisure.

'In previous years it often happened that I received, from other sources, Broederbond documents for perusal. What I read in these documents convinced me in an increasing measure that they were aimed at making use of the Church for political aims.'

Geyser argued that the Broederbond was 'making the Church, which is the Bride of Christ, a handmaiden of politics. And above all, I observed in these documents the kind of quasi-Biblical arguments that I encountered during my trial. For this reason I decided that the only way to frustrate these aims and views would be to make them public.

'There was a second reason for my decision: I was aware that three-quarters of the clerical judges at my heresy trial were Broederbonders. I was also aware that the heresy charges brought against me came remarkably soon after I had published a condemnation of secret organisations, including the Broederbond.

I also realised that extracts from the Bond documents in my possession would assist me greatly in my defence.

'I photographed the documents and gave the negatives to a person whose good faith I did not doubt. This person had for a long time been collecting Broederbond documents. We had an agreement to exchange facts that we had gathered about the organisation. I knew that he was a journalist.

'Two officers, one from the Security Branch, paid me a visit on November 11, shortly after they had been to see Mr Naudé. Our conversation was short and to the point and I answered all their questions and in my turn asked them whether they were members of the Broederbond, which they denied. Then I asked them how it was that a member of the Security Branch had been entrusted with the investigation of a charge of theft and house-breaking, where, in the first place, there was no question of theft and house-breaking, and secondly, when the State was not involved.

'I asked them this because I was wondering whether the publication of Broederbond documents was tantamount to undermining the safety of the State and whether the security machinery of the State was being used to keep a secret society secret.'[16]

It emerged that the man who launched the investigation into the Broederbond, Charles Bloomberg, had left the country to study in Britain. The *Sunday Times* had then called in Hennie Serfontein, an Afrikaner and public relations officer for the opposition Progressive Party. For a while Serfontein had helped to write and translate subsequent published articles in the Broederbond series. He was later to join the newspaper, and became a well-known journalist in the fields of Afrikaner politics, the Broederbond and the Afrikaans churches.

Beyers realised that many Afrikaners would never forgive him. 'The Afrikaner people felt, consciously or unconsciously . . . that I had betrayed them. When the whole picture became clear, I realised that I had left the Afrikaner *volk* . . . in those days most Afrikaners felt that you could leave the NG Kerk, even leave the National Party, but that you must not touch the Broederbond. Because if you touched the Broederbond, then you were tearing at the heart of the Afrikaner *volk*, and everything that it stood for. Anyone who did that committed treason.'[17]

The Broederbond episode, combined with Beyers's decision to join the Christian Institute, had disturbing repercussions on his family. Their large circle of friends dwindled. One of Beyers's sisters severed all contact with the Naudés. The family received so many abusive telephone calls that Ilse told her children not to answer the telephone in her absence. Beyers also began receiving vicious anonymous letters. His daughter Liesel, who was by then attending high school, had to endure snide remarks about her father from some of her teachers. It was perhaps for Ilse that the adjustment was most difficult. After years of happy and busy service in her church she was suddenly cut off and alone.

Once the family had moved to their new home in Greenside, they became members of the nearby Parkhurst congregation and Ilse decided she needed to be involved in church work once again. 'I could not live in a vacuum, not knowing who was sitting next to me in church, so I became a Sunday school teacher. Beyers went to church with me, but he also preached around a lot. I could not often go with him because of my Sunday school work, and in that I did not feel the break from the church as he did.'

Their son Hermann remarked: 'My mother was terribly hurt when friends ostracised them. It made a deep impression on her and it took her a long time to reassess who her real friends were.'[18]

Of this whole time Beyers commented: 'The two youngest children also went through a very difficult period . . . it was made clear to them that their father had betrayed the Afrikaner people and that they were not welcome to remain in Afrikaans-medium schools. At that stage, they did not convey much of this to my wife and I. They felt that we were suffering enough and they did not bring it into the open. It was only later that they began to tell us of the traumatic and painful effects which this had on their lives.

'But if I look back today at that period, I would say however painful it was, it was necessary. It was a period in which I personally had to rediscover the deepest roots of my life, of my convictions, of my commitment to the whole cause of justice and love in South Africa.'[19]

The Broederbond affair had serious consequences for the Christian Institute. It heightened the hostility of the NGK towards the new ecumenical movement, and many Afrikaners, even those who had previously been sympathetic, became very suspicious of the CI. Several explanations would be proposed about what exactly had occurred between Beyers and Albert Geyser. Some claimed that they had deliberately leaked Broederbond documents to attract support for the CI. Others pointed to the incident as an example of how Beyers sometimes allowed himself to be manipulated. Geyser needed the documents in his fight against the Broederbond and he used his influence with Beyers to gain access to the secret information.

But while Beyers might have handed the documents to Albert Geyser in good faith, he was naïve to believe the information would remain confidential. He was to regret very deeply the way in which the organisation had been exposed. 'I made a mistake and I have publicly apologised for it. What I should have done, I should have gone to the Broederbond and said, "This is where I disagree with you, here are my reasons and I now want to notify you that I am duty bound to make this known. You may shoot me or you may kill me if you want to, but this is what I feel I must do." I should then have released the information to the public as I saw fit. That was the mistake. I should have had the courage to do it on my own. I did not have it.'

10
A New Ministry Unfolds, 1963–1965

It was ironic that the inaugural service of the Christian Institute took place on the same weekend that Afrikaners were marking one of their holiest days, the Day of the Vow, when Voortrekker forces defeated the Zulus at Blood River in 1838. Beyers Naudé delivered his inaugural address on 15 December 1963 at the Methodist church in Johannesburg before a multi-racial congregation. The next day a senior Afrikaner politician, Senator Jan de Klerk, father of the later state president, addressed an all-white gathering at the Voortrekker Monument in Pretoria. Both men directed their speeches to Afrikaners but the messages were fundamentally different – De Klerk assured Afrikaners that God was on their side, while Beyers Naudé exhorted Afrikaners to place themselves on God's side.[1]

Most of the people present at the inaugural meeting of the CI were firm supporters of the new organisation, but some attended out of curiosity. The service certainly made an impact on many. For one Afrikaans woman the event was so traumatic that two years later she wrote to *Die Transvaler* describing what took place. Her horror at the racial mixing which she witnessed at that church service showed precisely the almost unbridgable gulf between Beyers Naudé and the people he was hoping to reach. Her anonymous letter read: 'I was also present at the inaugural address of Mr Naudé as director of the Christian Institute in the Methodist Hall, Johannesburg. I had known Mr Naudé for many years as an endearing minister with a lovely personality. He always commanded respect. That is why I could never understand where all the strife came between the NG Kerk and Mr Naudé, and I decided to go with an open mind to listen to his inaugural address.

'Outside the church, a multi-racial mob of people had gathered, but we expected that one part of the church would be for whites and another part for non-whites. Inside the church, we noticed that people were indiscriminately sitting anywhere. White women, followed by their servants, came in and sat down next to each other. I can just mention what went through my mind: I wondered about the relationship outside the church. It couldn't be any different!

'A Bantu [African] choir sang at the service. Some were late while others just left their places. I thought about the dignified atmosphere which you always find in the NG Kerk to which Mr Naudé was also accustomed. And here was anything but order. I thought: Suppose Mr Naudé and his helpers triumph over the present "old-fashioned" religion of the Afrikaans churches, how our places of worship would be desecrated. . . . I decided to write to describe what I, an ordinary *Boeredogter*, saw and experienced, and imagined what could happen to the church where I took my first small steps. The church, which for many others is the Way to Eternal Life, and which today is not good enough for . . . Mr Naudé and his supporters.'[2]

Beyers and his CI colleagues frequently encountered such attitudes, but they were nevertheless filled with hope and were determined to make a success of their new venture. The offices of the CI were established in Dunwell House in Braamfontein, near the city centre, and close to the offices of the South African Institute of Race Relations (SAIRR), where Fred van Wyk still worked. Van Wyk played an extremely important role in the practical arrangements of the CI in those early years, serving on the board of management and board of trustees and helping in the running of *Pro Veritate*. He later joined the CI as its full-time administrative director, strengthening the organisation in an area in which Beyers was considered weak. Beyers's staff felt that he often became engrossed in the problems of people who flocked to see him, to the detriment of routine chores, such as keeping his correspondence up to date. There must have been many times when this upset Fred van Wyk. When he finally decided to return to the SAIRR, he seems to have done so not only because he felt the CI was becoming 'too radical', but because he disagreed with Beyers's style of working. In spite of these differences, Van Wyk showed his respect for his friend by continuing to address him as *dominee*, when most people called him *Oom Bey*, or just Beyers.[3]

The CI had an initial membership of about 150, but through steady recruitment, this figure had risen to well over a thousand by the end of 1964. Its emphasis in those early years was on establishing study and prayer groups. Regional meetings were held at various centres in the country to organise members of all races into small groups. Study groups were required to meet nine times a year and were provided with Bible study material related to South Africa's racial and church problems. It was still very difficult to find suitable venues where black and white Christians could meet freely. Church halls belonging to the English-speaking denominations were often used, but frequently Beyers held meetings in his own home, as did other CI members.

A theological library was established for the use of members. With the help of local and overseas donations, the CI built up a valuable collection of books and articles over the years. All this was lost when the police raided the CI in October 1977.

Beyers's early goal was to develop inter-racial contact between Christians, to promote the ecumenical movement, and to provide Afrikaners with an alternative to their conventional set of beliefs. He had the enthusiastic support of several English-speaking church leaders, such as Dr J. B. Webb and

Archbishop Joost de Blank. Beyers had hoped that this strong support for the work of the CI would be shared by ordinary members of the English churches. However, he soon discovered latent forms of discrimination in these churches. Not only were the leadership positions almost exclusively in white hands, but he realised that ordinary white churchgoers were not prepared to challenge the racist society in which they lived. Speaking of this problem, Beyers remarked: 'It was not only just the Afrikaner people we had to convince. More and more I was discovering the attitudes of English-speaking people. It was a revelation and a very deep disappointment when I realised how superficial the non-racial claim in the English-speaking churches was.'

For most white people the message of the Christian Institute was startlingly new, and it ruffled many feathers. Apart from its promotion of dialogue and understanding between races, the Institute's strong stand on demonstrating Christian unity by including a Catholic, Mrs Margaret Malherbe, on its board of management created an uproar among conservative, Reformed Afrikaners. Beyers said of this issue: 'We insisted that the cause of Christian unity had to transcend the confessional and denominational differences. That is why from the beginning I insisted that Catholics had to be included. I knew full well that it would cause an horrific reaction on the part of the NGK. It was referred to as the *Roomse gevaar* . . . and it was one of the main arguments used by the NGK to have the CI declared heretical in 1966.'

Soon after the CI's launch, Beyers announced that he and Ilse would visit the United States in April and May 1964 as guests of the US government. Beyers also planned to use the opportunity to visit the Netherlands and England, and acquaint himself with the ecumenical movement overseas. Fred van Wyk's excellent network of foreign church contacts stood Beyers in good stead on that visit. In the years that followed, Beyers developed his own circle of friends in the United States, the Netherlands, England, and other European countries, who became important supporters of the Christian Institute. His engaging personality and persuasive style would make him an excellent fundraiser, and for many years the CI's main programmes functioned as a result of this overseas support.

Beyers and Ilse maintained an exhausting schedule in America in 1964, visiting Atlanta, Phoenix, Los Angeles, San Francisco, Chicago, Rochester, New York, Boston, Philadelphia and Washington DC. The trip provided Beyers with numerous valuable opportunities to speak on the work of the Christian Institute. Parallels with the work of civil rights activists like Martin Luther King stimulated interest in Beyers's cause. He was also able to re-establish important contacts with leading officials in the World Council of Churches, including Bob Bilheimer.

Beyers's impulsive and determined nature was evident in his decision to cut short his American and European trip in order to attend the Mindolo Consultation on Race Relations in Kitwe, Zambia, at the end of May 1964. Still in the United States, he wrote to Fred van Wyk, who was running the CI in his absence, to inform him of the change in plan. Van Wyk was dismayed and sent Beyers two letters advising him to keep to his original schedule. In one he urged:

'you must complete your programme in the United States, England and Holland rather than . . . rush to Mindolo. You will be able to make contact with the Church in Africa later, but you probably won't get the opportunity in a hurry to go to England and Holland.'[4]

Beyers chose to ignore this advice but assured Van Wyk that he had been able to meet all his commitments in the United States. Displaying his customary energy, he wrote: 'It will probably be of interest to you to know that yesterday and today I was able to see . . . all the people who were on my list and that from Monday to Wednesday afternoon I have a further 10 appointments with various people and groups.'[5]

Beyers had correctly gauged the importance of the Mindolo conference, which coincided with the granting of independence to the former British colony of Northern Rhodesia. The mood of a new, post-colonial Africa pervaded that consultation in its focus on South Africa and other southern African countries still under colonial rule. Mindolo was the first major church conference since Cottesloe to examine South Africa's race policies so closely. While church leaders were divided in their support for measures such as sanctions and the armed struggle to end white rule in South Africa, all felt strongly that discrimination on the basis of race could no longer be condoned.

What Beyers learnt at Mindolo was that the English as well as the Afrikaans churches bore a major responsibility for the race problems in South Africa. Writing in *Pro Veritate* on his return to South Africa, Beyers said: 'this meeting was of considerable importance for two reasons: First, because everyone present received a clear picture of the race situation in various parts of Southern Africa, and secondly, because through honest self-examination, it brought to light the weakness and guilt of the church. While this guilt was firstly seen as that of guilt by virtue of silence, . . . we would mention another form of guilt: that of ambiguity. With regard to South Africa, the Afrikaans churches, if they want to be honest, must acknowledge that their guilt in the area of race relations is their silence about many forms of injustice which no Christian, in the light of the Word of God, can defend or approve of with a clear conscience. . . . With regard to the English-speakers, there is also a heavy burden of guilt – the shame of making decisions or policies which carry the message of justice, while in practice . . . these are so watered down that they present no real challenge to the racial attitudes of thousands of their members.'[6]

On his return from Mindolo, Beyers continued to attract regular press publicity in South Africa. To the English press he was a courageous, popular figure – a man who had been martyred and maligned by the Afrikaans community. The Afrikaans press portrayed him as a troublesome, controversial man with many new and suspect 'communist' or 'liberalistic' views. These press images made it impossible for Beyers and the Christian Institute to reach ordinary Afrikaner people.

Publicity surrounding Beyers Naudé's troubles with the NGK was typical of media treatment of the controversies surrounding him at this time. The English press depicted him as the target of unfair victimisation while the Afrikaans press, through several hostile reports and letters, conveyed the impression that he was probably getting what he deserved.

In February 1964, he made a fresh appeal against his church's decision to deprive him of his status as a minister, but the synodical commission of the Southern Transvaal NGK declined to review his case.[7] He encountered further problems after his election as an elder of the Parkhurst NGK. Beyers and Ilse had joined the Parkhurst congregation when they moved to their new house in Greenside. Their minister, Dr Jan van Rooyen, was overseas completing his doctoral thesis at the time, and another colleague, Dr Ben Engelbrecht, was deputising for him. Beyers handed in his certificate of membership to Engelbrecht, and at a church council meeting in May 1964 was elected onto the council as an elder. Another member immediately objected because of Beyers's work with *Pro Veritate* and the Christian Institute. Two members of the Parkhurst church council resigned in protest and lodged appeals against his election with the Johannesburg circuit of the NGK.[8]

The problem confronted Van Rooyen on his return to the country in June 1964. For the quiet, reserved Van Rooyen it was the start of a thirteen-year battle with the church leadership. The general synod of the NGK would eventually censure Beyers for his work with the CI, but Van Rooyen felt a member of the church could only be censured if he had sinned against God, not against the political views of the church.

In July 1964 the Johannesburg circuit declared Beyers's election invalid, but there was an immediate appeal by six NGK ministers to the synodical commission. Among those who sided with him were his old friend Dr Willie Jonker, then chairman of the Johannesburg circuit, and the secretary, Dr A. J. Venter. Others included Ben Engelbrecht, Jan van Rooyen, and another close friend, the Reverend Roelf Meyer.[9]

The election saga dragged on, with appeals and counter-appeals. Coming hard on the heels of the controversy about Beyers's status as a minister, it was an extremely embarrassing episode for the church leadership. After the manner of Pontius Pilate, the various bodies asked to rule on his election tried to wash their hands of the problem. The synodical commission refused to hear the appeals that had been lodged, and referred the matter back to the Johannesburg circuit. The Johannesburg circuit in turn referred the matter back to where the dispute started – the Parkhurst church council. In February 1965 the Parkhurst council under the leadership of Dr Van Rooyen once again approved Beyers's election as an elder. He was inducted at a service in March 1965 after the church council had rejected a new complaint against him. The matter was then taken up by two other NGK ministers who lodged complaints with the synodical commission. Finally in May 1965 the commission declared his election as elder invalid, a decision which had seemed inevitable from the outset.[10]

To observers, the row over Beyers Naudé's election to the church council seemed petty, but symbolically it was important. As an elder, Beyers could have been elected to attend church synods, and his opponents wanted to make quite certain that he would never again have an official platform from which to air his views. For Beyers and his supporters a matter of principle was involved. In

A new ministry unfolds

Beyers's view, his removal from the church council was invalid in terms of church law, and he was angry and saddened by the outcome.

Right from the establishment of the CI, attacks were made in parliament, from pulpits and the press. Especially after the revelations about Beyers's involvement in the Broederbond exposés, many seemed to think he was fair game, and suggested the CI was a 'communist' organisation. As 1964 drew to a close the campaign against Beyers and his supporters showed no signs of easing. Under great pressure, several members of the NGK began resigning from the CI, and its hope of reaching Afrikaners receded even further. Displaying incredible hope and patience, Beyers wrote numerous letters to the Afrikaans press, trying to defend himself against venomous reports and letters.[11]

Although in the 1960s and 1970s the NGK gradually began to shift away in its official utterances from claims that the Bible justified apartheid, the church continued to support the government's policy of 'separate development', insisting that apartheid provided a just dispensation for all races in South Africa. This stand sharply contrasted with the views of the CI, and an open clash was inevitable. *Die Kerkbode*, still under the editorship of Andries Treurnicht, kept up a steady attack on the CI. In January 1964, for example, it hit out at the 'alarming trend' of having a Roman Catholic on the CI's board of management.[12]

If 1964 was a difficult year for the CI, 1965 was wellnigh impossible. Wave after wave of attack was mounted on Beyers in church, media and political circles. Yet in the midst of this fray, the CI continued to expand and grow. By April 1965 Fred van Wyk had taken up his position as full-time administrative director of the organisation. Clerical staff were employed, and the CI began to look for a full-time black fieldworker to increase awareness of the Christian Institute in the black community. Young ministers, like James Moulder and Danie van Zyl, were also now working for the Institute. In the fourteen years of its existence, the CI was to have a high turnover of staff and board members. Some left when they moved to new jobs and towns, but many broke away because they were opposed to the direction the CI was taking or did not like its organisational structures. Although Beyers never ran the CI in a dictatorial way, his style as director determined the trajectory the CI took. Many of Beyers's former colleagues questioned the impulsive way he hired staff and felt he often displayed poor judgement of character. While there were several disastrous appointments over the years, Beyers also attracted a number of very talented, creative people to the CI.

The composition of the board of management in 1965 reflected the mixture of South Africans who supported the Institute's work. The English churches and the Christian Council of South Africa were well represented by people like Basil Brown and Bill Burnett, while individual Afrikaans Reformed ministers still enjoyed a high profile, notably Ben Engelbrecht and Albert Geyser. Notable by their absence from the board, however, were any Afrikaner ministers in important positions of leadership in their churches. Black representation on the board was expanded to included ministers like J. C. M.

Mabata and S. A. Mohono, in addition to long-time supporter E. E. Mahabane.[13]

One of the first goals in 1965 was to increase support by means of a membership drive. It was Beyers's aim to enlarge membership from about 1 200 to 2 000 by the end of that year, and work in other parts of the country, like Durban and Pietermaritzburg, was accelerated. At that stage, the CI operated some 35 discussion groups throughout the country. New Bible study material was prepared by a group of volunteers and permanent staff members.[14]

From 1965 an important new dimension was added to the life and work of Beyers when the separatist or indigenous black churches approached the CI for assistance. Beyers's direct involvement with these churches was to absorb a great deal of his time, and spanned more than ten years. In many ways Beyers failed to reach his goals in helping the indigenous churches improve their position. However, his eagerness to respond to their unexpected appeal for help was typical of his enthusiastic approach to new projects. Beyers and the CI were pioneers in recognising the need to reach out to these rapidly growing churches, isolated from mainstream Christianity, which already had millions of followers in the 1960s.

While it is difficult to generalise about so complex a phenomenon, it can be said that the separatist or independent churches had their origins in black Christians' disillusionment and unhappiness with the missionary churches, and their desire to pursue their faith unhindered by white control. Broadly speaking they fell into two categories, the Ethiopian churches which often retained much of the doctrine and liturgy of the missionary churches but stressed the idea of 'African churches for Africans', and the Zionist groups which emphasised the charisma and strength of their prophet leaders, incorporated some traditional African ideas and placed great importance on the power of the Holy Spirit and on faith-healing and baptism by immersion. Members of separatist churches mostly came from the very poorest communities, and their ministers and prophets, often with only a few years of schooling, usually eked out a precarious living. In December 1964 a group of leaders, wanting to upgrade their theological education, approached the Christian Institute for help. Since historically these separatist churches had kept their distance from any white structures, the request for assistance came as a surprise to many.

Anthropologist Dr Martin West, who spent two years under the auspices of the Christian Institute studying the separatist phenomenon in Soweto, believed it was highly significant that the African independent churches trusted Beyers sufficiently to approach him. 'The AI churches had been going for a hundred years at that time and had a reputation of being . . . very cautious and sceptical about involvement with whites and mission churches. They felt inferior and were always worried about being looked down upon by the conventional churches. It is quite extraordinary and an enormous tribute to Beyers that a number of them were prepared to cooperate with the CI when they were not prepared to do so with others. . . . I attributed this to two factors. Firstly, the CI was not a mission organisation, nor a denominational organisation, as the AI churches were cautious about falling under the wing of a particular denomination. The fact that it was an ecumenical body was one of the attractions. The second factor was the political aspect – the fact that the CI was non-racial and got some political flak for being non-racial.'[15]

Beyers, with his strong commitment to evangelism and his growing awareness of the need to reach out to the indigenous churches, did not hesitate when they asked for help. 'My interest was a deep personal one but it was also a theological one. I realised that it was a challenge to the other historic mission churches in South Africa – that if they could not meet the legitimate needs and aspirations of the AI churches, with their two and a half million members, they would never be able to become an indigenous church in the biblical sense of the word. . . . That was the beginning of a very long, difficult, but in a certain respect rewarding association between the CI and the AI churches.'[16]

Working with men like the Reverend Z. J. Malukazi, a minister from an independent church, Beyers began making contact with other leaders to try to identify their needs and problems. Beyers realised that to achieve anything with the AI churches, it was necessary for them to maintain their independence and so he agreed to assist them, providing they set up their own organisation with which the CI could deal.

In January 1965 an exploratory conference attended by about 75 church leaders was held in the black township of Daveyton, east of Johannesburg. A resolution was adopted giving 'our fullest confidence to the Christian Institute of Southern Africa and inviting its director, the Rev. C. F. B. Naudé to guide us through every difficulty in the Christian field'.[17] Two months later the CI's board of management officially agreed to help the AI churches, and in June 1965 the African Independent Churches Association (AICA) was formed in Queenstown in the Eastern Cape.[18]

The CI and AICA worked out an ambitious programme for setting up Bible study correspondence courses, refresher courses and vacation schools. A committee to coordinate assistance efforts was set up, consisting of representatives of the CI, AICA, the Christian Council of South Africa (forerunner of the South African Council of Churches) and other black churches.[19] A parallel woman's organisation was also established, which with the help of advisor Els te Siepe functioned well for several years.

James Moulder and later Danie van Zyl took much of the responsibility for AICA, but the work also absorbed a great deal of Beyers's time – solving internal disputes, fundraising and arranging conferences. The major problem which was to lead to the collapse of AICA by 1974 was related to disputes over money and position. From the start Beyers insisted that members of the AICA board of management should be given financial compensation for travelling to meetings. For people with little or no fixed income, representation on the board was to become very important and lead to endless disputes and the formation of breakaway organisations.

Commenting on this aspect, West remarked: 'In my view there was a lot of financial mismanagement in AICA, not in a criminal sense, but in the way things were organised, which was part of the downfall of AICA and was a mistake on the part of Beyers and which Els te Siepe did not allow to happen to the women's organisation. The men were always fighting over money and the women not. . . . The expenses paid to the men to attend meetings were something they could not afford to lose and it added a dimension to AICA politics. It wasn't just being thrown out of the presidency or the board of management, it was actually the loss of the money. Money was the root of evil in the whole thing, and the women's organisation handled it better. I don't think they paid the same sort of expenses and they did more practical things with their money, the men didn't. Much of it was used on travelling about and on politicking at a local level. . . .

'One of Beyers's strengths and weaknesses was that he could never say no. I was there often where he would say: "There is no more money, it's finished, you've used it all up," and they wouldn't believe him, and the money would come. Every time he delivered the goods it made it worse, he just could not say no. It stemmed out of a positive aspect of his character, but it became a negative thing.'[20]

Although the AICA venture was to end in failure, many constructive achievements were made. In the first six years, theological refresher courses were held in major towns around the country. These lent credibility to what AICA was trying to achieve and provided a forum for church leaders to meet. A correspondence course was also launched but was not run properly and failed to get off the ground. One of the major goals was to establish a theological college. By 1967 the Christian Institute came to an arrangement with an existing theological college, the R.R. Wright School of Religion in Evaton, Transvaal, to serve as a seminary for AI ministers.[21] This did not prove satisfactory and the CI conducted negotiations with other institutions. AICA's long-term goal, to open its own seminary, was reached in 1970, when, after considerable fund-raising and great expense and trouble, a seminary was opened at Alice in the Eastern Cape.

The work with AICA provided Beyers with his first experience of close interaction with a black organisation. His open, sympathetic approach enabled him to develop relationships of trust with many of the individuals involved in the separatist churches. Danie van Zyl has described this aspect of Beyers's personality: 'I think the one outstanding feature of Beyers is the way in which he was trusted. People believed in him and they trusted him. I saw this specifically in terms of the black people who really trusted Beyers. Regardless of the conflict within the AICA groups, they all trusted him. . . . Beyers was good at holding things together when it became very difficult. He would call them all in and they would sit and talk. They would not resolve a thing, but we would say we won't do anything until we have at least met again. And then Beyers would be overseas. And in four months' time they would still be there. . . . Even when Beyers had little to do with this whole [AICA] thing, because he got so involved in other things, he remained the important figure in the background.'[22]

While AICA added a new dimension to the Christian Institute's work, Beyers was still preoccupied with efforts to reach out to the Afrikaner community and moreover responding to the campaign of vilification against him and his staff.

A major problem was that he had no opportunities to speak to ordinary Afrikaans congregations or audiences. NGK ministers dared not invite him to preach at their churches for fear of falling foul of the Afrikaner establishment, and anyone who attempted to do so immediately joined the ranks of the outcasts. It was against this background that an ugly incident occurred in the Johannesburg suburb of Belgravia. One of Beyers's surviving NGK friends was Roelf Meyer, then minister of the Belgravia congregation; through Meyer's efforts, the church council agreed that Beyers could address the church youth group, the *Kerk Jeugvereniging* (KJV), on the subject of 'the church and politics'.

This caused a controversy in the Belgravia church and in the broader NGK. It was claimed even that Beyers's speech would influence the outcome of an upcoming provincial election. As a result of mounting agitation against the meeting, Roelf Meyer announced from his pulpit that Beyers's address had been moved forward by two weeks. This infuriated conservatives in the church who felt that Meyer was outmanoeuvring them in their efforts to have the meeting cancelled. The night before Beyers was due to speak, an extraordinary meeting of the church council decided to cancel the original invitation to Beyers. Roelf Meyer, however, declared the church council meeting invalid and urged Beyers to come to the church at 7 p.m. on 9 March 1965, as arranged.

When Beyers arrived at the church that night, several members of the church council had gathered, determined to prevent him from addressing the KJV. Beyers parked his car, waited outside for a few moments, and then crossed into the church yard. He was immediately met by an angry crowd. A representative of the church council demanded that Beyers leave and several other people began shouting, some accusing him of trying to split the NGK and others of trying to influence their children. By the time Roelf Meyer arrived on the scene, the mood of the crowd was angry, and he was unable to persuade them to let his guest into the church. Two men then grabbed Beyers by the arms and marched him outside the church gate. Roelf Meyer had by then called the police, but the bewildered policeman who arrived was unable to resolve the dispute. Finally, the small number of KJV members who had turned up for the meeting departed with Beyers and Roelf Meyer to hold the meeting at a private house.[23] But Beyers's opponents had been successful in preventing him from addressing a public meeting of the KJV, the youth organisation which, ironically, he had helped create.

The Belgravia incident hurt Beyers very deeply, but the NGK showed few signs of remorse for the display of bad manners of its members. The Johannesburg circuit frowned on the incident, but *Die Kerkbode* refused to condemn unconditionally the use of force against a former minister. In an editorial it piously declared that the incident could not be seen as a very 'happy' one, but went on to say: 'The fact is that our brother has taken standpoints and has involved himself with an institute which our church has spoken out against. We cannot deny someone the right to their views or to belong to organisations. But where church channels are searched for and are offered with the idea of promoting those ideas, then in our opinion there is reason for dissatisfaction and efforts must be made to ensure healthy order is maintained in the church.'[24]

It was not only the church that showed an interest in maintaining 'healthy order'. In May 1965 the security police carried out their first raid on the CI on the pretext of searching for documents relating to 'communism and the ANC'. The raid came three months after *Pro Veritate* had mentioned a book which was banned for distribution in South Africa. After the 'offence' had been pointed out to Beyers, all remaining copies of the February issue were censored to remove the offending title. This, however, did not satisfy the authorities and so in a dramatic raid, eight members of the security police searched the offices of the CI as well as the Naudé home in Greenside. Beyers himself was asked to empty his pockets and was then 'frisked' by a policeman looking for incriminating evidence. The police haul consisted of a few copies of *Pro Veritate* as well as copies of a controversial report on South Africa by the British Council of Churches.

Beyers and his supporters were well aware that the raid would further tarnish the image of the CI in the eyes of many white churchgoers. A futile attempt was made to minimise the damage by emphasising that the police action was not connected to the new organisation.[25] The English press, however, rose to Beyers's defence, accusing the police of becoming involved in a political vendetta. Opposition politicians demanded an explanation for the raid in parliament. The then Minister of Justice, John Vorster, said the purpose of the raid had been to gain evidence for an alleged contravention of the Suppression of Communism Act.[26]

In the midst of all this, Beyers left for the first of many trips abroad to raise funds for the AICA movement. During his absence, the 'unrest' in the NGK continued. One church council demanded that the CI issue be considered at a special synod of the Southern Transvaal NGK. This request was refused, but the synodical commission finally did hold a special meeting to discuss the various controversies surrounding Beyers and the CI. With Beyers unable to defend himself, the meeting approved a report which condemned the CI and any minister or church council member who belonged to it. This statement was distributed to all member churches in the Southern Transvaal area, and placed new pressure on NGK ministers to resign from the CI. On the basis of this report the Johannesburg circuit terminated Beyers's position as elder of the Parkhurst congregation.

Ben Engelbrecht was one of the ministers who came under strong pressure because of his support for the CI. After Van Rooyen's return to Parkhurst, Engelbrecht took up a post in a nearby parish, but he was criticised because of his links with Beyers. Several members of his church council lodged an official complaint with the Johannesburg circuit over an article he had written for *Pro Veritate*, and some members of his church council resigned. Engelbrecht eventually joined the CI to work on *Pro Veritate* and also lost his status as a minister.[27]

Although Beyers had become accustomed to pressure and adverse publicity, the police raid on the Christian Institute shocked and angered him. He was overseas when the news of the police action appeared in South African newspapers and he was obviously concerned about the impact it would have on the CI. He had long reflected over the parallels between Nazi Germany and South Africa and, while still abroad, wrote the first in a series of controversial articles for *Pro Veritate* in which he called for the creation of a confessing church movement in South Africa.

The confessing church movement was to have an important influence on Beyers's thinking. In the 1930s the German Evangelical Church, which represented the majority of Protestant Germans, compromised with the Nazi regime because of the close historical links between church and state. But there was also a strong group of pastors who rejected this compromise. In 1933, some 6 000 pastors joined an emergency league to reject the church leadership's support for the Third Reich. 'Free synods' were held in various centres in Germany where the foundation for the confessing church movement was laid. The name 'confessing church' came from the desire of the pastors to restore the true confession of the Evangelical Church and root out the false doctrine planted by the Nazis. These efforts culminated in the holding of a national synod in Barmen in 1934. The synod adopted the famous 'Barmen Confession' – a six-point statement which reaffirmed Christ as the highest authority from whom all human freedom derived and rejected the notion that the church should serve or be controlled by the state.[28]

Out of the Barmen declaration came the idea of a national confessing church. Its leaders never sought to establish a new church, but claimed that Christians who supported it constituted the true German Evangelical Church. The years which followed were characterised by a long and complicated church struggle. The Nazi regime succeeded in gaining control over the 'official' church, which resulted in its ultimate destruction. The confessing church movement, struggling with increasing repression as well as internal problems, was nevertheless a small light in Nazi Germany during the war years and served as a witness to Christians all over the world.

Beyers's first article calling for a confessing church movement in South Africa appeared in the July 1965 issue of *Pro Veritate*. He argued: 'It should be clear to anyone who is familiar with the development of the church situation in the Third German Reich, and, looking at events in our country affecting the church and the state, that there are more and more parallels between Nazi Germany and present-day South Africa.

'This parallel is not just found in the methods used in South Africa, not just in the creation and spreading of slogans in the press and on radio, but also in the general reaction of fear on the part of an increasing number of Christians. This fear leads to untenable compromises and unacceptable silences, and strengthens the power of an authority which . . . because of the race philosophy underlying its policy, can do no other than to apply increasingly stronger measures against anyone – including the Churches and Christians – who act out of pure Biblical and Christian convictions and condemn unchristian elements in our race policies.

'If I think about all these signs, then it is clear that the time has arrived for a Confessing Church in South Africa. . . . I want to make it clear . . . that this has nothing to do with establishing a new church . . . but that it means that

Christians of the various faiths . . . should call on their churches to take an unambiguous stand and deliver a fearless witness based on the Word of God.'[29]

The article unleashed a storm of protest in Afrikaans church circles.[30] *Die Kerkbode* described the Nazi label 'misplaced'. 'Those who want to attribute to us the German sins of a quarter of a century ago can do so only out of ignorance or with other motives, but such a person has no hope of arousing a sincere feeling of guilt in us about sins which we have not committed. . . . Our church is not too proud to confess our failures and sins. But we find unfair and abhorrent the insinuation that we are being taken into tow by an evil dictatorship.'[31]

In another article for *Pro Veritate* Beyers admitted that the situations in Nazi Germany and South Africa were not identical, but said that there were certain parallels. He compared Nazi Germany's concern with racial purity and discrimination against Jews with the Afrikaner's obsession to maintain a racially pure *volk*. He described how the German Christians had used the Bible to forbid intermarriage between Aryans and Jews – and compared it with the Afrikaner's use of Scripture to forbid racial mixing.

He also argued that in Nazi Germany there was close identification between church and nation, and that eventually the church was expected to serve the ideals and aspirations of the people. He warned that letters and articles in newspapers in South Africa demonstrated this same tendency of wanting a close relationship between church and *volk*, and expecting the church to support the political vision of the people.[32]

In the final article on this issue, Beyers identified further parallels between the situations in the two countries. Highlighting intimidation in Nazi Germany, he asked: 'Is it necessary to quote examples of the situation in South Africa? . . . I think of scores of NGK ministers and laymen who have told me that they are frightened to speak up about their deepest Christian convictions . . . because, if they are white, they will either be ostracised or lose their jobs . . . or if they are black, face possible intimidation from the authorities.'

Beyers also drew a parallel between the 'sinful silence' of German Christians on the issue of the persecution of the Jews and injustices suffered by black people in South Africa. He ended with the claim that the confessing church in South Africa had already arrived. Its voice was still small and uncertain, but there was already a new life and spirit in the church.[33] He was obviously thinking of the CI. Most South African theologians would disagree that a true confessing community was ever established in South Africa, and would probably cite the practical difficulties involved or say that a disillusioned 'confessing element' already existed. But in some respects the CI did fulfil the role of bringing 'confessing' elements in the various churches together by giving support to individual Christians in their struggle against injustice as well as backing important Christian-motivated projects. As theologian John de Gruchy put it: 'What the CI did . . . was to provide resources and an *ad hoc* supportive community for those who were at the cutting edge of the churches' witness. And this proved an immense strength to those involved.'[34]

As 1965 drew to a close, Afrikaner hostility towards Beyers and the CI continued unabated and he was forced to step down as chairman of the governing body of his daughter's school.[35] In another attack, *Die Kerkbode* editor Andries Treurnicht used the first in a series of radio broadcasts on 'The Afrikaner and His Church' to criticise Beyers. Referring to the call for a confessing church movement in South Africa, Treurnicht said: 'The intention is to create unrest among the Afrikaner in regard to his church membership and the unity of the *volk*. It is not the first attempt to estrange the Church and the *volk* or to replace the Afrikaans churches, with their particular role in the life of the *volk*, for another religious organisation. . . . The target is clear – control of the Afrikaners. And to get control of the Afrikaner, control of the churches is necessary.'[36]

In a final, desperate effort to counter this 'organised campaign' (as they saw it), Ben Engelbrecht, Beyers Naudé, Fred van Wyk and another member of the Christian Institute, J. D. Smith, sent an open letter to 1 500 NGK ministers in South Africa. The strong influence of the confessing church idea came through in this letter – it warned Afrikaners that they were abandoning their confessional basis in favour of a *volksteologie*. The letter identified a 'new development' in Afrikaner church circles: 'The development which is taking place before our eyes is that a point of view or attitude which is held by someone in respect of its permissibility, integrity, acceptability and Christian character, is no longer tested against the Word of God, but against a political ideology, which no matter how well-intentioned it originally may have been, . . . becomes in many of the ways in which it is applied, increasingly less able to stand the test of the Word of God.'

The letter continued: 'Christians and the Church in South Africa will not allow themselves to be blinded by all that is happening against *Pro Veritate* and the Christian Institute. The time has come to realise the deadly seriousness of the situation. It is no longer a political game with a relatively harmless meaning. Absolute contradictions are taking shape. There are two Gospels, two Lords, two Christs, which have come to oppose each other in our national life. . . .

'In the name of the Lord we would beg your deepest consideration of what we have brought before you. We do not ask your sympathy and support for the Christian Institute and *Pro Veritate*. . . . We ask you to consider the position of the Church in South Africa, to see and to mark, to hear and to understand that the political ideology wants also to blind the Holy Ghost to rule over the living God and His Word, to threaten the freedom of the Church in her preaching the Word of her Lord. We beseech you to realise that you may wait no longer to take a considered position and make it known.'[37]

It was a letter written from the heart and sent in faith, but it was to no avail. The following year would bring the final, irreconcilable break between Beyers and his church.

11
Years of Struggle at the Christian Institute, 1966–1968

By the mid-1960s Beyers had accepted the fact that the CI had not made progress with the Afrikaner churches and realised that his organisation would have to find a new direction if it wished to become relevant in South Africa. Yet he had no clear strategy, and in the next few years the CI's work would branch out in a random, almost erratic way. Some of Beyers's closest friends felt that the 'mushrooming' of the CI was a fault and that Beyers failed to consolidate sufficiently. Peter Randall, a writer and publisher who was to work closely with both the CI and the SACC in the late 1960s and early 1970s, said: 'One of the greatest strengths of the CI was that it was constantly grappling at the theoretical and practical level with issues as they arose, experimenting with styles of organisation. But if I had a major criticism of the CI, it would be . . . that at times it seemed to be too open to every new influence, to new demands made upon it. I was considerably frustrated at times at the CI's apparent inability to set a clear order of priorities.'[1]

The style of the CI's operation reflected to some extent Beyers's own personality; he himself has been described by friends as *konsekwent*, in a typical Afrikaner way – displaying stubbornness and a step-by-step logic that led him inexorably from one action to another. However, Beyers's actions and the CI's programme must be seen in the context of the political climate in South Africa. The decade from the mid-1960s to the mid-1970s, the core years of the Christian Institute, was also the era of supreme white confidence and the years of grand apartheid. Beyers Naudé and other staff members were constantly challenged to respond to the problems and crises of the time.

An example of these problems was the government's relentless programme to eliminate any 'mixed-race' areas in South Africa. The destruction of District Six in Cape Town, and the forced removal of about 30 000 Coloured people, encapsulates the anger and misery this policy caused. In February 1966, District Six was proclaimed a 'white area'. The housing shortage for Coloureds in Cape Town already exceeded 9 800 families, and in spite of bitter protests, appeals and petitions, the government was adamant – the Coloured people of District Six had to move.[2] On the pretext that District Six was a slum and that it wanted to provide better housing for Coloured people, the government moved out every single Coloured inhabitant and bulldozed the district to the ground. The destruction of this suburb and other forced removals and re-zonings in Cape Town caused massive upheaval. While the government later developed new, uniform townships for Coloureds, these were far from the city in the desolate area of the Cape Flats.

Writing about District Six in *Pro Veritate* in March 1966, Beyers said: 'There is a dark shadow lying over District Six – a shadow which will remain like a ghost over the area for many years to come – long after the Coloured shanty houses are cleared and replaced by flashy offices for white occupants and investors. It is a shadow, not of a laudable deed of urban renewal, . . . but of an action which forms part of a policy which wants to force people apart and keep them apart simply because they are a different colour. . . . Eventually we as whites are going to suffer most because of our unwillingness to protest and to witness. Our dehumanisation of our neighbour, which humiliates the Coloured, will eventually destroy us.'[3]

In spite of the CI's concern about the suffering of black South Africans, it still remained a white-dominated organisation which relied on the support of mainly white English-speakers. Black membership was small while Afrikaner support was falling. Indeed, there was no let up in the opposition from within mainstream Afrikanerdom to the CI. Opponents continued with their insinuations that Beyers was a communist – a rumour that was fuelled when it was revealed that communist trialist Bram Fischer had sent him a letter while on the run from the police. The letter was intercepted before it reached Beyers, but this did not deter police from conducting a thorough search of his home on the pretext that they were looking for the note.[4]

Beyers was angered by these attacks but refused to become embittered. 'This was firstly because of my understanding of the gospel and of Christ's demand. I read many of those passages, especially in the New Testament, of what Christ demanded of those who act in this way. . . . I realised that if there is really a sincere love of your fellow human being, including your enemies, then that love must express itself in the willingness to at least not allow anger and aggressiveness and vindictiveness to lay claim to your life.

'I realised that in the long run if I allowed this to happen to me, I would lose and drain so many of my emotional, spiritual and intellectual energies which I knew that I would need for the future struggle which lay ahead. I think I understood the Afrikaner people much better than they understood themselves. I thought of my own home, of the deep bitterness which at times my mother expressed about what had happened to the Afrikaner people in the Anglo–Boer War, of the 26 000 women and children who had died in the concentration camps. . . . I had to admit that there were legitimate reasons why the Afrikaner people felt this terrible bitterness towards anybody whom they saw as crossing over to the other side. They regarded that person as a traitor, just as they regarded Jan Smuts and others as traitors. . . . I realised this was the way in which the Afrikaner people had been brought up, had been taught to look at anybody who, from their viewpoint, betrayed them. I could never agree with this or support it, but it made it bearable. I realised that if I allowed that same kind of vindictive, aggressive, unforgiving spirit to take hold of my life it would destroy me.'

On many occasions not only Beyers, but other CI staff members were able to see the funny side of what seemed a bleak situation. Beyers's wry sense of humour was noted by many of his friends. Martin West recalled one incident: 'Beyers and I were walking somewhere in town and he met and greeted an old acquaintance in the street. We continued walking and suddenly Beyers started laughing out loud. I asked him what was so funny and he said to me: "That guy still gave me the old Broederbond handshake!" So he still had those links with the authorities.'[5]

Beyers was cordial and good-mannered even with his fiercest enemies – including the security police. Danie van Zyl recalled: 'I went with Beyers on one occasion when he was summonsed by a senior policeman to John Vorster Square in Johannesburg. Beyers walked into his office and shook his hand. He saw a photograph of his son and he immediately began asking him about the boy and the rest of his family. I saw this policeman, who had been ready to have a real confrontation with Beyers, suddenly dissolve. Even when Beyers met his greatest enemies, like Koot Vorster or Kosie Gericke, he would shake their hands and talk to them as if they were the best of friends. It was not that Beyers was being insincere. He would talk to anybody, debate with them and try to change their minds.'[6]

Despite the problems the CI faced, Beyers continued enthusiastically with his work. In the early years he travelled extensively to promote the CI. Early in 1966, he undertook a four-week trip to the Cape Province where he visited all the major towns and spoke at various meetings.[7] While gradually over time the focus of the CI would swing away from Afrikaners and the white community in general to concern itself more with black issues, Beyers's method of operation never really changed. As head of a very small organisation with limited means of communication he had to spread himself very thin, making contact with as many people as possible. Thus extensive travelling, speaking engagements and meetings with numerous groups and individuals became the pattern of his life. By September 1966 membership of the CI stood at about 1 700 and discussion groups had grown from 33 to 45. Bible study material was being issued to many churches and was generally well received. The CI also initiated several public symposia where topical issues were discussed.[8]

One major ecumenical initiative in which Beyers was involved in the mid-1960s was the restructuring of the Christian Council of South Africa. For years, the Council had operated as a rather ineffective body, ill-equipped to deal with the critical developments facing the South African churches, and it was not taken particularly seriously by the member churches. This troubled church leaders, and after the retirement of Basil Brown as general secretary, they searched for a successor who had vision, an understanding of the problems facing South Africa, and influence among the English-speaking churches. Finally it was decided to approach Bill Burnett, Anglican Bishop of

Bloemfontein.⁹ Burnett, as the new general secretary, assisted by people like Fred van Wyk, took the lead in restructuring the Council, while behind the scenes Beyers also made an important contribution. The Council was to be renamed the South African Council of Churches (SACC) in 1968, to emphasise that it had been established by the churches for the purpose of inter-church cooperation. In the next decade the SACC would grow rapidly, adopting numerous programmes and responsibilities.¹⁰ Another goal of the new body was to foster closer ties with the NGK but it was an effort which never came to fruition – largely because of political differences.

Beyers regarded the restructuring of the Council as of major significance. 'The Christian Council did not really operate with the authority of the churches, while the SACC did. We realised that if we really wanted the Protestant churches to play a significant role in the struggle for change in the situation of racial injustice, then it would have to be organised on a more structured basis and that this could only be done through a council of churches instead of a Christian council.' A sign of the growing cooperation between the Christian Institute and the Christian Council was the decision to affiliate the CI to the Council during 1966, and Beyers served on the SACC executive for many years.¹¹

In July 1966 Beyers and Bill Burnett attended the historic World Council of Churches conference on Church and Society, in Geneva, which was to set the debate on Christian involvement in social issues for the next decade. In its final statement the conference condemned racism in churches, urged Christians to oppose the myth of racial superiority, and demanded that all races have equal rights in society.¹² It also laid the foundation for the adoption in 1970 of the WCC's Programme to Combat Racism, which was to cause so much upheaval for member churches in South Africa. As John de Gruchy put it: 'Geneva confronted the churches with the cry of millions of people, particularly in the so-called Third World, for a just world. It was at Geneva that the question of Christian participation in the revolutionary struggles of our day was first raised at such a high level for the Christian church.'¹³ Beyers, who served on the working group on The Action of the Church in Society, placed great significance on the Geneva conference. 'I realised that a very important development was taking place because it was leading us to the wider area of social and economic justice, of getting to grips with the deeper roots of the situation of racial oppression and injustice in South Africa. It helped me to expand and widen my thinking of how we would have to deal with the racial situation in South Africa.'

In 1966 Beyers also travelled to the Netherlands, and extended his contacts in church and political circles. His champion was Professor J. Verkuyl, an influential figure in the Gereformeerde Kerk in Holland. Verkuyl had spent many years in the former Dutch colony of Indonesia as a missionary, where he had been concerned with the problems of racism and the struggle for power at the time the Indonesian people were fighting for independence. Verkuyl, who had returned to the Netherlands in 1963 and who was then working as general secretary of the Netherlands Missionary Council, recognised that Beyers and the CI were tackling the very issues which the world churches ought to be confronting. He was influential in helping to lead his own conservative and insular Gereformeerde Kerk out of its isolation, and he was equally important in mobilising support and interest for Beyers during his Dutch visits.[14]

Largely as a result of the efforts of men like Verkuyl, Beyers was introduced to prominent politicians, journalists and churchmen during his trips abroad.[15] Beyers's fluency in Dutch, his Afrikaner credentials and his orthodox Reformed views were crucial in his ability to influence and impress the Dutch churchmen. He so impressed them that the Hervormde Kerk promised to donate a sizeable sum for the CI's work with the African Independent churches.

One of Beyers's oldest Dutch friends and supporters, Jone Bos, remarked: 'Like most of Beyers's Dutch friends, I was brought up in a Reformed family . . . and we had a very friendly attitude toward the Boers. We admired Paul Kruger and all the old Boers in their battle against the British. . . . During one of Beyers's first trips to the Netherlands, Professor Verkuyl phoned me and said: "This afternoon a certain Dominee Beyers Naudé will be at the synod of the Hervormde Kerk. I am bringing him there and I would like you to be there too." That afternoon a lot of important people, including a man from the Netherlands Bible Society, the chief editor of our Christian newspaper *Trouw*, and one member of parliament met Beyers. They were very impressed and said they wanted to help. And that was the start. . . . Beyers corresponded to the images of my youth – a *dominee*, a Boer, friendly and proud. Verkuyl told me that the CI needed money and I was appointed a sort of secretary to an unofficial committee to help the CI. . . . In the 1960s Beyers would come to the Netherlands two or three times a year and he always came for money and help.'

Jone Bos was closely involved in raising funds for AICA as part of the massive *Kom oor de Brug* fundraising campaign. He noted: 'Beyers could get any amount of money because of his personality. There were a lot of strange projects, of course, but it was the personality. He deeply convinced men with his expression of strong convictions. . . . It was not always the great impression that his projects made on us . . . it was his personality. First of all, you felt that he would never get rich out of it, you knew that he would stay forever at his house in Greenside. . . . It was also an immense advantage that he spoke our language, and also our religious language. . . . Of course his trips to Holland were very difficult for the people who had to organise his programme, because he would never refuse anybody time or an interview.'[16]

In the latter part of 1966, on Beyers's return from Europe, the Christian Institute and the Christian Council began to plan holding regional conferences to consider the Geneva message for South Africa. But while cooperation was steadily improving with the English churches, there was no contribution forthcoming from the Afrikaans churches, and the tension between the CI and the NGK continued to build up.

One of the weaknesses in the NGK's campaign against the CI was its refusal to subject the Institute to a thorough theological examination. In the three years of its existence, the CI had repeatedly asked the NGK to substantiate its criticism, and in anticipation of the NGK's general synod which was meeting that year, the board of management of the Christian Institute in May 1966 issued a formal invitation to the NGK's *breë moderatuur* to investigate the CI.

In his letter to the secretary of the *breë moderatuur,* Beyers assured the synod that the CI 'welcomes any investigation by the NG Kerk into the aims and activities of the Christian Institute and that there is nothing the Christian Institute desires more than that the NG Kerk should judge the Institute on the basis of the only criterion which should bear weight with the Church, Scripture and Confession.' Apart from an official acknowledgement of this letter, there was no further response.[17]

While fully expecting the synod to take a strong stand on the CI, Beyers was taken aback by the severity of the resolution that was adopted by the synod. The general synod, which met in Bloemfontein in October, based its decision on a flimsy report compiled by the *breë moderatuur*. While taking 'note' of Beyers's letter of invitation, it accepted, with only one dissenting vote, a resolution declaring the CI an extra-ecclesiastical organisation that acted in competition with the church and professed to perform the task 'better than the church did itself'. The resolution also noted that the CI, by including Roman Catholics within its membership, was denying the Protestant confession. Furthermore, it claimed that the CI opposed the NGK's mission policy, had a 'highly questionable church concept and view of ecumenism', and moreover was creating discord in congregations. The synod accused the CI of having 'heretical tendencies' and instructed office-bearers and members of the NGK to withdraw from the CI 'out of loyalty to their church'.[18]

Beyers was determined to challenge the decision. He and three other members of the CI who were also members of the NGK informed the church that they would not resign. The statement sent to the NGK, signed by Beyers Naudé, Ben Engelbrecht, Fred van Wyk, and the CI's publicity officer, Dr Bruckner de Villiers, declared: 'It is our deepest desire to remain members of the NGK, the church of our fathers, but we do not find it in our hearts and consciences to resign as members of the Christian Institute and thus deny the Scriptural truths and principles for which the Institute stands. . . .

'We find the fact that the NGK could take such a decision a most disturbing indication that the Church is in the process of removing itself from the reign of Christ and lapsing into the grip of human arbitrariness.'[19]

In the wake of the decision the press began to speculate about a witchhunt in the NGK directed against laymen or ministers who dared to defy the synod. This did not materialise. Most remaining members of the NGK withdrew from the CI, and only a few 'survivors', resigned to the inevitability of conflict with their church, remained. Beyers and Ilse, and Ben Engelbrecht and his wife, continued to attend the NGK in Parkhurst.

The NGK's decision brought immediate support for the CI from the English-speaking churches. A Christian Council statement, reflecting the gulf in the attitudes between English and Afrikaans churches in South Africa, expressed 'complete confidence in the Christian Institute as a sincere attempt on the part of individual Christians of all denominations and races to meet, study and confer together.'[20]

By contrast an editorial in *Die Kerkbode*, delighting at the synod decision, repeated the claim that the 'liberal' SAIRR had been responsible for the founding of the CI.[21] The editorial so infuriated Beyers that he and Ben Engelbrecht flew to Cape Town to meet editor Andries Treurnicht, moderator Kosie Gericke and actuary Koot Vorster. After three and a half hours, the two sides parted company, more at odds than before.

If one looks back at that synod decision, there must be many NGK members who, even though they opposed Beyers Naudé, doubted the wisdom of the challenge. It had the effect of marshalling support for the CI both in South Africa and, perhaps even more important, overseas. Overseas Reformed churches were in effect forced to choose between the CI, which preached against racial injustice and in favour of Christian unity, and the NGK, which was determined to maintain its racially separate churches and to support apartheid. Professor Bennie Keet recognised the NGK's error at the time. 'It has been an unwise step for the Synod to force the issue, and it will cause a great deal of ill-feeling and harm. The resolution taken by the General Synod of the NGK is quite wrong. . . . The whole objection to the CI is that it wants to work with other churches. I am very sorry that the step was taken by the Synod because it tells members of my church what to do and think. It is against the freedom of thought of the entire church.'[22]

Perhaps the most important consequence of the general synod's decision was the effect it had on the NGK's relationships with the Dutch churches. The issue featured prominently in the Dutch press and several newspapers strongly condemned the decision. The Dutch newspaper *Trouw*, for example, editorialised: 'It is not a theological decision. . . . It is a political decision in favour of the policy of apartheid of the South African government. The synod has set foot on an iniquitous road which can only lead to further disaster.'[23]

The Hervormde Kerk in the Netherlands, the spiritual 'mother' church, was equally disturbed. Cabling for clarification, the board of the general synod of the Hervormde Kerk said: 'Relations between the Nederlandse Hervormde Kerk and the NG Kerk will become so strained that it is questionable whether the Nederlandse Hervormde Kerk can continue to recognise the NG Kerk as a church.'[24]

The extent of overseas concern about the synod's decision was evident when fourteen leading academics from the Free University and the Theological Seminary in Kampen wrote a letter of protest to the NGK.[25] This strong reaction from the Dutch churches and universities had serious implications for the NGK. The latter still placed a high premium on academic exchange between South African universities and Dutch institutions such as the Free University, and valued the opportunities its ministers and theologians had to study abroad. During the course of the next decade the doors would close. As fewer and fewer opportunities arose for white ministers to study abroad, their places were taken by ministers of the Dutch Reformed 'daughter' churches, and Beyers, together with figures like Professor Verkuyl at the Free University, were influential in opening doors for these young African and Coloured ministers.

The NGK's action also led to increasing support for the work of the CI from churches in other countries. In the next decade, the budget and operations of the CI would expand rapidly – largely as a result of the growing sponsorship from the overseas churches.

The general synod's decision caused great controversy in the NGK. The issue was argued at interminable meetings of the various church forums, recalling the petty manoeuvring which had taken place earlier to deny Beyers his status as church elder. Beyers was determined that the church would have to expel him – he would not leave voluntarily. After a formal investigation of the synod's decision, the Parkhurst church council issued a statement rejecting action against Beyers and Ilse Naudé and Ben Engelbrecht and his wife. The council had based its decision of the NGK's own Church Order, as well as the Heidelberg Catechism and the Netherlands Confession, and argued that a member could only be censured if he had sinned against God.[26] Formal complaints were laid against the Parkhurst council, but in spite of this and accusations that it was guilty of 'mutiny', the council, under the leadership of Dr Jan van Rooyen, refused to back down.[27]

Andries Treurnicht, writing in *Die Kerkbode*, stoutly defended the decision of the general synod and criticised certain churchmen for their disobedience. Beyers wrote a strongly worded reply in *Pro Veritate*, warning that the inability of the *breë moderatuur* to provide Scriptural grounds for rejecting the Christian Institute was damaging its credibility. 'This decision has placed the church on a road, the outcome of which is uncertain. This is not in the first place about the Christian Institute, but about a cardinal principle which determines whether the church wishes to be and will remain a church. The question is – what is the yardstick which is recognised by the church as the highest and final authority . . . the Word of God, or the word of a synod?'

Beyers accused Treurnicht of basing his attacks on political rather than biblical principles. 'The editor has used a church newspaper to promote a decidedly party-political view of the Christian Institute, covered by a thin veneer of religion. . . . Our deepest concern is that *Die Kerkbode* has been used as the launching pad for the flight from Church to politics. In this exercise, Dr Treurnicht has been regularly and faithfully supported by Dr J. D. [Koot] Vorster. . . . It was these two brothers (brothers-in-arms in the ideological struggle they are conducting), who in their . . . teamwork in the church, are so close to the views of a current political extremism which is being carried further and further into our Church and which is going to plunge our Church further and further into misery.'[28]

The determination of individuals like Koot Vorster to 'get' Beyers Naudé was matched by the antagonism he encountered among some of his own family members. When his mother died in 1967, Beyers was on a visit to Cape Town and made special arrangements to fly to Graaff-Reinet to be present at the funeral. Even at this time of grief, some members of her family would not put aside their bitterness towards him. At the graveside they crowded around the grave, refusing to allow Beyers to approach.[29]

One striking success Beyers achieved in defending himself and the CI was the libel suit which he and Albert Geyser instituted against arch-conservative Adriaan Pont, Professor of Christian History at the University of Pretoria. Pont was one of the CI's fiercest critics, and as early as 1964 he attacked Beyers Naudé and Albert Geyser during a *volkskongres* on communism held in Pretoria.[30] Pont pursued his 'red smear' campaign in 1965 in a series of articles which were published in the Hervormde Kerk journal, *Hervormer*. He claimed that the CI had openly sided with 'Communist-inspired and directed Pan-Africanism'.

One particularly disturbing article in the *Hervormer* declared: 'The Christian Institute is in its deepest essence a carefully planned and well-equipped front organisation – a means whereby leftist and Communist thoughts are being spread into the South African church world.' Another article dealt with the Mindolo church conference which Beyers and Albert Geyser had attended in 1964. It said that the 'fellow theologians' who had participated in the conference had 'sold themselves to the Devil' and that they were 'traitors to God and their churches, traitors of their country and people'.[31] Pont also insisted that the CI's membership drive, based on the principle of establishing small 'circles', was similar to the 'Communist cell system'.[32] Pont even went so far as to accuse Albert Geyser and Beyers directly of supporting communism. They threatened to sue unless an apology was published in the *Hervormer*, but Pont was unrepentant and continued his attacks on the CI.[33]

The case against Pont began in the Rand Supreme Court on 15 February 1967. It dragged on for 40 days, absorbing an enormous amount of Beyers's time and energy. Beyers and Geyser were demanding R40 000 damages – an exorbitant sum in those days – as a result of the articles written by Pont in the *Hervormer*. The plaintiffs argued that it was clear Pont had been referring to them in several articles when he accused 'fellow theologians' of being communists and supporters of sabotage, war and revolution against South Africa. Beyers and Geyser also claimed that Pont had painted them as people with despicable moral standards who had betrayed their country, their people, their church, their faith, and who only pretended to be Christians. Although Pont denied the charge of libel, it became obvious during the trial that he had not really changed his mind about the two men – he sincerely believed that they had betrayed the *volk* and were helping 'the communists'.[34]

On 9 June 1967 Mr Justice Trollip awarded Beyers and Geyser R10 000 each plus costs – the highest amount ever awarded until then for libel in South Africa. The judge said he had awarded a large sum to vindicate the right of the two theologians to advocate their views in public and to establish and support organisations like the Christian Institute and journals like *Pro Veritate*. Professor Pont appealed against the award, but this was dismissed with costs by the Appeal Court.[35]

For Albert Geyser and Beyers Naudé the outcome of the case was a triumph. Beyers felt that not only he and Geyser, but the Christian Institute itself had been on trial, and he was grateful for a public vindication from the courts. Beyers and Geyser wrote to Pont requesting a meeting to iron out their differences, indicating that they would be prepared to reconsider the full payment of damages.

After a series of letters between the two parties, Pont rejected a meeting and the two sides remained unreconciled. Shortly after judgment had been handed down a writ of execution was served on Professor Pont. Pont handed over assets worth only R332, claiming that he had no further moveable possessions. Finally, Beyers and Geyser accepted an offer that he pay off the amount at R65 a month – which did not even cover the interest on the debt. On several occasions Beyers and Albert Geyser offered to write off the debt if Pont would publicly apologise for his remarks. He refused to do this and continued to make monthly payments for more than 20 years. Since Beyers had raised the bulk of the money for their court costs from overseas churches, neither he nor Geyser took any of the money. Instead, the money was placed in an ecumenical trust fund to assist individuals and organisations.[36]

Looking back at the Pont case, Beyers said: 'Albert Geyser felt very strongly about it because Pont was a minister of the Hervormde Kerk. I think he felt that in exposing Pont he was exposing the distorted theological and political approach of his church. I think the outcome of that trial certainly rattled the Hervormde Kerk and made it clear to some of them that they were on the wrong track as far as their theological and political outlook was concerned.'

In April 1968, Beyers left for a three-month tour of Europe to promote the Christian Institute and to raise more funds for the CI's rapidly expanding work with the African Independent churches. He had by now gained wide recognition in many countries and gave numerous lectures and sermons in the Netherlands, Denmark, Norway, Sweden, Switzerland, England and West Germany. In his addresses, he frequently appealed for more contact between South African and European churches, and described South Africa's isolation as one of the main causes for the development of apartheid ideology.[37]

The Afrikaner establishment, having done its best to destroy the CI's reputation in South Africa, was becoming very concerned about the support that the Institute and Beyers were attracting abroad. While the NGK had severed ties with the World Council of Churches, it was still sensitive to criticism from the Reformed churches overseas. It was thus deeply shaken in 1967 by the strong condemnation of apartheid which the Reformed Church of America issued in a statement. In reply, the NGK's director of information, Dr Willem Landman, wrote a book in 1968 entitled *A Plea for Understanding*. Since this was essentially an apology for the government and the church's race policies, it is hardly surprising that the South African government's Department of Information provided backing for the book.[38]

While the government's propaganda projects were later to achieve a high level of sophistication, in the late 1960s some of their attempts proved embarrassingly amateurish. Beyers himself was witness to one of these bungles when he attended the 1968 Uppsala assembly of the World Council of Churches which focused partly on South Africa's racial policies.[39] During the conference South African agents dropped two Department of Information 'fact sheets' outside the door of each Uppsala delegate, and for good measure also left copies of Landman's book.

Referring to the incident on his return to South Africa, Beyers summed up the damage the propaganda bid had created. 'This action caused very serious harm to the witness the NGK wished to give through the book. Delegates were also deeply upset by the fact that this gave the impression that while the NGK had withdrawn from the World Council – and had therefore officially ceased . . . dialogue – it was now presenting its case through unknown individuals.'[40]

A further blow to the Afrikaans churches came a month after the Uppsala assembly when the Reformed Ecumenical Synod (RES) met in Lunteren, in the Netherlands. The synod issued a statement on race relations, which while couched in moderate language, posed a direct challenge to apartheid theologians by declaring that Christian unity should be expressed through 'common worship, including holy communion, among Christians regardless of race'. The resolutions attracted widespread publicity because they directly confronted the two white South African members of the RES, the Gereformeerde Kerk and the NGK, with the need to reconsider their race policies.[41]

While the CI enthusiastically endorsed the Lunteren resolutions, calling on the NGK to do the same, the latter put the issue on the back-burner by appointing the Landman Commission. This delayed issuing a report until 1974. The NGK faced further discomfort when one of its 'daughter' churches, the *Sendingkerk*, endorsed the Lunteren resolutions. The NGK's refusal to reassess its support for apartheid was to lead to increasing tension and conflict with the daughter churches.[42]

Increasingly in the late 1960s the CI and the SACC came to work jointly on projects. While the relationship deepened, it was not without tension. There was a vast difference in operational styles and the CI was considered far more radical than the SACC. This was mainly because of Beyers's leadership, and because the CI could take quick decisions while the SACC had first to obtain the support and approval of member churches.

James Cochrane, who belonged to the staff of the CI for several years, wrote: 'The Christian Institute was aberrant in the sense of deviating from many of the norms and standards of the contemporary South African "way of life," a fact which made it unwelcome and treated with suspicion, even sometimes within the churches officially supporting it. It was best to distance oneself even while agreeing with the basic direction of its witness. . . . One often heard in those days the phrase: "Yes! But really don't go too far!" '[43]

Peter Randall also detected a faint resentment towards Beyers in liberal circles. 'I first met Beyers in 1964 when I had joined the SA Institute of Race Relations as assistant director. I was very conscious among some of the English-speaking white liberals of an almost condescending attitude towards this Afrikaner, as well as, possibly, a certain element of jealousy. Race Relations had been plodding away for donkey's years, it was pleasantly asleep on its feet, and suddenly Beyers Naudé appeared on the scene and stole all the thunder. And got all the press coverage. I used to sense quite regularly this almost resentful feeling on the part of the English liberal establishment and I wondered whether this was also reflected in the church scene.'[44]

John Rees, who became general secretary of the SACC in 1968 when it was formally constituted, commented: 'The CI had more freedom to act and far more money than the SACC in those days. An inevitable tension arose when the SACC was perceived to be dragging its feet, when in fact it was held up by a much more cumbersome decision-making procedure. There was a love-hate relationship with Beyers as a person as far as the church leadership was concerned, particularly when he made statements either critical of the churches, or when he made statements on behalf of the CI and the SACC without sufficient consultation. I think there were also people in those churches who disagreed particularly when, in their opinion, Beyers became confrontational in his challenges to the authorities. There was also a resentment relating to money. The SACC wanted to do things and it never had the funds, and the world church seemed to be pouring money into the CI. . . .

'But the CI had a very important role to play at a period in the history of South Africa, of calling Christians to a rejection of apartheid and to a more radical commitment to Christ. It gave people opportunities in the midst of a tightening apartheid situation to meet non-racially. Those were important things, because they served as leaven within the churches. Beyers's opinion was also very much valued within the context of the SACC. His was a very articulate position on the aspirations of black people and that was important because in the initial stages the SACC was dominated by whites.'[45]

One joint SACC–CI project which assumed importance in the life of Beyers was the issuing of a Christian declaration challenging apartheid, entitled *A Message to the People of South Africa*. As early as 1967, the CI and Christian Council had arranged a series of regional church conferences to explore the church's role in ending racial injustice. This culminated in a national conference on church and society held in Johannesburg in February 1968. The conference, which had considerable input from the laity as well as from theologians, tried to define how South Africa could become a more just society.

In the same spirit the SACC established a theological commission to consider 'what obedience to God requires [of] the Church in her witness to her unity in Christ in South Africa'.[46] Its three chief members, John Davies, Ben Engelbrecht and Calvin Cook, were also leading members of the CI. The *Message* was finally released at a press conference in September 1968. The six-page document sought to show that apartheid was contrary to the Christian message and that Christ had made reconciliation between people possible and essential. 'The Gospel of Jesus Christ declares that God is love; separation is the opposite force of love . . . apartheid is a view of life and of man which insists that we find our identity in dissociation and distinction from each other; it rejects as undesirable the reconciliation which God is giving to us by His Son; it reinforces distinctions which the Holy Spirit is calling the people of God to overcome; it calls good evil. This policy is, therefore, a form of resistance to the Holy Spirit.'[47]

The *Message* did not simply reject apartheid as unchristian but warned that the system of racial segregation presented a threat to the church itself. Christians could not ignore what was happening in the wider society and were 'under an obligation to live in accordance with the Christian understanding of man and of community, even if this be contrary to some of the customs and laws of this country'.

The *Message* earned high praise from many quarters, as well as criticism from some dissenting Afrikaner theologians who argued that it did not spell out an alternative to apartheid. Baptists in turn criticised it for confusing man's eternal salvation with political issues. To the Baptists apartheid was merely a political policy; to the drafters of the *Message* it had become a rival gospel in South Africa and therefore had to be resisted.[48] Later, a radical critique of the *Message* would emerge that questioned the document for being a white initiative which had stopped short of understanding the gospel as a call for the oppressed to take their future into their own hands.[49] But in its historical context the *Message* represented a significant challenge to many Christians and churches. What is more, it worsened relations between the English-speaking churches and the NGK, and angered the government.

Prime Minister John Vorster took a personal stand on the declaration when he warned churchmen not to 'disrupt order in South Africa under the cloak of religion'. He declared that if anyone had ideas 'about doing the kind of thing here in South Africa that Martin Luther King did in America' they had better 'cut it out, cut it out immediately for the cloak you carry will not protect you if you try to do this in South Africa'. In response Beyers and a number of other leading figures in the CI and SACC sent an open letter to Vorster, insisting that as long as the government tried to justify apartheid in terms of the Word of God, they as Christians would deny and challenge it. Vorster's reply to this was: 'It does not surprise me that you attack separate development. All liberalists and leftists do likewise. It is with the utmost despisal, however, that I reject the insolence you display in attacking my Church as you do. This also applies to other Church ministers of the Gospel . . . who do in fact believe in separate development. . . . I again want to make a serious appeal to you to return to the essence of your preaching and to proclaim to your congregations the Word of God and the Gospel of Christ.'[50]

As 1968 drew to a close, the Christian Institute and its supporters felt a sense of frustration, mostly because of its inability to attract Christians from the Afrikaans and black communities. As the CI's board chairman Calvin Cook put it in his address to the August 1968 annual general meeting: 'How frustrating to those who have shown such faith that we have produced so little to justify their hopes. . . . There is a growing suspicion that our influence was like King Log: one big splash, then a few ripples, and finally a tranquil pond once more. Despite the Institute, South Africa remains the most stable country in Africa: a financier's dream. Again, the close scrutiny of the Institute's affairs showed that the fears of Professor Pont were completely unjustified: what he saw in the dark was not even a paper tiger; it was a domestic tabby. We seem headed for the limbo that awaits the politically unsuccessful: will Beyers Naudé end up in some niche alongside of Tielman Roos and Robey Leibbrandt?'[51]

Yet there were also some hopeful signs. One of them was the increased interest and support for the Christian Institute from the European church community. Another was the flickering interest in the CI from the black communities. Beyers, with his deep faith and optimistic view of life, was preparing to change gear and search for new ways to be obedient to God.

12
The Challenge of Black Consciousness, 1969–1972

As a new decade began to dawn in South Africa significant changes were occurring on the political landscape. The Black Consciousness movement, led by a crop of dynamic young leaders who were affirming the power and dignity of black people, made its appearance. The BC leaders issued a challenge not just to supporters of apartheid, but also to white liberals: black people were asserting a pride in their blackness and potential, and in their determination to struggle for liberation on their own. This came as a shock even to the CI, which was then shifting its emphasis from white Afrikaners to the black majority.

Beyers's ultimate acceptance of the BC philosophy – which resulted in his second political metamorphosis – confounded many of his white friends. What made this transformation even more curious for many was the fact that he never looked like a 'radical'. Part of his charm, especially to white English-speakers and overseas admirers, was the fact that in his dress and mannerisms he was still very much the Afrikaner *dominee*. He favoured the popular Afrikaner dress – a short-sleeved 'safari suit', and with his black-rimmed bifocal spectacles and thick, neatly combed-back hair, he appeared indistinguishable from many of his former NGK colleagues.

It is difficult to explain why it was that Beyers, unlike many of his other white friends, made the political transition from 'liberal' to 'radical'. Cedric Mayson, a former Methodist minister who worked closely with Beyers in the CI in the 1970s, had this to say about why Beyers changed: 'There is a beautiful, apocryphal story that drifts around the hazy, sentimental, religious world of Europe, which says that Beyers studied his Bible and there he discovered that his inherited attitudes to blacks was wrong. That is absolute nonsense. . . . A central theme in everybody who made that change, including Beyers, was that they got to *know* black people.'[1]

During the late 1960s and early 1970s much of Beyers's time was absorbed with the black ministers from the African Independent churches. Beyers's CI colleagues were often driven to despair by the high priority he gave to this work. Many former CI workers have cited instances where Beyers, instead of attending to pressing CI business, would be locked in inconclusive meetings with AICA representatives trying to resolve a leadership feud, or else negotiating with garages and mechanics for a new car for a black minister. It was not an uncommon sight at the CI's offices for seven or eight people – mostly AICA men – to be waiting to see Beyers about a problem. It was both a strength and a weakness that he could never turn any of them away. His genuine sympathy, and openness for anyone with a need, made it possible for him to understand and gain the trust of these black men.

When AICA finally collapsed in the 1970s Beyers had little to show for all his years of effort. Did he consider his struggles worthwhile? Said Beyers: 'If you think purely in terms of AICA as an organisation it wasn't worthwhile. But if you think in terms of the experience I gained, the wider insight and understanding of the religious and Christian perspective, it was worthwhile.

'We didn't achieve what we wanted to, we made serious mistakes, also because of my lack of really understanding the whole background of the African indigenous churches and of the African personality, African social standards, criteria and values which I knew absolutely nothing about and which I did not study properly and think about and analyse.'

One of the African Independent church leaders who developed a close relationship with Beyers was Bishop Harry Ngada of the African Methodist Episcopal Church. Ngada worked for the CI for four years and later for AICA as a literacy worker before founding his own Spiritualist Churches Association. 'I first met Beyers in 1967 when he helped me to get a scholarship to study at my church's seminary. . . . He became a precious friend, in some instances he was like a father, even a grandfather. If you went to Beyers with a problem you were sure, if he had a way of helping you, he would. . . . After I completed my studies I was stranded in the sense that the church couldn't pay me a stipend because the African Independent churches and their members are poor in the true sense of the word. I was in a desperate situation, with a wife and two children and a mother to support. Through Beyers and Brian Brown, who was the CI's administrative director, I was offered work with the CI. I worked there for four years and carried on with my ministry. The source of my strength during my involvement with all the struggles of this country came from Beyers and the CI.

'I don't think a day would pass without Beyers attending to an AICA problem. He dedicated his life to all those problems. . . . He always said that the African Independent churches were a very important part of the Christian church in South Africa. Most Christians in South Africa are members of these churches and they have been ignored. Through his base at the CI he tried his best to help. . . . He has been a father to us, in good times and bad. If the history of AICA is ever written, then Beyers should be described as the spearhead, because he introduced the idea of unity to the AI churches.'[2]

It was also on Beyers's initiative that work with the women in the African Independent movement was extended. Beyers appointed a Dutch woman, Els te Siepe, to work with them in an advisory capacity. In 1968 the Women's Association of the African Independent Churches (WAAIC) was formed. Later a second adviser, Lindy Myeza, was appointed as this project expanded. Motivated by a desire to lift themselves out of their desperate poverty and prove that they were able to handle their affairs independently, the women of WAAIC began to tackle practical projects such as literacy training, and health and nutritional courses. But WAAIC was not primarily about sewing and cookery classes. Their CI adviser, Els te Siepe, explained: 'WAAIC brought forward the cause of women; they developed a consciousness of their own worth, of their tremendous strength. One of the things the CI did was to give them the possibility of demonstrating that. And Beyers helped with that because he said: "Let's do something together with the women of the AI churches." He understood you don't do things for people, but you do things together. The women decided how and what they wanted to do and they did it themselves.'[3]

The relationship between the CI and AICA became increasingly troubled as the struggles for the leadership of the latter intensified. Each time board members or leaders were voted out of office they stood to lose their financial privileges, and there arose as a result bitter recriminations and disputes. This led to the formation of several breakaway groups.

Some elements in the Afrikaner churches were suspicious of the CI's work with AICA and in 1970 exploited the divisions in AICA by setting up the breakaway Reformed Independent Churches Association (RICA). Beyers's old enemy and critic, NGK minister Nico van Loggerenberg, initiated this with promises of a car, a theological school in Soweto, railway concessions and marriage licences for those AICA leaders who were prepared to form a new organisation. The split was widely reported in the Afrikaans press, which insinuated that the Independent churches were unwitting pawns used to further the political ambitions of the CI. Complaints of financial mismanagement and of poor theological education were also made. The political motives behind the establishment of RICA became apparent in the organisation's constitution, which had been drawn up with the help of Van Loggerenberg. It included a 'security clause' which stated: 'RICA is a non-political organisation to promote the Church work among the Bantu on separate lines to the honour of the Kingdom of God, and to work in harmony with the State.'[4] One of the most prominent leaders of the breakaway RICA group was Bishop Isaac Mokoena, who later claimed to have 'millions' of followers; he emerged as a strong critic of the SACC and undertook several overseas tours in the 1980s to oppose sanctions and disinvestment.

Many members of RICA eventually returned to AICA, but leadership problems and disputes over money and successions continued to plague the latter body. The CI had always maintained AICA's records and budget because the organisation lacked administrative skills but by 1972 Beyers felt that this arrangement could not continue. Unhappy with AICA's inability to spend its funds wisely, and influenced by the prevailing sentiment in the Black Consciousness movement and by the wishes of overseas donors who wanted AICA to have financial autonomy, Beyers moved to reduce AICA's dependence on the CI.[5]

Recommending that AICA hire a qualified bookkeeper and other administrative staff, the CI handed financial control over to the organisation in January 1973. Martin West summarised the demise of AICA after the CI pulled out:

'AICA did not appoint a qualified accountant, and following mismanagement of funds (including the purchasing of motor cars and the increasing of salaries of all officials) it used up its resources in nine months. By the end of 1973 AICA had virtually collapsed, the college and correspondence courses had been closed down, and the Reverend [E.] Maqina had been deposed as president. After supporting AICA financially for six years and making good regular deficits, the Christian Institute finally withdrew support entirely, and there did not appear to be any hope that AICA could be revived.'[6]

Another CI worker who was closely involved with the AICA work was Methodist minister Brian Brown. Born in Cape Town, Brown had studied accountancy for four years before entering the ministry. He joined the CI in the late 1960s and became one of Beyers's closest colleagues and friends, faithfully serving the CI until its closure in 1977. Of his and Beyers's involvement with the Independent churches, Brian Brown commented: 'I think AICA is a success story on one level and a disaster on the other. The success story is that the CI had created an image of openness and sensitivity which enabled people to come to Beyers and seek a relationship which had either not been sought, or had been sought and denied, within the historic churches. . . . The CI churches were as a result of this in a large measure put on the map . . . they became part of the body of Christ and even in my time we stopped talking about separatist sects and talked about the Independent churches. . . .

'On the negative side one was dealing with a community which was having its first attempt at togetherness whereas the divisiveness had been the pattern all the way along. . . . Now suddenly the CI was saying, "Let's reverse the trend." That was one of the difficulties. The other difficulty was we tried to bring together these wide extremes of Zionist and Ethiopian sects . . . there was a whole dimension we did not understand.'

Brian Brown partly agreed with the criticism that Beyers was not firm enough when it came to requests for money. 'We were in a situation of professing a Christian ideal, which was to allow democracy to prevail, and doing so in the context of a society where white paternalism had always determined black responses. Beyers was trying to break away from that. The kind of strength of response which could be called correct and responsible in healthier societies was so easily viewed as either paternalism at best or racism at worst in the context of the CI. And if I am to defend ourselves and damn ourselves, we did not want to be racists and so we yielded in terms of financial disbursements when we were not always happy that they were being properly used. So the criticism of Beyers is legitimate but it has to be seen in the context of the bedevilment of interpersonal relationships in South Africa, by the history of white domination and by the enduring reality of racism, and it was in that vice that we were crushed.'[7]

By the late 1960s many of the original initiatives of the CI were in decline. The Bible study groups, which had been one of its central features in the early years, were showing signs of stagnation. In 1969 there were some 55 groups, and while by the next year this number had risen to 78, there was a feeling among members that the groups amounted to a great deal of talk but no concrete action. The aim of the groups had been to encourage inter-racial and inter-denominational contact between Christians, but the major problems experienced were apathy, the distances between white and black residential areas, and intimidation by official church and state bodies. The centralised structure of the CI, and the fact that all major initiatives were taken by staff rather than by members, contributed to the decline. Several people were brought into the CI to try to strengthen this work, and for a time, under a talented communicator, Anne Hope, it seemed as if the group work would expand. But it was an aspect of the CI's ministry that never lived up to expectations.[8]

Another sign of the change in the character of the CI was the steady decline in Afrikaner membership. By August 1969, Beyers admitted that there were only about 150 NGK members who still belonged to the CI. While initially between 40 to 50 ministers of the NGK had joined the CI, by 1969 there were none left. Subscriptions to *Pro Veritate* by Afrikaners were also falling.[9]

The waning influence of Afrikaners was also seen in the departure of several prominent Afrikaans-speakers from the staff of the CI. The two most important staff members to leave in 1970 were Ben Engelbrecht and Fred van Wyk. Another founder member, Albert Geyser, also withdrew. Van Wyk continued to serve on the CI's board of trustees for several years and, in spite of certain reservations about the CI's direction, he remained on good terms with Beyers in his new position as head of the Institute of Race Relations. The parting between Beyers and Engelbrecht was not as cordial.

Engelbrecht is one of numerous figures who for many years featured prominently in Beyers's life, and then suddenly disappeared. Engelbrecht's decision to leave the CI and join the University of the Witwatersrand's faculty of divinity, which Albert Geyser headed, was prompted by dissatisfaction with the changes that were occurring within the CI. The break between Engelbrecht and Beyers was also the result of personal clashes. Beyers's breezy optimism sharply contrasted with Engelbrecht's somewhat depressive nature.

Engelbrecht said of Beyers: 'My first disappointment with Beyers Naudé was the fact that when I came into the CI, he didn't want to hand over the editorship of *Pro Veritate* to me. . . . It was very reluctantly that he later stepped down. It was only for the sake of being editor that he clung to it.' Engelbrecht also felt that Beyers was not 'consistent' in his behaviour and that he 'exaggerated' South Africa's problems overseas, by insisting that there was no hope for a peaceful solution. 'It seemed that Beyers Naudé developed more and more in the direction of radicalism. When I left I never ever looked back. I just closed the door behind me and didn't want to have anything to do with *Pro Veritate* and the CI. Looking back I think that I was quite right. After my departure from the CI everything became so radical: the viewpoints, the way they acted. It was throwing down the gauntlet to the state.'[10]

Engelbrecht's statements give an insight into the feeling of bitterness among some of Beyers's Afrikaner friends who felt he had betrayed their cause. John Rees, who observed many of these reactions, commented: 'They accused him of having started the CI with one aim in mind, and then changing it when he was unable to succeed with his original goal. They were not being totally fair since it was a very difficult job to change whites, but that is how they perceived it. Beyers evoked strong reactions and there were some who hated him. But his role as the conscience of Afrikaners was still crucially important. Afrikaners were quietly beating tracks to his door all the time. Even though some of them disliked him so much, they still used to call him *Oom Bey*.'[11]

The departure of Ben Engelbrecht from the CI signalled a gradual change in the character of *Pro Veritate*, which he had edited. He was replaced by another Afrikaner theologian and long-time worker at the CI, Bruckner de Villiers. Although he also came out of the NGK, De Villiers had broader and more progressive political and theological views than his predecessor, and under his editorship the journal's circulation steadily increased. When De Villiers left after two years his place was taken by another former NGK minister, Roelf Meyer. Abandoning its previous, rather dry, theoretical approach and emphasis on Afrikaner Reformed theology, *Pro Veritate* began to devote more attention to social issues and current affairs. The journal also followed the progress and course of the Black Consciousness movement, by giving prominence to Black Theology and Black Consciousness ideas. By August 1972 there were almost 3 200 subscribers, including a small group of interested foreign churchmen.[12]

A vacancy which Beyers found difficult to fill was that left by the departure of Fred van Wyk. There were successive, largely unsuccessful appointments to the post, and it was only later when Brian Brown took over the administrative department that it ran smoothly again. The CI, which by 1970 had a staff complement of 25, continued to have a high personnel turnover. There were numerous remarkable individuals, who, for a time, made important contributions to the CI. People like Elfie Strassberger, Cosmas Desmond, Anne Hope, Mark Collier, Oshadi Phakati and Horst Kleinschmidt, were just some of the many talented and strong-willed individuals who worked at the CI during the 1970s and who all, in some way, had an impact on the life of Beyers Naudé.

One of those who had a great influence on Beyers was Theo Kotze, who in 1969 became director of the CI's newly established Cape Town regional office. Kotze had been the Methodist minister of a successful parish in the affluent white suburb of Sea Point in Cape Town. Like Beyers, Theo Kotze came from an established Afrikaans family, but he had been spared the classic NGK upbringing because of his father's non-conformist views on religion. His marriage to Helen Clegg, daughter of a Methodist minister, and his decision to enter the Methodist Church himself, led him to question the Christian's responsibility in apartheid society. For a brief period he also served as Methodist pastor to prisoners on Robben Island and performed this task with directness and compassion. He met and ministered to PAC leader Robert Sobukwe and ANC leader Nelson Mandela (both Methodists) until prison authorities relieved him of his duties on the ground that he 'did not know how to conduct himself with prisoners'.[13]

As a member of the CI, Theo Kotze developed a close friendship with Beyers; Beyers was frequently a guest in the Kotzes' home during his trips to the Cape, and in 1967 he was invited to preach in the Sea Point Methodist church. Kotze's involvement in the CI deepened after he agreed to head the CI's Bible study group in Cape Town and to serve on the CI's board of management. It was decided that the CI should open a Cape regional office and the funds for the project were raised from the Methodist Church in the USA.[14]

In offering the post of Cape director to Theo Kotze, Beyers gained a very warm-hearted and able colleague and a valuable asset to the CI. Kotze had a quick sense of humour, a sharp intellect, and a charisma which enabled him to build up a lively CI constituency in the Cape. Always loyally supported by his wife Helen, Theo Kotze made an important contribution to the CI until, like Beyers, he was served with a five-year banning order in 1977. The relationship between Beyers and Theo Kotze was not without pain – there were many moments of tension over the years, with Theo often feeling that Beyers did not consult him sufficiently or take his views into consideration. But in the end, in spite of all the difficulties, the two men retained a deep affection for each other.

Speaking of Theo Kotze, Beyers remarked: 'Theo was the one person at that time who, as a Methodist minister, was willing to stand up, to be counted and to pay the price for his convictions. He was a deeply loyal person and a friend who stood by me, as I tried also to stand by him, through these years. Theo also had a link, a personal association and comradeship with black Christians which I did not have. I learnt how to let those friendships grow through my personal experience of Theo's relationship towards them. He also had administrative and organisational abilities which we very urgently needed in the CI, and he made a contribution which was tremendously significant. He built and created for the CI a stand and an acceptance and an influence, first in the Western Cape, and then later in the whole of the Cape Province and which also extended to Namibia.'

In addition to expanding the CI in the Cape, Theo Kotze also helped to promote the organisation during many trips abroad. By the end of 1970 he had raised sufficient funds overseas to open an ecumenical centre in the Cape Town suburb of Mowbray.[15]

A new development of critical importance to the CI at this time was the launching of the Study Project on Christianity in an Apartheid Society (Spro-cas) in March 1969. Sponsored jointly by the SACC and the CI, it was to play a decisive role in advancing Beyers's thinking on political issues. Spro-cas was meant partially as an answer to criticism from the government and its supporters, who argued that the *Message to the People of South Africa* had not spelt out an alternative to apartheid. Spro-cas set out to examine various aspects of South African society, including political, social and economic, and consider strategies for change.

Speaking about the origins of Spro-cas, Beyers remarked: 'When we issued the *Message to the People of South Africa*, we saw for the first time that a new note of anxiety, hesitancy, uncertainty had crept into the previously overconfident attitude of the government and the NGK. I felt very strongly that we had to show that there were alternatives which were more just and Christian than those of apartheid. . . .

'The CI was the moving force behind Spro-cas because Bill Burnett had found that many of the member churches of the SACC would not go beyond a superficial stand against apartheid. . . . It would have been very difficult for the SACC to sell the Spro-cas programme to the churches and get approval for the project to start. I made the point time and again that if we had to wait for the approval of all the synods of the member churches, we would never get the project off the ground. And so the CI took the lead. . . . I believe that the Spro-cas effort became one of the most important and significant projects ever undertaken by any church or ecumenical group in South Africa.'[16]

The man appointed to head Spro-cas was Peter Randall, a teacher by profession, who had worked for five years as assistant director at the South African Institute of Race Relations. Randall came from a liberal English-speaking background, and although he had a Methodist upbringing, he had no strong claims to being a practising Christian. He nevertheless shared the concerns of men like Beyers Naudé and Theo Kotze about the unjust society in which they lived, and was keen to take on the challenge presented by the Spro-cas project.

Not everyone in the SACC was happy with the choice of Peter Randall as director of Spro-cas, because of his 'lack of Christian commitment'. Beyers, however, insisted that he was the best man for the job. For someone who had, at one time, practised his faith so piously, Beyers's openness on this point might have surprised many. But he had come to accept and work with people of different backgrounds and religious convictions. 'There were people who said, "Kindly find a committed Christian for Spro-cas." And I said if you can find such a person who has the same capability of handling this effectively from a purely academic viewpoint, then bring him, let him do the job. If not, then I am not bothered by such nonsense. . . . To me the important thing was the intrinsic value, the capability of a person, and his commitment to our goal. That was the crucial test.'

So Peter Randall got the job. Starting with little more than an empty office, a secretary and a lot of ideas, he faced the enormous task of advancing the church's critique of apartheid, contained in the *Message to the People of South Africa*, many steps further. The *Message* had been based on five biblical principles: faith in human dignity, acknowledgement of individual responsibility and commitment to uplifting the oppressed, to working for constructive social change and to building a shared society. On this basis, the *Message* had condemned apartheid as unjust and unchristian. The guiding idea behind Spro-cas was to use this biblical commitment to social renewal in order to present alternatives to apartheid in six crucial areas of South African society – economic, educational, church, legal, political and social. Six study commissions were set up to analyse these areas and propose alternatives. Randall set out to recruit experts from various fields to serve on them, and 130 people were ultimately drawn into the Spro-cas studies at various stages. Spro-cas was to last almost five years, during which time the commissions released their reports as well as many occasional papers, books, posters and study aids. The Spro-cas commissioners began their exploration well aware that it would not lead them to the solution to South Africa's ills, and even conscious that, during the course of their studies, they might encounter many new problems.[17]

Typical of liberal initiatives of that time, Spro-cas met with hostility from both the Afrikaner and the black communities. An indication of how government supporters viewed Spro-cas was the reaction of *Die Vaderland*, which dismissed it as an attempt to replace the 'WHITE REPUBLIC where whites are sovereign with a WESTERN state, where everyone who complies with Western values will be given equal rights'.[18]

A more immediate problem was black reluctance to participate. Randall approached numerous important black figures to serve on the commissions, but the prevailing suspicion of white liberal initiatives made it very difficult for him to attract more than a small number of black panelists. In spite of this, the Black Consciousness movement had a profound effect on Spro-cas and the CI. Beyers said of this: 'Even though the number of black participants was not as high as we would have wanted, the discussions we had in the different commissions revealed very clearly the nature and depth of the differences in the English-speaking churches between a reformist and a more radical stand. It also became very clear that for us to gain acceptance with the black community, we would have to move forward and to take a more radical stand.'[19]

The recognition shown by Beyers, Peter Randall and others of the need to adopt a more radical approach did not always accord with the findings of the Spro-cas reports. As Peter Walshe has pointed out, the Spro-cas project was limited by its origins and the composition of the study commissions, and contained many contradictions. Commenting on the Spro-cas Economics Commission report, *Power, Privilege and Poverty*, Walshe said: 'The report made a genuine attempt to envisage a more egalitarian society. It accurately described many of the structures of injustice and offered a series of recommendations, which, if applied, would have gone a long way in eradicating racial discrimination in the economy and establishing a colour-blind welfare state. On the other hand, the Commission was apparently oblivious of the radical black critique of capitalism, and it made no attempt to present the insights and vision of what was becoming a black consciousness movement. It only hinted at the need for structural changes in capitalism itself. Moreover, it was over-optimistic in its expectation that white initiatives would be as important as black initiatives in dismantling apartheid and ushering [in] a new social order.'[20]

The Political Commission also revealed in its report the dominance of white thinking. While the commissioners eloquently described the lack of political rights of black South Africans and warned of further polarisation and confrontation, they rejected the option of a black majority government. Instead they favoured a federal-style government in South Africa, with 'proportional representation', 'regional autonomy' and pluralism as a 'necessary counter-weight to the power of government and as a necessary base for a free society'.[21] Black Consciousness leader Steve Biko remarked of the Spro-cas studies: 'the Spro-cas commissions are . . . looking for an "alternative" acceptable to the white man. Everybody in the commissions knows what is right, but they are looking for the most seemly way of dodging the responsibility.'[22]

The church study perhaps came closest to appreciating black demands. Calling for confession of the church's failure to promote inter-racial communication and understanding, the Church Commission spelt out how patterns of inequality and discrimination were ingrained not only in the Afrikaans churches, but also in the multi-racial English-speaking churches. It found that in some churches white domination was maintained by a disproportionate weighting in the supreme church courts and by the packing of important committees and commissions.[23] In spite of these inequalities, the Christian church stood in a unique position to promote inter-racial contact. It could become an important agent for social change provided it put its own house in order and took the risks necessary to ensure its renewal. Specific recommendations included redistribution of funds to promote community development and the launching of a programme to re-educate church members. The Commission also called for parity in pay scales of black and white ministers and recommended that black churchmen undertake crash training courses so that they could assume leadership positions in the churches.[24] Many of these recommendations were put into practice in the next decade.

It is difficult to assess accurately the influence of the Spro-cas reports. Although the Afrikaans press and the government ignored them, the Spro-cas publications sold very well. The process had an impact on many of the politicians, academics and theologians who served on the commissions; they included André Brink, Zach de Beer, André du Toit, Bennie Khoapa, Fatima Meer, Alan Paton, Rick Turner, Desmond Tutu, Frederik van Zyl Slabbert, Ernie Wentzel and Francis Wilson. Beyers, who was a member of the Political and Church commissions, remarked: 'Spro-cas was important in that it presented the views and convictions that were the seeds of new ideas and thoughts and directions in South Africa. It directed many of the participants to think about the future in a different way. It also conveyed to the black community the message that here was a group of white people in South Africa who were beginning to take seriously their claims for the future.'

Spro-cas helped the CI to understand the new challenges confronting the church in South Africa. However, in the late 1960s and early 1970s the Institute was still battling to make the adjustments and the transitions this involved, and was coming under strong pressure from its overseas donor bodies to take a stronger, more active stand against apartheid. Referring to this in his 1969 annual report, Beyers said: 'We are deeply grateful for the moral and financial support which we receive from . . . [overseas] bodies and groups and we are aware, sometimes with trepidation, of the expectations they hold of our witness and work. In the past two years, partly because of the increase and strength of the militant Black Power and anti-apartheid groups throughout the Western world . . . the feeling against South Africa, because of our racist policies, has been steadily mounting, and calls for violent action have been made from within Christian groups who see no other way to resolve a situation of serious discrimination.' Rejecting this option he proceeded: 'yet our path is clear:

despite criticism from some overseas groups of our being too conservative (and exactly the opposite indictment from many whites in South Africa . . .) we will have to pursue the course of obedience to God and His Word as we understand it through Christ.'[25]

Opposition by the white Afrikaner churches towards the CI was tinged with disquiet about Beyers's influence and relations with churches overseas. When the Gereformeerde Kerk in the Netherlands met in synod at Lunteren in March 1970, tensions between the NGK and the CI came to a head. The most important issue to be debated at the synod was the resolution on racism adopted by the Reformed Ecumenical Synod two years earlier. Representatives from the white NGK and Gereformeerde Kerk in South Africa, as well as one conservative representative from the black NGKA, were invited to attend the synod. The CI's Bruckner de Villiers was present as an observer.

At Lunteren numerous Dutch churchmen spoke out strongly against Christian collaboration with apartheid, and it was clear that the heat was on the white Reformed churches from South Africa. But instead of addressing the issue, the NGK delegation tried to swing the emphasis away by launching an attack on the CI and on Beyers. During his address to the synod, NGK actuary Koot Vorster claimed that the CI was misappropriating funds intended for the African Independent churches and further insinuated that Beyers was an immoral person for allowing himself to be addressed as *dominee* when his church had defrocked him. This attack was rebutted by Bruckner de Villiers, who was permitted to speak because of the severity of the accusations that had been made. To demonstrate that the NGK was 'reasonable', moderator Kosie Gericke intimated that his church was prepared to enter into dialogue with the CI.

In this climate, in which Dutch churchmen thought they detected a slight softening in the attitude of their South African sister church, a decision was taken not to condemn the policy of apartheid outright, for fear of jeopardising future talks. In the end the synod adopted a moderate condemnation of racial discrimination without any direct reference to South Africa. Mindful that the white NGK might use this resolution as 'proof' that the world did not condemn apartheid, the synod also sent the South African church a letter containing a plea to reconsider its racial policies and to begin negotiations with the CI.[26]

Although in Holland the NGK had seemed willing to meet with the CI, Gericke promptly denied this on his return to South Africa. Frustrated by these developments, Beyers wrote: 'There is a serious contradiction; the Gereformeerde Kerk in the Netherlands has formally taken notice of the undertaking of the NGK to a discussion, while Dr Gericke immediately denies it. It can only give the impression that leaders of the NGK are willing, when confronted overseas, to make certain promises in order to prevent criticism from members of sister churches, but they are then anxious to evade the responsibility of giving a hearing to the Christian Institute.'[27]

While the NGK might have won a little more time at the Lunteren synod, its refusal to speak plainly on apartheid would ultimately result in its complete isolation. The NGK lost further ground when the late-1970 assembly of the

World Alliance of Reformed Churches in Nairobi, Kenya, strongly condemned the NGK's practice of apartheid.[28]

These resolutions pointed to a new spirit that was sweeping the world church community: a desire to take active steps to end racism and a determination to put pressure on churches which supported apartheid. The CI's commitment to these principles won it strong support in the ecumenical community. This was evident when Professor Verkuyl, widely regarded as a leading Dutch theologian, visited South Africa shortly after Lunteren as a guest of the CI and the SACC. He was accompanied by Jone Bos, secretary of an inter-church aid agency in the Netherlands. The two men were members of a new Dutch organisation, known as the Kairos working group, which promoted awareness of South Africa's race policies in the Netherlands and lent moral and financial support to the CI. Kairos, which had been formed at the request of Beyers, was headed for several years by Professor Verkuyl and was important in mobilising support for the CI in the Dutch church community.[29]

Numerous colleagues and friends have identified Beyers's responsiveness to change as one of his most notable character traits. It is difficult to pinpoint exactly when shifts took place. Very often an ambiguity seemed to creep into what Beyers was saying and doing. In seeking to win people over to his side Beyers would avoid long debates on issues that could cause conflict. This often led people to believe that he actually agreed with them when in reality he was much further ahead in his thinking. A complicating factor was the reactionary political climate in South Africa. Statements and projects that were considered moderate and even conservative in overseas or black circles were often considered revolutionary and subversive by white South Africans. Thus Beyers sought to play down issues that would further alienate white South Africans, and this sometimes gave the impression of contradictory or even duplicitous behaviour.

Kor Groenendijk, head of the Kairos group in the Netherlands for many years, said of this: 'Everybody had his own idea of Beyers. People would visit him and speak to him and come back and say that Beyers agreed with them. What usually happened is that Beyers would listen to people and not say very much, he would be kind and not disagree. They did not understand his understatement or the fact that he was often in a difficult position in South Africa.'[30]

The row over the 'Ulvenhout consultations', which erupted in South Africa in 1970, provides a good example of the dilemma Beyers often faced. Determined to smear him with the claim that he supported violence and 'terrorist' organisations, the Afrikaner establishment pounced on Beyers's participation in these talks. Beyers strongly suspected that the 'evidence' against him had been dug up by the security police.[31]

In letters to *Die Burger*, Koot Vorster claimed that he had come across minutes of a secret church meeting which Beyers had attended in Ulvenhout in the Netherlands, in October 1969. He said that participants, including Beyers Naudé, had agreed that they should help unite the South African liberation movements and should start negotiations with them. Vorster suggested that Beyers, by being present at the meeting, was cooperating with the country's 'enemies'.[32] What in fact had occurred was that Beyers met with eight churchmen at a private house in Ulvenhout for informal talks about South Africa. Far from being 'threatening' as Vorster had suggested, participants actually showed a great deal of sympathy for maintaining cultural and sports links with South Africa – provided this was on a multi-racial basis. Most participants spoke out in favour of making contact with the South African liberation movements and of trying to resolve the differences between the ANC and PAC. They also expressed support for the CI, the Spro-cas project and the Black Consciousness movement.[33]

The finer points of the Ulvenhout discussions never featured in the hysterical reports carried by the Afrikaans press. Beyers, desperate to minimise the damage of these reports, produced a letter from the secretary of the meeting which declared that Beyers had actually disagreed with the suggestion of making contact with the ANC and PAC. The letter noted that Beyers had not supported communication with organisations that used 'violence' to achieve their ends.[34] Beyers was in a no-win situation. Government supporters ignored his claims that he was opposed to contact with the liberation movements while his overseas friends were confused by his position.

An issue which became a crucial test, not only for Beyers, but for the entire church community in South Africa, was the World Council of Churches' decision to create a practical programme to root out racism. The Programme to Combat Racism (PCR) was proposed at a consultation held at Notting Hill, London, in 1969 and was endorsed by the central committee of the WCC at Canterbury later that year. The idea was to tackle racism in all spheres of life and to give active aid and support to oppressed communities. This included support for the idea that Christians were entitled to use force as a last resort to end injustice. The SACC, affiliated to the WCC but still largely dominated by whites, expressed strong reservations about these proposals.[35]

The opposition from South Africa did little to sway the WCC. In August 1970 the central committee of the WCC agreed to set up a special fund to provide humanitarian aid for liberation movements as part of the PCR programme. The PCR consisted of many other, less controversial projects but the main focus was on the special fund. In the first year $200 000 was distributed to nineteen organisations, with most of the money going to liberation movements fighting racism and colonialism in the southern African region.[36] Beneficiaries included the PAC and ANC (representing South Africa), ZAPU and ZANU (Zimbabwe) and SWAPO (Namibia).

This decision provoked an emotional response in many parts of the world, and especially in South Africa. The 'outrage' was deplored in white pulpits and political platforms around the country. Beyers, in his first reaction, again anxious to shake off any suggestion that the CI supported the use of violence, also expressed reservations about the WCC's plans. The SACC was another to criticise the grants.[37]

There was little rational debate or reflection on the issues involved. No one seemed to be concerned with the view of black Christians, and it was left to *Pro Veritate* to try to provide some balance. A special issue of the journal published in full the decision of the WCC, as well as all available points of view. While at first the CI opposed the grants, there was evidence that Beyers and his organisation had begun to give more thought to the matter. In a perceptive article on the PCR's special fund, he wrote: 'I venture to suggest that this decision . . . will be a catalyst, a parting of the ways, not only for the world churches, but also for the churches in South Africa; the consequences of this decision cannot yet be foreseen.

'The general reaction of whites, who have, with saintly indignation, raised their hands to the heavens, as if they have no part in the guilt . . . as if they have no injustices to right, no involvement in the situation which has led to this decision – this reaction has widened the gulf between them and the world community. . . .

'In the middle of all the storm . . . there has been a great silence . . . the silence of the more than 18 million voices of the black population of South Africa. . . . Those of us who have had the opportunity and the privilege of contact with some of these non-white leaders, know and understand: they dare not speak out about their true feelings.'[38]

Beyers, after consultations with black people, had begun to reconsider his position. It would be many years before his new views on the black liberation movements would crystallise; but his willingness to consider why black people had resorted to an armed struggle was an important pointer to the change he was undergoing.

Not since Cottesloe had a church event angered the South African government as much as the announcement of the WCC's plan to support South African liberation movements. After Cottesloe, Hendrik Verwoerd had succeeded in bludgeoning most of the NGK 'strays' back into line, and his successor John Vorster hoped to do the same with the SACC. Ordering South African churches to withdraw from the WCC, he thundered: 'If they do not decide to abandon their membership, I will be failing in my duty if I do not take action against them.' Vorster also took the opportunity to launch a blistering attack on Beyers, deliberately linking the WCC to the CI in South Africa. Ignoring the fact that Beyers had already provided a letter to his brother Koot Vorster about the Ulvenhout consultations, Vorster accused Beyers of supporting violence, and declared: 'He owes South Africa an explanation.'[39]

While the SACC member churches all criticised the WCC's Programme to Combat Racism, the SACC elected to stay in the WCC, believing it important to keep open the lines of communication. The churches' obstinacy angered the government, which then blocked a proposed meeting between the SACC and WCC representatives to discuss the PCR. The state also refused visas to any foreign visitor from the WCC, ending a long tradition of close contact between South Africa and the Council.[40]

The government was furthermore determined to crush clergymen who were 'undermining the security of the state'. This it did by confiscation of passports, bannings, deportations, raids and even criminal charges. In January 1971 *Pro Veritate* published a list of seven South African ministers whose passports had been seized and seventeen foreign church workers whose residence permits had been withdrawn or who had been refused entry to the country.[41] The following month the CPSA Dean of Johannesburg, G.A. ffrench-Beytagh, was detained amid speculation by the Afrikaans press that he was masterminding the distribution of overseas funds for 'terrorists' and political opponents of the South African government. Security police then raided scores of offices and homes, including the offices of the SACC in Johannesburg, Cape Town and Port Elizabeth, as well as the CI's Cape Town premises. Dean ffrench-Beytagh was later charged with three counts of terrorism for inciting people to commit revolutionary and violent deeds and for accepting funds from the Defence and Aid Fund in London for the legal defence of political prisoners. The Dean was found guilty and sentenced to five years' imprisonment, but the conviction and sentence were later set aside by the Appeal Court.[42]

Several of the people who came under state pressure were members or workers belonging to the CI. In February 1971, for example, the CI's group worker, CPSA minister Colin Davison, was deported. Cosmas Desmond, then a Catholic priest working for the CI, had his passport confiscated and was later banned for five years and placed under house arrest. Desmond had spent three years writing and researching the effects of the mass removal of black people for his book *The Discarded People*. Although – or perhaps because – it was banned, the book drew worldwide attention to one of the most cruel and destructive features of apartheid policy and practice.[43]

In 1972, Colin Winter, the CPSA Bishop of Damaraland, in Namibia (then South West Africa), had his work permit withdrawn after he had tried to intercede during a workers' strike in Ovamboland. Winter, who had worked closely with Theo Kotze in opposing the illegal South African occupation of Namibia, was later deported. Two other clergymen who had taken up posts with the CI, Basil Moore and David de Beer, were also banned in 1972. In April 1972, *Pro Veritate* listed well over one hundred cases of severe action against church people.[44]

Writing about the conflict between church and state, Beyers asked: 'The crux of the matter is: what does the State regard as dangerous to its national security? Is the State in danger when a churchman, in obedience to God and his conscience, carries out the biblical command of love, social justice and compassion across the colour line? Or is the problem not rather that the authorities recognise a conception of religion, which, with regard to race relations, is in direct conflict with those church leaders . . . who regard apartheid as unchristian?'[45]

Beyers called for an urgent meeting between churchmen and the government to discuss the growing conflict, but this appeal was dismissed. *Die Vaderland* editorialised: 'We wonder whether Mr Naudé does not realise that he is testing the patience of South Africans to their limit. What does he mean that the government should meet with church leaders "without delay"? . . . Why does he use the word "conflict"? Mr Naudé is presumptuous to demand a meeting to try to "reconcile different points of view" when his Christian Institute is the backer of the attack on the government's education policy which the 14 members of the Education Commission of Spro-cas have made.... They make the same old tattered plea for a fully integrated education for whites and non-whites.... Does Mr Naudé really expect any serious South African – let alone the Cabinet – to swallow this ridiculous nonsense? To us, it looks as if this organisation which calls itself Spro-cas fell asleep in some sleepy American town in 1954 and forgot to hand in their report to the American Supreme Court on how schools in the South should be integrated. Mr Naudé, we live in South Africa, not in America!'[46]

In the midst of the WCC controversy the NGK held its general synod in October 1970. Four years having elapsed since the NGK had ordered its members to withdraw from the CI, the small number who had in fact defied the order faced disciplinary action for their 'disobedience'. The focus was especially on the Parkhurst NGK for refusing to act against CI members, and a resolution to this effect had been tabled under the rubric of church discipline.

Before the synod met, Beyers and 33 fellow CI members wrote to members of the synod appealing to them to reverse the 1966 decision. Affirming their commitment to the Reformed faith, the signatories declared: 'All of this has done nothing to change our devotion to the Reformed faith and our love for the NG Kerk.... It is unthinkable... that there should be no place for us in the NGK. Our plea to the synod is to show us and all those whose eyes are on the NGK, that the Church, which is led by Christ, has enough place to accept us with joy and willingness.'[47]

Conscious of the attention of the world Reformed community, especially after the promise to enter into dialogue with the CI at the Lunteren synod, the church leadership was anxious to avoid an embarrassing and protracted debate on the CI. It came as no surprise to Beyers when the synod shelved the CI debate by referring the issue to a permanent commission on current affairs. A special three-man committee was appointed to investigate the representations made by the Parkhurst church council and the CI members.[48] Nothing further came of the proposed NGK–CI talks.

Although Beyers had by the early 1970s come to regard the Black Consciousness movement as central to the struggle for justice in South Africa, this recognition had not come easily. For many years he shared the suspicions of many white liberals that the Black Consciousness movement amounted to 'black apartheid'.[49]

An important speech given in May 1971 showed that he was developing new perceptions of the political situation in South Africa – although he still harboured fears about Black Consciousness, or Black Power as it was then commonly known. Speaking in Pietermaritzburg on the topic, 'Black Anger and White Power in an Unreal Society', Beyers reminded his audience that he was talking under the shadow of real demonstrations of black anger – violence had erupted at the Gelvandale township outside Port Elizabeth, while black homeland leaders had also expressed frustration and anger at white selfishness.

'From every quarter of our country many voices are heard which prove how rapidly (almost overnight) and how widespread the concept of black power has grown. . . . Think of SASO [the South African Students' Organisation], the black counterpart of Nusas, already operating over a fairly wide field. . . . Think of the new mood amongst African clergy as reflected in the call for black clergy to stand together for the ideal of a united black church. . . .

'More and more Coloureds are rejecting the Afrikaans language as the language of the oppressor; more and more young Coloureds are calling for closer links to be forged with the African and Indian communities in the solidarity of a common black front against the white. The circle is now complete: white power has created its counterpart of black power, white identity has now led to the emphasis on black identity and white separate rights have now developed an impetus for black separate rights. The Frankenstein creation is now slowly turning against its creator.

'In such a situation it is inevitable that white power, privilege and prestige must assert itself in order to curb any dangerous growth and to contain the possible development of bitterness and anger which could so easily lead to violence. The tremendous political, economic and military power held by whites has strengthened their belief in the inherent and undisputed supremacy of their own kind; it has created a sense of security in their position and has developed an attitude of indifference to the suffering of the blacks. This in turn has increased the frustration, bitterness and anger in the hearts of many blacks which must eventually steer towards a collision course. Black anger as a reaction against white supremacy is like a rumbling volcano which could erupt at the most unpredictable moment in the most unpredictable way.'

Beyers went on to predict further rapid growth in popular support for Black Consciousness organisations and institutions. Referring to the challenges this presented to white organisations and white people like himself, he said: 'The position of organisations usually described in the terms "white liberal" or "white-controlled" will increasingly become unenviable . . . there will be an inevitable withdrawal of active participation and support, not because of disagreement with the ideals and goals . . . but because . . . there were too many whites in these institutions who, with the best of intentions, never fathomed the depth of humiliation and rejection which the blacks experienced for so long . . . and secondly because many blacks, in the growing consciousness of their own dignity and identity, would rather go it alone with the possibility of failure than do it together in the white man's way. It seems to me there will be a certain period of temporary rejection or estrangement from such organisations until the black community feels that it is strong enough to move back as equals, or unless these organisations are willing to change their understanding and methodology in order to meet the legitimate demands and to deal wisely and sympathetically with the unreasonable demands which a racial relationship such as South Africa's inevitably calls forth.'[50]

Although some of Beyers's pronouncements were awkwardly put and undoubtedly jarred both Black Consciousness activists and white liberals, he had essentially arrived at the truth that while most white South Africans were oblivious of the smouldering tensions, sooner or later black anger would explode. He was correct in forecasting a period where blacks would go it alone and had understood the two options available to white liberals – to stay the same and become irrelevant to the liberation struggle, or to become radicalised by accepting the demands of black South Africans.

In his political development, Beyers was influenced by numerous people, both inside and outside the CI. Former CI worker Danie van Zyl explained this by saying: 'Beyers began from a conservative point of view. In the early days I don't think he would have supported universal franchise, a basic liberal thing. Yet he had an intuitive feeling for the needs of the oppressed. Very often it was as if it was this that led him, and he had to fit his intellectual patterns and plans to fit that feeling. I saw him again and again latch onto ideas that other people had raised, and sometimes I said: "But, Beyers, you are just taking over somebody else's thought." Until I discovered that it was not that at all: he was seeking to work out intellectually that which he somehow already felt intuitively. . . . I saw it in his dealing with SASO. He had a real feeling for the needs of those students, although at that stage I don't think his political or social philosophy was at that level at all. . . . I remember the address he gave on black power, which he had worked on with Peter Randall. At the time I said to Peter: "That's not Beyers's thinking, he's not there yet." But afterwards, looking back at it, in a sense Beyers was there without having thought it through. . . . Maybe this is why in a true sense people have called him a prophet in South Africa. . . . Because he has got this feeling about where people are and what their needs are . . . and he could feel with them and have the courage to change.'[51]

A key influence on Beyers was the University Christian Movement (UCM) and its founder and general secretary, white Methodist minister Dr Basil Moore. Moore and a small group of committed white students founded the UCM in 1967 in an attempt to unite Christian students of all races in the study of the social implications of the gospel and in working for change in South Africa – issues which made the UCM highly unpopular with the authorities. With an approach to worship that was considered too 'free and easy' and a theology that was 'avant-garde', the UCM soon became more attractive to black rather than white students.[52] A Black Theology project focused on black experience and black consciousness in relation to the gospel of Jesus Christ, and several publications on the new ideas were issued.

Advocates of Black Theology believed that white colonialists and missionaries had succeeded in destroying African culture and economic and family life in the process of 'civilising' and 'converting' the indigenous people. But while in consequence rejecting traditional Western Christianity, they did not reject Christ. They found in the gospel, in Christ's identification with the poor, the suffering and the oppressed, signs of hope. The task of Black Theology was to 'Africanise' Christianity, to relate it to the history of black people and to help people recognise that they were equal in God's eyes.

A resolution of the Black Theology conference at Hammanskraal in 1971 stated: 'We understand the starting point of this theology to be Christ's declaration of His mission in the following words: "The Spirit of the Lord has been given to me, for he has anointed me. He has sent me to bring the good news to the poor, to proclaim liberty to captives and to the blind new sight, to set the downtrodden free, to proclaim the Lord's year of favour." Black Theology is a theology concerned with the future of the black man in the light of Christ as liberator.

'As a consequence we turn our backs on the biased interpretation of the Christian message which the white-dominated churches have been feeding to the black people. We understand Christ's liberation to be liberation not only from circumstances of internal bondage, but also a liberation from circumstances of external enslavement. Christ's message therefore, to Black Theology means taking resolute and decisive steps to free the black people not only from estrangement from God but also from slave mentality, inferiority complex, distrust of themselves, and continued dependence on other men culminating in self-hate.'[53]

Black Theology became a 'liberation theology' and provided the foundations for the development of Black Consciousness as a political philosophy. A strong black caucus soon emerged in the UCM led by student leaders such as Steve Biko and Barney Pityana. As the urge to establish an all-black students' organisation grew, political restiveness increased on the black university campuses. At the University of Fort Hare, for example, a peaceful student demonstration was broken up by police, and the UCM was banned on campus. The state expressed its antagonism by banning UCM literature and confiscating Moore's passport. The white church leadership was also alarmed at the radicalisation of the UCM. The Methodist Church showed its disapproval by transferring Basil Moore from the student chaplaincy at Rhodes University in Grahamstown. When he then joined the staff of the CI he was deprived of his ministerial status.[54]

As the UCM became radicalised most remaining white support melted away, leaving only a small group of whites still prepared to engage in discussions about Black Theology and Black Consciousness.[55]

The seeds which led to the founding of an all-black students' movement were sown at a UCM conference in July 1968 attended by Steve Biko and other black student leaders. The South African Students' Organisation (SASO) was officially launched in December 1968 – as a breakaway from the multi-racial National Union of South African Students. In December 1971 SASO took the initiative in establishing an umbrella organisation for black organisations in the form of the Black People's Convention.

This growth in the BC movement coincided with mounting state harassment of the UCM, and in 1972 the organisation decided to disband. In spite of the UCM's failures, Basil Moore made an important contribution to the promotion of Black Theology and Black Consciousness. As Peter Walshe pointed out, though Black Consciousness was propelled by its own leadership and momentum, Moore was an important early catalyst.[56] He was also influential in helping Beyers and other white people adjust to the new political reality. Beyers's close association with Basil Moore began in 1971 when the UCM leader was appointed director of the theological correspondence course of

AICA. But it was not to last – in 1972 Basil Moore was banned for five years. From then on, the Moore family was subject to various forms of harassment – at one time their pet kitten was skinned and left at their front door – until finally they decided to leave the country.

Speaking about his gradual acceptance of Black Theology and Black Consciousness, Beyers said: 'There were a large number of significant people who helped me to change. . . . In the Spro-cas studies we entered into discussions and dialogue with the leaders of the Black Consciousness movement who told us why they could not participate officially. . . . That in turn led to very meaningful debate amongst ourselves about where we were in relation to the demands made by the BC movement. We spoke about this with the leaders of the UCM, with Basil Moore, for instance. We had fascinating discussions about the place of the Christian church, and how it could be reconciled with the demands of the BC movement. That stimulated my understanding of the Christian faith and challenged me. I was aware a totally new dimension had entered the life and future of South Africa.

'In the beginning, much about Black Consciousness was strange; it was totally new and I had to re-evaluate. I had to ask myself to what degree this could be seen to be in conflict with the basic truth and assumptions of the Christian faith and to what degree this was due to the fact that we as Western Christians had certain traditional concepts, both theological and political, which we took for granted as being the only valid ones. Here were people, coming from a different background and perspective, telling us that from their experience, as black Christians, they saw South Africa's future to be totally different. This required an extensive re-evaluation of my understanding both of the reality of what was happening in the country and of the role which the church had to play.

'I was being re-educated, with every new phase of life and development in the country; every new crisis was a reassessment and a re-evaluation. I think the reason why problems arose with some of the others in the CI is that they were willing to go up to a certain point but not willing to go any further. I felt I had to approach as honestly and objectively as possible the challenge which was being presented and ask: What is the validity of this? Am I prepared to face this honestly, and if so what is my response?'

The general reaction of the white church establishment, however, was one of suspicion and disdain. Writing about racism in South African churches, a black minister, Zolile Mbali, remarked: 'There was a hostile reaction from some white theologians to Black Theology. None of the Afrikaner theologians who contributed to a book on *Black Theology* viewed it in a positive light, but one essay "recognised black theology as a judgment on white Christianity in South Africa." . . . Another writer called Black Theology "the scream of the child." . . . The predominant tone of the DRC comment on Black Theology was to view it as reactive, and exponents of it were chided for being unappreciative. . . . However the exception to this Afrikaner mistrust of Black Theology was, as might be expected, Beyers Naudé . . . even while the whites were . . . ignoring possible black reaction to the PCR, the Christian Institute together with some of the staff at SACC were beginning to take note of Black Consciousness leaders.'[57]

Beyers's support for Black Consciousness and for black liberation did not mean that he had ceased to regard himself as an Afrikaner. Many people who became involved with him in the struggle against apartheid have been struck, and some even irritated, by his commitment to his people. According to Charles Villa-Vicencio, Beyers believed emphatically that the Afrikaner ought to be part of his new vision for South Africa. 'He has an almost disturbing attachment to his own, *die eie*, he clings to it in a way I cannot quite comprehend. He is an international man, but his roots are deep in the Afrikaner community. This is not necessarily a contradiction, but if it is, it is a disturbingly powerful contradiction. He is an Afrikaner to the enth degree.'[58]

Elia Thema, a minister from the NGKA who has had a long association with Beyers, said: 'I have never heard Beyers trying to be anything other than an Afrikaner. . . . He would always say: "I am not trying to be a black man, I don't have that experience . . . I am crying for my Afrikaner people. I am trying to say to them that they will never have a future unless they are prepared to live with others." This is what Beyers always tried to do.'[59]

Beyers would often remind people of his own roots. An article he wrote for the Afrikaans newspaper *Ster* in November 1970 began: 'I am writing as a Christian and as an Afrikaner: As a Christian who, though realising numerous short-comings and failings in my Christian witness, nevertheless knows that obedience and loyalty to Christ's word . . . towers above other love and loyalty. But I also write as an Afrikaner who, on account of my love for my people, wants to try to direct their attention to the catastrophic results of a racial policy which is threatening the future and continued existence of the white man (and particularly the Afrikaner) on account of its moral unacceptability and practical unfeasibility – and the continued application of which will cause more damage, harm and misery to the Afrikaner than to any other South African population group.'[60]

Despite, or perhaps because of, Beyers's commitment to the Afrikaner, his actions in the 1970s were motivated by concern for the oppression of the black majority – and in his opinion the Black Consciousness movement represented the best way to tackle injustice in South Africa. The CI's commitment to Black Consciousness became evident as the Spro-cas project entered its second phase. The individual Spro-cas commission reports had largely based their recommendations for change on the assumption that whites and white institutions would be prepared to make the necessary adjustments, but increasingly Beyers Naudé and Peter Randall recognised that the future of the country depended on black initiatives. In the final Spro-cas report, *A Taste of Power*, Randall wrote: 'fundamental change . . . will be initiated by blacks, and . . . the white oligarchy, which . . . has exercised a virtual monopoly of political and economic power will increasingly have to respond to black initiatives. We are in the early stages of a new historical phase in South Africa, in which the initiative for change is passing into black hands. The tempo of this process can only accelerate, no matter what temporary setbacks black initiative may receive and no matter what efforts are made to thwart it, so that it is possible to discern already the beginnings of a transference of power. Blacks have begun to have a taste of power, and whites are not going to be able indefinitely to prevent them from enjoying a full meal.'[61]

When overseas sponsors began inquiring about a follow-up project to the Spro-cas studies, Peter Randall and Beyers Naudé discussed the issue with various organisations. Finally it was decided that Spro-cas should adopt an action programme, designed to translate the recommendations of the Spro-cas reports into concrete deeds. The new programme, Special Project for Christian Action in Society, became known as Spro-cas 2. According to Peter Randall, 'Spro-cas 2 was formulated with the help of Black Consciousness leaders like Bennie Khoapa and Steve Biko. It was divided into two programmes, a white consciousness programme and a black community programme. . . . This again meant very close cooperation with the CI and with Beyers in particular, and I think it had a considerable influence on him.'

While Spro-cas 2 was officially sponsored by both the CI and the SACC, the latter was more cautious about the radical nature of the project. Once again it was the CI that provided the main support, with Beyers acting as chief fundraiser. The foreign funding of Spro-cas was criticised both by government supporters who saw it as foreign interference and by some opponents of the government who felt it was dangerous to become reliant on this source. The 1969–1973 Spro-cas budget came to just over R200 000. Apart from a R22 000 donation from Anglo American's Chairman's Fund, most of the big grants came from the Dutch, German and Scandinavian churches.[62]

Referring to this criticism, Beyers said: 'We did everything in our power to raise the major part of our funds in South Africa. I spent weeks approaching a number of funding agencies, organisations and companies. The reaction on the part of some, like Anglo American, was reasonably positive and I was grateful for the support. . . . We also received funds from a number of individuals, but by and large the response did not meet our needs and therefore I had no hesitancy or qualms of conscience in accepting money from the overseas churches. I took the same viewpoint as I had done with the CI. I saw the Christian church as a universal one. . . . What was happening in South Africa, with the Christian churches, would have a vital effect on the witness and the life of the church in the world as a whole. I felt it was incumbent on the Christian church in other parts of the world to support a weaker member. . . . I knew it was politically unacceptable, that it would lead to criticism of the CI. I knew that eventually action could be taken against us. . . . But the money was given with no strings attached. When I raised those funds I made it clear that there was no way I could predict the outcome of the study project. They had to leave us the total freedom to make our own conclusions on the basis of our own insight.'[63]

Peter Randall was appointed director of Spro-cas 2, and the main focus was on trying to bring about change in the fields of education, labour, church and social issues.

The decision to create separate black and white programmes had been taken in the prevailing political climate and out of a recognition of the different needs and problems of the divided communities. The goal of the white community programme, run by Peter Randall together with former student leaders Horst Kleinschmidt in Johannesburg and Neville Curtis in Cape Town, was to help white people recognise their own often racist attitudes, to help them change their values and to work for a redistribution of power in South Africa. The black community programme, based in Durban and headed by black social worker Bennie Khoapa, aimed at helping blacks become aware of their identity and power. The idea was to enable the black community to analyse its own needs and problems and to develop black leadership and potential.[64]

The white programme had little hope of succeeding. White South Africans had never shown any signs of wishing to change their attitudes or give up their power, and it was unlikely they would be persuaded to do so by a small group of over-optimistic Spro-cas workers. Several significant projects were nevertheless launched, including a campaign to highlight poor living conditions among black workers. Later, the white consciousness programme supported the campaign against the destructive effects of apartheid on black family life. In December 1972, eight pilgrims led by the Reverend David Russell embarked on a 900-kilometre walk from Grahamstown to Cape Town to protest against the polices of migrant labour and the pass laws. They were joined on the final stage of their pilgrimage by Roman Catholic Archbishop Denis Hurley of Durban, and by Beyers Naudé. Later the two men addressed a crowd of several thousand which had gathered at the Rondebosch Common to adopt a six-point Charter for Family Life, which called on the government to allow black workers to live in the cities with their familes. A Family Life Office was established to continue to promote this cause, but it was finally disbanded because of white apathy.[65]

In spite of the disappointing response to this campaign and other projects, the CI launched a new white programme in 1973 – the Programme for Social Change (PSC). The programme's organisers hoped to create a coordinated base for whites working for change, and through publications and conferences tried to promote alternatives to the existing social order. The overall results of the programme were once again disappointing and by mid-1975 it was disbanded. Beyers, who served on the PSC's advisory committee, said: 'We were aware of the fact that we were trying to achieve the impossible. There was no naïvety, no utopian idealism. . . . We were fully aware that we would be up against a stone wall of either indifference or prejudice in the white community. . . . But the black community was challenging us and saying: "Your first and primary task is towards your own white people." So we said: "OK, we accept the challenge, we will try." '

While the white programmes were still in progress, Spro-cas 2 began to focus attention on the black community programme. The BCP had greater potential for success in that it contained a promise of hope and action for black people. To start with, the BCP identified more than 70 different black-controlled organisations, in its desire not to create duplicate bodies, but rather to support existing ones such as SASO and the Black People's Convention. It also hoped to create networks through which black trade unionists, political leaders, students and churchmen could communicate, and to act as a catalyst in advancing black consciousness.[66]

The programme attracted several important BC leaders, including Bennie Khoapa, Barney Pityana, Bokwe Mafuna and Steve Biko. It seems odd that at the height of Black Consciousness, leaders of this calibre were prepared to be involved with an initiative sponsored by a white-run organisation. This was made possible by the way in which Beyers Naudé and Peter Randall worked – they provided the BCP with the resources and then left them to do their job without interference. Black Consciousness writer Sam Nolutshungu said of the BCP: 'It was politically important from the start, since it published most of the material produced by and about the Black Consciousness movement, and provided employment for key SASO militants after they left university and a framework within which they could continue to work towards their political objectives. . . . It also provided a model of politically minded, public action independent of white South African liberal patronage and hostile to official policies and plans.'[67]

One area where the cooperation between the BCP and Spro-cas was particularly successful was in the field of publishing. A publishing company, Ravan Press, had been formed by Peter Randall, Beyers Naudé and Danie van Zyl to handle Spro-cas reports and papers, and it was used by the BCP for their publications. These included an annual survey *Black Review* and a quarterly magazine *Black Viewpoint*. The popularity and success of these publications brought increasing attention from the government in the form of bannings of both the publications and the writers. By March 1973 all the leaders of the BCP had been banned, which made circulation of their publications illegal.[68]

Before the bannings in 1973, the BCP had met some of its goals. Apart from successful publications, it channelled funds to BC organisations so that they could hold conferences and seminars on a variety of issues. As Peter Walshe has noted, the BCP encouraged and helped legitimise black caucusing, and this signalled the emergence of a more assertive black leadership in the mainline English churches.[69]

Beyers developed good relationships with several of the BCP workers, including Steve Biko. Speaking about Biko, Beyers said: 'I learnt so much from him about the feelings and the aspirations of the black community. . . . We supported the actions of the Black Community Programme, and gave our blessing when the Black People's Convention was formed. . . . The point we wanted to make to the white community was to say: "The time has arrived where the future initiatives of the country can no longer remain in white hands. It has to be an initiative emanating from the black community, and we as whites . . . must find a new role – a supportive, complementary role, to get rid of the old spirit of paternalism, of white liberalism, to say to the black community: Over to you." To the vast majority of whites that attitude was treason: treason in the real sense of the word. And that is why the government increasingly began to take action against the Christian Institute. . . .'[70]

13
State Pressure Intensifies, 1972–1974

The negative image of Beyers held by many white South Africans was in sharp contrast to his growing stature abroad. He made history in May 1972 when he became the first South African invited to preach at the seat of the Church of England, Westminster Abbey. While he visited several European countries on that trip, the time spent in Britain had the greatest impact. Apart from delivering the Westminster sermon, he met with leading politicians and government leaders. Well aware of the importance of these meetings and speaking engagements, Beyers concentrated on two key issues which would so often dominate debate on South Africa in the years to come: the question of violence and economic sanctions as a means of changing the status quo.

These issues had been placed on the international agenda by the WCC Programme to Combat Racism. The WCC central committee voted as early as August 1972 to withraw its funds from corporations which invested in or traded with South Africa, South West Africa (Namibia), Rhodesia (Zimbabwe), and the two Portuguese colonies of Mozambique and Angola.[1] In the early 1970s Beyers, like almost all white South African liberals, was opposed to sanctions. During his trip to Britain he pleaded with a group of British peers, members of parliament, businessmen and industrialists to use their financial leverage to help black South Africans improve their economic position. 'I believe we should use all legal means to improve conditions and advance our black labour force economically.' Yet he also showed an awareness that the pressure for sanctions would grow. In a letter to *The Times* he warned that a world economic boycott of South Africa would gain strength unless racial equality was rapidly achieved, and he repeated his call for British firms to act as agents for change.[2]

Sections of the Afrikaans press deliberately distorted Beyers's message. *Die Vaderland*, for example, announced in a headline that 'Beyers Naudé Calls for a Boycott of South Africa'.[3] His actual position at the time was far more conservative and was summed up in an interview he gave on his return to South Africa: 'Give our blacks a better share of South Africa's wealth. It will stem the tide of economic resentment towards us and help us economically.'[4]

Beyers had often expressed his views on the issue of violence. As early as 1966 he had warned that unless negotiations were begun with recognised black leaders, the confrontation in South Africa would eventually become a violent one.[5] He had also frequently called for the churches to take the lead in a non-violent campaign against apartheid, citing the example of Martin Luther King.[6] And, while opposing force in all its forms, he had also pointed out that the church was often selective in its condemnation of violence.[7]

Dealing with this issue during his sermon at Westminster Abbey, Beyers said that while it might give partial or short-term answers to racial injustice and oppression, violence raised more problems than it solved. Violence produced an endless spiral, 'the mounting force of which draws both victor and victim, both conqueror and conquered into a vortex of endless bitterness and enmity'. Non-violence, which demanded a voluntary acceptance of suffering on one's own side, had failed, not because it had been tried and found wanting, but because it had never been tried by the Christian community on a universal scale.[8]

Beyers's frequent references to the potential for conflict in South Africa also provoked a strong reaction. In September 1972 *Die Vaderland* published a series of vituperative articles about him and the CI, which took particular exception to a warning he had given that if black anger eventually erupted in violence, then whites, and particularly Christians, would be to blame for consistently ignoring black demands and suffering.[9] *Die Vaderland's* political staff wrote: 'Mr Beyers Naudé . . . is becoming increasingly dangerous in his outbursts. . . . His accusation . . . that any violence by non-whites will be the fault of whites . . . can create a dangerous climate. His remarks can sow seeds of unrest in fertile soil. Ideas and thoughts are created when one speaks loosely about violence. To blame whites in advance for violence means that non-whites are cleared of all blame. By implication, any deed of violence by non-whites is justified. If violence does take place, then Mr Naudé must share part of the blame.'[10]

Beyers and Ilse had themselves lived with threats of death and violence since 1960 when he had taken part in the Cottesloe deliberations, and these forms of intimidation became a permanent feature of their lives. The abusive phone calls, the hate mail and occasional broken windows affected Ilse particularly, for beneath her seemingly tough exterior was a highly sensitive person.

Right-wing thugs were even more active in Cape Town, and Theo and Helen Kotze suffered continual harassment as part of the broader intimidation of anti-apartheid organisations and activists, mostly carried out by a two-man group called 'Scorpio'. Pressure on Theo Kotze intensified after he became involved in student protests against apartheid education. The Kotzes suffered abusive phone calls, petrol-bomb scares and slashed tyres, and shots were even fired at their house. The hammer and sickle sign was painted on the CI's Mowbray office on several occasions and two attempts were made to burn it down. In September 1972, vandals set fire to an Anglican church hall in Cape Town shortly after the end of the CI's annual meeting, and the same month the *Cape Times* listed 21 acts of violence against CI members or supporters, none of which had been solved by the police.[11]

While these indiscriminate acts were distressing enough, even more troubling was the government's mounting attack on the CI and other multi-racial bodies. A new level in this psychological war was reached in February 1972 when Prime Minister John Vorster announced that he intended appointing a parliamentary select committee to investigate the objects, activities and financing of organisations suspected of 'subversion'. The bodies against which he was convinced a *'prima facie* case' existed were the University Christian Movement (which disbanded the same year), the National Union of South African Students, the South African Institute of Race Relations and the Christian Institute.[12] The prime minister's decision would lead to one of the most significant church–state confrontations since the Cottesloe crisis.

The CI and the other targeted bodies responded to the announcement with indignation. The initial objection to the committee was that its investigations would be conducted by party politicians operating in complete secrecy under the cloak of state security. At first Beyers had been willing to cooperate, albeit reluctantly, with the select committee. But he became increasingly disturbed by the secret nature of the inquiries – and this would later form the basis of the decision taken by him and other CI staff members not to give evidence before the inquiry.

Beyers sent a telegram urging the government to appoint a public judicial inquiry. Determined instead to have the *'prima facie* case' tried secretly, the government went ahead with its appointment of a select committee. National Party MP Mr Jimmy Kruger, who would later become Minister of Justice and Police, was appointed chairman. Four months later Kruger requested that the committee be broadened into a commission of inquiry with wider terms of reference and powers to investigate any organisation or person connected in any way with the suspect bodies. It was decided that the commission would sit *in camera* and that the full evidence would not be published. No information about the proceedings could be divulged by witnesses or other persons present during the inquiry. Members of the organisations under investigation would not be entitled to view evidence which had been submitted against them, nor would they be permitted to cross-examine witnesses, lead their own evidence or call their own witnesses. Participation by counsel would be limited to advising clients of their legal rights.[13] When Jimmy Kruger had to step down as chairman on being made a deputy minister he was replaced by Nationalist stalwart Alwyn Schlebusch, after whom the commission came to be commonly named. Chairmanship would later pass into the hands of a politician who had been a deacon in Beyers's church council in Potchefstroom, Mr Louis le Grange, future Minister of Police.

One unforeseen consequence of the commission of inquiry was the conflict it created in the opposition United Party (UP); it later became a key factor in the party's collapse. UP leader Sir De Villiers Graaff was uneasy when the commission was announced and urged the government to appoint a judicial commission rather than a select committee. When this request was ignored, three UP members nevertheless agreed to serve on the commission along with six National Party MPs, on the grounds that it would give the party a say in the selection of witnesses and would enable them to form a balanced opinion of the organisations. Mrs Helen Suzman, a veteran white liberal and then a member of the Progressive Party, sounded a prophetic warning at the time, arguing that the UP was making a mistake by serving on the committee. She said if the UP refrained and left it to the Nationalists, it 'would make it clear what a farce the whole thing is going to be'.[14]

The first target of the Schlebusch Commission was the National Union of South African Students, whose members agreed under protest to cooperate with the inquiry. In an interim report issued in February 1973 the commission recommended that no action should be taken against Nusas as a body, but it named eight student leaders as a threat to the security of the state. The same night the students were issued with five-year banning orders under the Suppression of Communism Act. These contained severe restrictions, including a bar on their Nusas activities and on attending university. The United Party limply protested against the bannings but continued to participate in the Schlebusch Commission.[15] Among those banned were several people who had been involved with the CI and Spro-cas, including Neville Curtis and Richard Turner.[16] Shortly thereafter eight leading members of the black South African Students' Organisation and the Black People's Convention were also banned – including BCP workers Barney Pityana and Steve Biko. The director of the BCP, Bennie Khoapa, suffered the same fate a few months later.

The action against Nusas confirmed the CI's suspicion that the Schlebusch Commission was merely a vehicle enabling the government to take arbitrary action against its opponents. Thus when the commission began to turn its attention to the CI, Beyers and several other staff and board members decided not to give evidence.

Beyers's leadership of the CI has sometimes been described as excessively individualistic, but Brian Brown, who by that stage was working as the CI's administrative director, has pointed to the decision on the Schlebusch Commission as an example of how Beyers was often guided and influenced by other staff and board members. 'There was a lot of free-talking in a body like the CI. You didn't have people like Colin Gardner (chairman of the CI board for many years), Margaret Nash (board member), Manas Buthelezi (CI Natal director), Theo Kotze, Peter Randall and Beyers coming together without having a few sparks flying. I think that while Beyers's leadership was a one-man band in some measure, he also led in the context of a very competent, gifted and powerful CI board, and so it was not as if he could just paddle his own canoe. There was always the need for reference in terms of policy, and a beautiful instance of this need for endorsement and consensus was in our response to the Schlebusch Commission. It was partly bound up in my being in the invidious position that as administrative director I was being asked to hand over the books to the commission. I had to go to the board and say: "I need guidance." I was the one they were going to come to and must I hand our books over? . . . It was a very democratic debate. I remember going home and writing something at the behest of the board which was brought back and which became, after polishing, amending and approving, our statement of defiance.'[17]

The statement, adopted at a CI board meeting in March 1973 with seventeen votes in favour and four abstentions, affirmed support for CI members who refused to cooperate with the commission. 'The recent action taken against student leaders by way of arbitrary banning orders confirms our initial impression that the thinking behind the appointment of the Parliamentary Select Committee is calculated to permit punitive measures being taken under the guise of democractic procedure. . . . We reaffirm our conviction that the investigation . . . should be undertaken through a judicial commission which can ensure impartiality. . . . We fully support those of the board and staff . . . who decided that in conscience they cannot co-operate with a Commission of Enquiry which they consider by its constitution and mandate to be a denial of the democratic process and judicial procedure. . . . While we confidently affirm that we have nothing to hide, we also affirm that there is much to preserve by way of our Christian heritage of fairness and the evidencing of justice, which such a Parliamentary Commission palpably erodes.'[18]

This statement of defiance signalled a new phase in the conflict between the CI and the state, but CI members and Beyers himself felt strongly that their decision was primarily a Christian and moral stand and not a political one. In arriving at their decision, the CI members had raised the issue of the right of Christians to resist an unjust government. Drawing on theologians such as Karl Barth, Reinhold Niebuhr and John Knox, Beyers and four other leading CI members drew up a document entitled *Divine or Civil Obedience?*, which argued on the basis of the Scriptures their right to resist unchristian governmental authority in the name of Christ. On the ground that the prime minister and chairman had shown prejudice against the organisations even before the inquiries began, and because of the secretiveness of the commission and the subsequent state action against student leaders, the document argued that the government's clampdown was unchristian. 'The believer in Christ not only has the right, but the responsibility to harken to the Word of God and His righteousness rather than to the government, should the government deviate from God's will. Does not the responsibility lie with the Christian not to cooperate with the government in a matter which is in conflict with the Gospel? By doing so is he not witnessing to Christ and his righteousness? . . . In refusing to testify and cooperate with the government in a matter such as this, those who cannot cooperate on grounds of Christian conscience do not wish to pose as heroes or martyrs (as a section of the Afrikaans press had implied); they are concerned about obedience to Christ [as] the highest authority.'[19]

Speaking of the Schlebusch Commission, Beyers remarked: 'That was the turning point in the history of the CI. The battlelines were clearly drawn between the CI and the government. . . . We knew that from then on our position would become increasingly difficult, but we also experienced, for the first time, increasing support from the black community because many of them saw for the first time that we were prepared to pay the price for our convictions. . . . Some people said to us: "You people are foolish. Are you really going to take on the power of this mighty state?" We said: "No, we are not going to take it on, but we are going to give a testimony of what we believe to be right and that, in the course of time, will have its own effect.'[20]

Some critics have claimed, particularly with reference to the early 1970s and the Schlebusch Commission, that the CI seemed constantly on the defensive, unable to set its own agenda – merely reacting to pressure from the government. Brian Brown, in answer to this criticism, has summed up the feelings of those close to the CI in those turbulent times. 'I would acknowledge that in the 1970s the CI was far more responsive than freely creative, and I would see that on one level as a criticism, certainly a weakness, but I wouldn't say it was all weakness, nor would I wish to simply criticise without putting it in the context of the South African situation where any body or organisation which is committed to a vigorous anti-apartheid stance is of necessity engaged in a response to the power of the state. . . .

'While the Schlebusch Commission was the extraneous factor impinging upon our programme, by deliberate choice the CI chose to make it an issue. It became a matter of not just responding to the Schlebusch Commission, but asking: What is legitimate action against an organisation? Can there be a non-judicial action which is just? Is the rule of law being violated by the commission? Is the testimony that is being solicited being used against others to their detriment? If this is a violation of the rule of law, if this is an exercise in the darkness calculated to injure others, if this gives a semblance of impartiality to structures that are wickedly partial, then ought we to be participants? . . . So what could be regarded as a rather pathetic responsiveness to the uncontrollable forces of the state became in effect, in some measure, gaining the ascendancy.

'It gave us a vehicle, a platform, and using that platform in order to do what no manner of writing at that time would have achieved. And we saw in that process that the editorial stances of the liberal press changed. Initially there was an almost irritation with the Christian Institute. But as the significance of the event dawned, we found that the English press, which had after all been supportive of the United Party, began to criticise their participation. Suddenly we found that participation was causing the United Party more problems than the CI.

'As an organisation we dealt with the issue of participation very easily. But our stand was ultimately a prime factor in the dissolving of the United Party. We survived Schlebusch, they didn't. They were utterly discredited by their participation and it led to a split which was so weakening of an already weakened party, that politically its life was doomed. I am not saying that we deliberately set out to bring the UP into dissolution, but it was a consequence of it and it showed in effect that there was an inherent impotency in white politics.'[21]

In April 1973 the Schlebusch Commission had released another of its reports, this time into the activities of the ecumenical Wilgespruit Fellowship Centre, situated west of Johannesburg. Expressing disgust at the centre's sensitivity training programme, the government deported Eoin O'Leary, who headed the centre's Personal Responsibility and Organisation Development (PROD) project. John Vorster ordered the SACC, which was one of the trustees of the centre, to clear up the 'nest of iniquity'. The commission's allegations were subsequently rejected by the trustees, and the PROD programme, without the controversial sensitivity training, was later resumed.[22]

In August 1973 the CI's executive, which consisted of Beyers Naudé, Theo Kotze, Brian Brown, Oshadi Phakati and Roelf Meyer, issued a formal statement refusing to testify. In all, nine people from the CI who were subpoenaed to give evidence before the commission refused to do so, and while the South African Institute of Race Relations eventually decided to cooperate with the commission, four individual members also refused to testify.[23]

Beyers and six other CI members appeared before the Schlebusch Commission in the old Raadsaal building in Pretoria on 24 September 1973. When it was Beyers's turn to appear he refused to take the oath, but handed in the document in which the CI members had set out their reasons for refusing to testify, *Divine or Civil Disobedience?* Beyers had planned to fly overseas the day after he had appeared before the Schlebusch Commission. After checking in his baggage at Jan Smuts Airport he realised that he had forgotten to note the expiry date on his passport and discovered it was no longer valid. When he explained his predicament to officials he was handed an undated letter from the Secretary of the Interior notifying him that his passport had been withdrawn. The bizarre way the government had seen fit to restrict his right to travel attracted a great deal of publicity, and the government's action was strongly condemned by the English press and by many churchmen abroad.

Die Vaderland, as always the loyal National Party mouthpiece, explained that the action against Beyers Naudé was 'standard practice' since criminal charges were being investigated against him for refusing to testify before the Schlebusch Commission.[24] What the newspaper failed to point out was that Beyers had not even been charged (he was finally summonsed three weeks later). The NGK also defended the government's action and, replying to a call from the Gereformeerde Kerk in the Netherlands to intervene in the issue, the moderature declared the government had acted 'completely within its jurisdiction and in the framework of the laws of the country. We cannot think of a valid reason whereby you can expect us to interfere in the matter.'[25] Within a few months, the passports of all those who had refused to testify were confiscated by the state. Then followed a series of police raids on the offices of the CI and Spro-cas, and financial records and other documents were seized.

All those who had refused to testify before the Schlebusch Commission were charged under the Commissions Act – which carried mild penalties of a maximum fine of R200 or six months' imprisonment. Most of those who had been charged felt they would rather go to jail than pay the fines, and so began the saga of the Schlebusch trials, which, with the long series of appeals and counter-appeals, dragged on for more than two years. The first person to be convicted was Ilona Kleinschmidt (Tip), and when she lost her appeal and opted for jail instead of paying her fine, it was mysteriously paid by an unknown person.[26]

Beyers's trial, which began on 13 November 1973, became the focus of interest, symbolising as it did the clash between Christians and the apartheid state. The trial was attended among others by Dr G. O. Williams, representing the British Council of Churches, and by Professor Antony Allott for the International Commission of Jurists. The International Commission later published a book giving an almost full transcript of the proceedings and discussing the legal and moral issues involved. The introductory remarks in the book by Professor Allott provide a clue as to why the case attracted worldwide interest. He wrote: 'An overcrowded magistrate's court in Pretoria might seem an unusual setting for a fundamental debate about just and unjust laws and the duty of a citizen to obey the one and disobey the other, and even less usual for a re-examination of the Christian Gospel in its contemporary South African context. Even the boldest author of moralising fiction would hesitate to include, in the proceedings of such a court, the preaching of a full-length sermon on the Christian conscience face to face with the racial situation in South Africa. All this and more, however, is to be found in the trial of the Rev Dr Beyers Naudé.'[27]

Beyers pleaded not guilty to a charge of contravening the Commissions Act when he appeared before magistrate Mr L. M. Kotze, in courtroom E, one of the smaller courts in the complex. Defence attorney Mr J. C. Kriegler admitted that Beyers had refused to take the oath or to testify before the Schlebusch Commission, but argued that on grounds of conscience there was 'sufficient cause' for his refusal. Over the next four days the story of Beyers's life would unfold in the small courtroom as the defence attempted to justify his plea of not guilty. The evidence described his personal journey of faith which had resulted in his decision to leave the NGK and to join the CI. It also dealt in detail with his beliefs, the principles of the gospel, the attitudes of the church in South Africa and the history and nature of the Christian Institute. As the trial progressed it became clear that this was the way Beyers Naudé had chosen to respond to the Schlebusch Commission. He was prepared to give a full account of his work – and to answer any questions put by the state – at this, a public hearing. Each day the court was packed with both supporters and security policemen, and on the third day of the trial it had to be moved to a larger courtroom to cope with the crowds.[28]

When Beyers was called to the witness stand he described his background, the nature of the CI and all the factors which had led him to challenge the NGK.

Attorney Kriegler then asked him: 'Mr Naudé, you have already explained to His Worship that the directorship of the Christian Institute was offered to you and how you applied to retain your status and that was refused?'

Beyers: 'That is correct.'

Mr Kriegler: 'Was it an easy decision for you to end the years of your ministry as minister of the NGK?'

Beyers: 'That was the most difficult decision which I have had to make in my life.'

His attorney then asked him to read the sermon he had delivered in September 1963 in which he announced his decision to accept the directorship of the CI. Beyers began to read those familiar words: 'We bring you this morning the Word of God from Acts 5: 29, "We must obey God rather than men." . . .' Clouds had been gathering all day outside the court and suddenly the thunderstorm broke, drowning out his words. When the storm subsided Beyers continued to read the sermon to the packed courtroom. When he had finished his attorney asked him: 'Now, Mr Naudé, in the ten years since you preached that sermon, have you had any reason to change you opinion in any way?'

Beyers replied: 'No, in the past ten years that opinion has only been deepened, broadened and confirmed.'

The defence then tried to show why the Schlebusch Commission could not be regarded as a 'neutral' inquiry, and why its secret method of operation had violated the rule of law. Beyers explained that he objected to the secret nature of the commission, and that his opposition to secrecy had deepened because of his experiences with the Afrikaner Broederbond. His understanding of the Scriptures had brought him to the conclusion that 'through the grace of God I should try for the rest of my life to do everything in the open and in public. This is not to say . . . that there are no circumstances and situations in which a person should not act confidentially, certainly there are many such situations in which confidential information is given, in which confidential relationships exist which a person would honour. But secrecy as a principle cannot be endorsed or supported by a Christian.'

During the final stages of Beyers's evidence he was closely questioned by the magistrate. In the words of Afrikaans journalist Rykie van Reenen, the court case was suddenly transformed into a conversation 'between two Christian Afrikaners who were trying to reach each other across a gulf'.[29] The questions posed by the magistrate summed up the attitudes of Afrikaners and their objection to Beyers Naudé. The magistrate noted that the state president had a legitimate constitutional right to convene a secret inquiry, and that Beyers, by refusing to testify, was challenging the authority of the government. Referring to the necessity for the government at times to appoint extraordinary commissions, the magistrate asked: 'Is it not true that it sometimes happens . . . that the government by necessity must take certain action based on certain information? . . . It can happen in the best democratic systems that certain measures are taken which give the executive wide powers to resist that situation.'

Beyers: 'I realise this and should it be announced in our country that such an emergency exists, and that because of it certain emergency measures are necessary, then I accept that a citizen, in so far as it is at all possible, must submit himself to those emergency measures. It remains the duty of the Christian, if he is convinced that those emergency measures are in conflict with his conscience and his point of view of the right of the authorities, to protest against it, and if it is necessary, to make it clear that he cannot go along with it. . . . It is of greatest importance that we should realise for the Christian in any case, all authority is given by God, that God gives this authority to the State to govern, he also gives the authority to the Church to . . . witness. The test is applied to both the Church and State to obey this authority which God gives. . . .'

The magistrate asked Beyers whether he did not hold a great deal 'against' the Afrikaans churches.

Beyers: 'I do not hold anything against the Afrikaans churches. I have something against the unbiblical points of view in our Afrikaans churches, in which it is my calling and duty as a Christian to bring to their attention everything which is in conflict with the Scriptures . . . and in particular to the church to which I belong, the Nederduitse Gereformeerde Kerk.'[30]

On November 1973 Beyers was found guilty as charged. The magistrate rejected the defence's argument that Beyers had 'sufficient cause' to refuse to testify before the Schlebusch Commission. He also rejected another more technical argument that the Schlebusch Commission had not been legally constituted since the state president did not have the right to impose secrecy on the commission.

Beyers was sentenced to a R50 fine or one month's imprisonment, with a further three months conditionally suspended. Leave to appeal was granted, and payment of the fine was deferred pending the outcome of the appeal. The initial appeal to the Transvaal Supreme Court succeeded on technical arguments, but this was overturned by the Appeal Court in December 1974.

The Schlebusch trial had been an emotional and exhausting time for Beyers, but the state was determined not to let up the pressure. Two weeks after his trial Beyers, along with Peter Randall and Danie van Zyl, as co-directors of Ravan Press, were charged under the Suppression of Communism Act for quoting a banned Nusas leader in one of their publications. They made several appearances in court before the charges were dropped for 'technical' reasons in 1974.[31] The fate of others who were charged for defying the Schlebusch Commission varied. Most received suspended sentences while in some cases the charges were withdrawn. Peter Walshe commented: 'The state had made its point in prosecuting, but the process stopped short of creating martyrs.'[32]

The Schlebusch Commission and the trials were an indication of the elaborate steps which the government was prepared to take to justify its actions against its white opponents. It displayed less subtlety and greater severity when it came to deal with black organisations. By the end of 1973 the staff and publications of the Black Community Programme had been banned, as had all important black student leaders. The CI estimated that by the end of 1973 altogether 28 whites and 186 blacks (including Coloured and Indian people) were banned. By January 1974 some 40 young leaders were being held without trial under the Terrorism Act, and later that year another 13 BC leaders were detained after they had attempted to hold a rally to celebrate the victory of Frelimo in Mozambique.[33]

This repression did not succeed completely. An important sign of black restiveness was growing industrial action at a time when workers were denied basic rights – including the right to form unions and to strike. A wave of wildcat strikes swept through Natal in 1973.[34] Until that stage Beyers and the white members of the CI had paid little attention to the demands of black workers and to economic inequalities on which South African society was structured. But gradually a new awareness would dawn about the nature of the conflict in South Africa. Beyers commented: 'For many years we lacked an understanding of the true nature of the struggle in South Africa. In the beginning the CI saw it mainly as a racial issue, where colour was the decisive determinant. We did not fully understand that during all those years the whites had very shrewdly and skilfully exploited colour. By and large it coincided with a lack of education and training. Colour was exploited as a principle of division, separation and discrimination. Even if the racial situation were to slowly change, the basic problem would remain, not of a racial struggle, but of a class struggle of economic disparity between the poor and the rich. The CI began to see this more clearly from 1974 onwards.'[35]

It would take several years for Beyers's new perceptions to crystallise into action. Besides the new attention to economic injustices, the CI began to consider seriously its role in a predominantly black society. The influence of Black Consciousness leaders working in the Black Community Programme had helped Beyers realise that blacks needed to be brought into the mainstream of the CI's work. But the CI's history as a largely white-run organisation made it difficult for the organisation to adapt. It nevertheless made a sincere if belated attempt, and an increasing number of black people were elected onto the CI's board of management and appointed as staff members. In 1973 the Reverend Manas Buthelezi of the Lutheran Church became regional director for Natal – bringing one of South Africa's most prominent black theologians directly into the life of the Christian Institute. His work came to an abrupt halt at the end of 1973 when he was banned for five years. The banning order was lifted the following year after he had managed to leave the country to attend a conference of the powerful Lutheran World Federation and successfully sue the government-funded *To the Point* magazine for defamation.[36]

Another new black staff member in the CI was nurse and social worker Mrs Oshadi Phakati, who was appointed community programme organiser for the Transvaal and Free State in 1973. Phakati, who was to have a close but troubled relationship with Beyers, had initially trained as a nurse in Durban. She then worked at Soweto's Baragwanath Hospital before moving to a clinic in Mamelodi, a black township on the outskirts of Pretoria. As a child welfare nurse and district health worker, she was exposed to the terrible living conditions under which most black people lived and found it impossible to divorce her job as a health worker from her social context.

During her years with the CI, Oshadi Phakati launched several community development projects in the Pretoria area, setting up self-help literacy programmes, day-care centres and first-aid and home-nursing projects. An adherent of the Black Consciousness philosophy, Phakati tried to use community projects to raise people's consciousness about the nature of their predicament. Explaining why she felt it worthwhile to work for a white-dominated organisation, she commented: 'I felt the CI's policies did not go far enough but I thought it would be possible to use the CI's resources to reach people. . . . For example, one of our projects was a self-help study group where students were encouraged to help one another. We used the opportunity to look at Bantu education in a critical manner. . . . We became well known in the community and we had a base from which to take action, for example when we held a church service to pray for the students who had been detained for organising the Frelimo rallies. . . .

'I took the initiative most of the time, but the CI was always willing to support me. If the CI made some contribution it was that they did not try to directly control what we were doing. We had our own programmes, but you could fall back on the CI for many things, including moral support. . . . Beyers was a very good fundraiser and a generous person, and he did not control too much. In fact, sometimes I thought he lacked control. I always said that Beyers and Brian Brown made a good team. Beyers could say yes too much, while Brian could say no and stick to it. But he could also say no too much and then you needed Beyers's influence.'[37]

By 1974 some of the old faces in Spro-cas and the CI had begun to disappear. Peter Randall, who had never considered himself a political activist, had a 'final fling' in active politics as an unsuccessful Social Democrat candidate in the 1974 white general election, on a platform that called for equal political and economic rights for blacks. From then on, he began withdrawing from the CI, but remained committed to one of the most successful spin-offs of Spro-cas, the publishing company Ravan Press. It was probably his involvement in Ravan that resulted in his inclusion on the list of banned people in the crackdown of October 1977.[38]

Beyers was himself moving closer to a new group of people in the CI, who in their political views and actions were regarded as more radical. One important figure was Horst Kleinschmidt, who had initially worked for the Spro-cas 2 project. Kleinschmidt, who was born in Namibia of German parents, came from a deeply conservative background. His views began to change at university, and his involvement first with Nusas and then as a youth worker for the Progressive Party in Cape Town brought him to a commitment to black liberation in South Africa. He joined the CI after he had left student politics, 'not because I felt the great image of Christianity looming in my face but because it was the group which I felt closest to, politically'. Kleinschmidt, friendly with both Theo Kotze and Peter Randall, became in 1975, at the age of 29, Beyers's administrative assistant. Shortly after this he was detained under the Terrorism Act for almost three months. He fled South Africa in April 1976.[39]

Horst Kleinschmidt, speaking of his involvement with Beyers in the CI days, recalled: 'I was made Beyers's assistant because he needed an administrative aide in the office who would support him. He had been through a long list of people who had been his deputies, but who in the end clashed with him quite seriously. There were some disastrous people. Many of them were also very nice people, but there were always problems. That is something you need to say about Beyers. His openness, his acceptance of people and of people's faults has often made him make unwise choices about the people he was going to work with. There were real organisational problems and I also had some difficulties in working with him. . . . There are many examples of what looked from the outside like Beyers's lack of consistency, yet today I feel that I can relate to these more philosophically.

'One example of this is the cars the CI used to loan to people in SASO, the Black Community Programme and the African Independent churches. The frequency with which these cars would be crashed and ruined was fantastically high . . . and eventually it was the CI's black staff who at a staff meeting challenged Beyers not to allow the CI's resources to be abused. . . . Finally after a long discussion the CI decided that in future it would not give out cars and it was my job to explain this new policy. . . . A few days later a theological student came to me for a car, and I gave the reasons why we could not comply. He stormed out of my office in fury and anger, and went down to Beyers, thumped his fist on the table and said, "That racist has no understanding of our needs, I need a car." . . .

'Beyers then told him that it was true that the CI had changed its policy and that cars were no longer available, but he then offered him one of his own cars. Beyers gave him the car, and he got as far as Uncle Charlie's [to the west of Johannesburg] before he crashed it. . . . I felt very angry about that and when I challenged Beyers, he said something that I had never heard him say before. . . . He described how difficult it was for him to say no when he had to come to terms with his guilt as a white person who, for so many years, had been part and parcel of oppressing blacks. For him the dividing line of keeping a good and honourable relationship with black people was something that he still had to learn about. . . .

'But this reflected on one extraordinary part of Beyers, and that in my experience was his infinite ability to say: "I have been wrong and I will have to learn what is the right thing to do." Beyers had a remarkable ability and facility to change.'[40]

Another person who was sometimes frustrated with Beyers was the CI's Cape regional director Theo Kotze. He said: 'I regard Beyers unquestionably as one of the most important prophetic voices in the country . . . but he used to do some very impulsive things that worried some of us. The one thing you have got to say about Beyers is his unquestionable, total sincerity, but it flies off in all kinds of directions. . . .

'I think he is a deeply compassionate man, but at one stage I also thought he was very self-centred. . . . Everything seemed to centre around him. . . . I suppose in my relationship with Beyers there has also been an element of jealousy, a feeling of "Why should he get all the glory and publicity?" But that is a human thing. But we also had a very natural, good relationship. . . . I also felt that Beyers, because he is a very open person, was careless sometimes and trusted people when he should not have. . . . I can remember Beyers would ask me to come up to Johannesburg because he wanted me to meet somebody he was thinking of appointing to the CI and then he would tell me that he had already made the appointment. . . . Having said all that there is no doubt about his very important role in history and that he was a very loving man.'[41]

Beyers also clashed at times with staff in the SACC. John Rees commented: 'The SACC's Dependants' Conference was caring for about 900 families at one stage and we could only afford to give them R25 a month. There would be people who would come and make representations for more, but our hands were tied. They would walk straight upstairs and get money from Beyers. That was very difficult and sometimes caused people to play us off against one another.

'Beyers never wanted to disappoint. He would agree with one group of people in one meeting but then he would do the same thing at a meeting with people with an opposing view. Beyers did not want to take sides, he always fudged the issue, and some regarded this as duplicitous. My view was that he found it very difficult to say no and he never liked a confrontational situation. I don't think he deliberately set out to hurt anybody, but he was never totally aware of the consequences of what he did. He became so concerned with a particular goal that its effect on another matter became peripheral. And when you pointed it out to him he was genuinely repentant. . . . Like so many African giants he had his strengths and weaknesses. A lot of Beyers's weaknesses were transparent, but because of his greatness in other areas, people tended to overlook them.'[42]

Charles Villa-Vicencio remarked of Beyers: 'I first met Beyers when I was studying in the United States in 1974. I drove to New York to hear Beyers speak when he was awarded the Reinhold Niebuhr prize. I spoke to him afterwards and immediately he offered me a job in the CI – that was typical of him. . . . Beyers is not a manager, not an organiser. He is a charismatic person, a prophet. He identifies visions and pronounces goals, and God help everybody else how they are going to get there. That is his strength and his weakness. . . . Beyers has a tremendous drive. Niebuhr once said that grace and ambition are intertwined. It is Beyers's ambition that makes him a channel of God's grace in a situation, it is God's gift to him.'[43]

Beyers's shortcomings, and the fact that some of his closest colleagues were critical of him, in no way diminish the significance of the role he played in the struggle against apartheid. As Horst Kleinschmidt said: 'Beyers is a landmark in the struggle against apartheid and took courageous strides at a time when other and organised forms of struggle were largely absent. Inevitably for those circumstances, he developed an individualistic approach. He could hardly help developing like this. He was, after all, a loyal and responsible member of his church for half his life and had operated in an independent way. When he joined the forces for change no checks or constraints existed. We should not expect the man who gave direction to the struggle to also be the one who provides a fully accountable structure.'[44]

While the CI had its fair share of problems a strong spirit of unity nevertheless bound the staff. There was a genuine love for the CI's at times idiosyncratic director, and for other members of the staff, each with his or her own particular foibles. Although not all CI workers were practising Christians, the Christian commitment infused the whole life and activity of the CI. It also remained Beyers's source of strength, and his daily habit of prayer and Bible reading never changed. And while the CI might have undergone many changes since the early days, morning prayers continued to form an integral part of the daily routine. The CI's Cape Town staff, under the leadership of Theo and Helen Kotze, also developed a close relationship, particularly as a result of their meals of fellowship together, which were known as the *Agape* or love feast. Formal communion posed a problem to the CI because of the presence of both Protestants and Catholics in the organisation, and so the *Agape* became an informal alternative.

Staff and CI members would meet to pray and to read the Bible, and then bread and wine was shared together as the 'food and drink of fellowship'.[45]

Speaking about the CI's spirituality, Brian Brown said: 'I think that it would have come as a surprise to our detractors that we gathered every morning at 8.30 for prayers. And both as a sign of punctuality of the staff and also as a sign of their willingness to partake in that discipline, Beyers Naudé's office was always packed with staff members as we gathered to consider the events of the day and the night and to pray. That was a focal point. . . .

'Another facet of the spirituality could be seen in the remarkable capacity of black staff members to recount the brutalities of the night which they might have witnessed or personally experienced, in the presence of white companions or colleagues in a very unselfconscious way, as if this is not remotely being said in order to embarrass you, to attack you, to impute guilt to you, and at no point need you interrupt and bare your soul and either apologise for white society or seek to exclude yourself from that society. . . .

'It wasn't the expectation that everyone coming into the CI should be a "born-again believer," whatever that phrase means, but it was a belief that we shared a commitment to the values of the Kingdom, the values of love, peace, justice, goodness, righteousness, truth and beauty, and that if you didn't have that commitment to the Kingdom values, then you had no part with us. You were self-excluded and that expression of commitment to the Kingdom values was invariably bound up with an intensely personal faith on the part of CI participants.'[46]

The year 1974 saw a new political climate emerge in southern Africa, with the collapse of Portuguese rule in Angola and Mozambique, the stepping up of guerilla wars in Namibia and Zimbabwe, and the resurgence of the South African liberation movements. In response, white South Africans rallied round the Nationalist government. While conscription of young white men had been compulsory since 1967, gradually the period of national service and the subsequent annual camps had increased. South Africa became rapidly militarised and the South African Defence Force later developed the concept of a 'total strategy' to deal with the so-called 'total onslaught'.

At the SACC's annual conference held in August 1974 at Hammanskraal near Pretoria, the churches had to face up to these issues when presented with a resolution on conscientious objection. The 63 delegates represented ten million members, 8,5 million of whom were black. Accommodation at the seminary enabled all the delegates to be housed together for the three-day conference, and this helped white representatives to develop a greater awareness of the concerns of their black colleagues.[47] Several South African churchmen had recently returned from the All Africa Council of Churches conference in Lusaka where they had been challenged on their stand towards the liberation movements – and this also heightened expectations at the SACC meeting.

During the conference several black delegates criticised the church's stand on the growing strife in South Africa: they referred to the government's threat to move 130 000 people forcibly in the black homeland of Lebowa as an example of the daily violence suffered by the black community. They declared that while the churches had all roundly condemned the World Council of Churches for giving aid to the liberation movements, they were silent about white participation in the conflicts on the country's borders – which they saw as violence being used to maintain a discriminatory society.[48] On the first day of the conference, the Reverend Douglas Bax, a white Presbyterian minister, asked whether the time had not come for the SACC to challenge young men to consider conscientious objection to military service. Bax then drew up a resolution on the issue, which was to be presented to the conference the following day. He decided to ask Beyers to second it to give it more impact. Beyers, then strongly attracted to the pacifist ideas of Martin Luther King, agreed immediately.[49]

The resolution consisted of a preamble and several items which were debated and voted on one by one. The preamble maintained that South Africa was an unjust and discriminatory society which was a threat to peace. Since Christians were called to 'obey God rather than men', they could not accept military service blindly but had to consider whether the cause was just. Defence of an unjust society was ruled out. The preamble also focused on the need for consistency by asserting that it was hypocritical to deplore the violence of 'terrorists or freedom fighters while we ourselves prepare to defend our society with its primary, institutionalised violence by means of yet more violence'. It questioned the basis upon which chaplains were seconded to the military forces 'lest their presence indicate moral support for the defence of our unjust and discriminatory society', and raised the issue of ministering to the 'other side'. The resolution then deplored all violence as a way of solving problems and asked the SACC member churches to consider 'whether Christ's call to take up the Cross and follow Him in identifying with the oppressed does not, in our situation, involve becoming conscientious objectors'. After a fierce five-hour debate, the preamble was carried by 35 votes to 10 and the resolution as a whole by 48 votes to nil.[50]

Beyers, probably more than anyone else, was aware that the resolution would provoke an outcry. 'The whole question of violence had been a constant theme through all the years and I had been doing a lot of private thinking about it. When Douglas Bax came with the motion I was immediately willing to support it. But I warned him. I said: "Douglas, do you realise the storm that this will create?", and he said: "I think so." But I doubt whether Douglas realised the measure of anger which would erupt, especially on the part of the government.'

Once again it was the press which was responsible for the initial frenzy. Even before the conference had debated the resolution, its contents were reported in the *Rand Daily Mail*. The conservative Afrikaans newspaper *Hoofstad* thereafter announced in a front-page story that Beyers Naudé had urged young men to refuse to serve in the Defence Force. This was followed by a barrage of hysterical reports in other Afrikaans newspapers. The SABC in radio broadcasts detected the 'evil influence of the World Council of Churches' and in one of its daily commentaries said about the Hammanskraal decision: 'In the past we have described the South African Council of Churches as unrepresentative and un-South African. It has now revealed itself as a menace to the security . . . of this country.... The stand taken by the Council is an offence to the common sense as well as the sentiment of the ordinary South African Christian.'[51]

The English press and white opposition parties also opposed the resolution, claiming that the country's borders had to be defended. John Vorster warned that 'those who play with fire ... must consider very thoroughly before they burn their fingers irrevocably'. The adoption of the Hammanskraal resolution coincided with a debate in parliament on the Defence Further Amendment Bill in parliament to extend the period of citizen force service. After the news of the SACC resolution, Defence Minister P.W. Botha introduced a further amendment containing harsh new penalties (a fine of up to R10 000 or ten years' imprisonment or both) for anyone who incited any person to avoid military service. When the law was finally enacted by parliament, maximum penalties had been reduced to R5 000 or six years or both, and the only party which had voted against it was the small Progressive Party.[52]

Just as in the debate about the WCC Programme to Combat Racism, the press and the government ignored the views of the majority of South Africans when they condemned the Hammanskraal resolution. Yet as Beyers pointed out in a speech soon after the conference, it was because of the strong black representation at Hammanskraal that the resolution had been adopted. 'I believe that in this resolution we are listening to the voice of authentic black Christian conviction and concern, not only because ... more than two-thirds of the delegates were black, but because of the convictions and feelings so clearly expressed in the discussion in the conference as a whole.'[53]

Hammanskraal presented an important challenge to the English-speaking churches, and although opposition was expressed by many rank-and-file white churchgoers, the resolution was later supported at many church synods. However, an effort to take the debate further at the SACC's 1975 conference, in the form of another resolution written by Douglas Bax and seconded by Beyers Naudé, was blocked by more cautious figures in the SACC. Nevertheless, the issue of conscientious objection had been firmly placed on the agenda of the churches and would assume increasing importance as militarisation and conflict increased in South Africa. Beyers and the CI and some leaders in the SACC had realised that it was not enough simply to criticise apartheid or condemn the violence of those who opposed the government. In a sermon delivered shortly afterwards, Beyers declared: 'As a Christian community we are commanded by Christ, not only to identify ourselves with those in suffering and distress, but also to take active and positive steps to prevent as far as humanly possible such suffering.... We are called not only to be peacelovers but even more – peacemakers. This is the crucial challenge which the situation of confrontation and conflict on our borders presents to us. Are we satisfied that it should develop into a dangerous, massive clash of open violence, bloodshed and warfare on and within our borders, or are we willing to seek active ways and means to discover true peace which can only be founded on justice? What are we prepared to do to find peace?...'[54]

At the same time that Beyers was trying to put this message across, the Afrikaans press practically accused him of treason. As one columnist wrote: 'We say to Mr Beyers Naudé: just what direction are you following? What inspired you to support a motion which amounts to telling a democratic country to sit back and allow communist-inspired murderers and men of violence to overrun it?'[55]

By contrast with the attacks were the honours and awards that came Beyers's way. In 1974 the University of the Witwatersrand decided to award him the honorary degree of doctor of laws. In his citation, Professor E. Kahn described Beyers 'as an international figure, the embodiment of the liberal spirit in this land'.[56] The same year the University of Chicago awarded him, together with prominent Russian dissident Andrei Sakharov, the Reinhold Niebuhr Prize for human rights. Beyers's passport was briefly returned in November 1974 to enable him to receive the award personally – and he made use of the concession by travelling first to the Netherlands. It was the last time for many years that he was permitted to travel abroad, and the opinions he expressed about his country's political future once again fuelled controversy in South Africa.

A large group greeted Beyers and Ilse on their arrival at Schiphol airport. He was interviewed by Dutch television, and featured prominently in press reports and in several radio broadcasts. In various interviews and addresses, he made it clear that the government should prepare the way for eventual black rule and begin negotiations with the country's legitimate black leaders both in exile and in prison.[57]

Beyers addressed these issues in a speech at the Hervormde Kerk synod in Driebergen. Quoting John Rees who had been present at the All Africa Council of Churches conference in Lusaka, Beyers said the African National Congress had warned that guerilla warfare would reach South Africa within two years. At a press conference shortly afterwards, Beyers was asked whether the CI would continue to act as a buffer between the races in the event of open confrontation. He replied that it would be impossible for any organisation to remain neutral and that the CI would side with the oppressed. These statements were simplified and distorted in reports. Quoting from a Dutch source, the Afrikaans morning newspaper *Beeld* then claimed that Beyers had 'sided against the whites', that he predicted terrorism in South Africa and that the CI supported the 'freedom fighters'.[58] The SABC then announced that Beyers Naudé and the CI supported violence, and this was followed by a public attack on him by Prime Minister Vorster. It was only after Dutch church leaders publicly refuted these reports and Beyers had issued numerous statements to the contrary, that *Beeld* admitted that it had misquoted him.[59]

While Beyers may have been misquoted, he had correctly understood that South Africa was on the brink of violent confrontation. He had also come to demonstrate a far greater commitment to black liberation and sympathy for the liberation movements, a view which he made public during his visit to the United States. An important shift in his public utterances was that he no longer condemned outright those who had resorted to armed struggle as a means of fighting to end apartheid. Yet he continued to search for another way. Accepting the Reinhold Niebuhr award, Beyers once again noted how often the institutionalised church had closed its eyes to immense human suffering and abuse of human rights. 'This is one of the crucial questions with which the Christian church . . . is faced. . . . Deep differences of conviction are being . . . expressed on this issue. . . . One is constantly reminded of the fact that long-existing situations and systems of oppression and violence called into being struggles where counter-violence was seen to be the inevitable answer to meet and overcome such existing forms of violence, and I do not think that Christ gives us the right to judge or condemn those who, in finding themselves in such situations of tyranny and oppression, have come to the conclusion that, having tried all else, there is no option left to procure liberation . . . through violence.

'But I hold the conviction that this is not, cannot be, and will never be the truly satisfying answer which God has made available to his children on earth. . . . I sense . . . that there is a dimension of divine power and moral force available to us as human beings which we . . . as a Christian community have not yet been able to grasp and act upon. In the tradition of . . . Mahatma Gandhi and Martin Luther King, I . . . believe that once this . . . moral force . . . is understood . . . it will . . . create a human initiative presently lacking in our society to resolve situations of conflict through means other than those of violence. One of the essential elements which would be required to operate in order to allow moral force to display itself is that of voluntary, individual or communal suffering on the part of those involved in the struggle for human dignity and human rights.'

In closing, Beyers referred to the Christian Institute, revealing an awareness that this organisation's time was running out. 'In 1963 a small body of deeply concerned Christians of all races and denominations in South Africa, called the Christian Institute of Southern Africa, started to join forces with the voices of protest and the pleas for fundamental, peaceful change. During the last eleven years our aims have been ridiculed, our activities have been made suspect, our pleas and warnings have been largely ignored by the majority of the white community in South Africa. . . . Whatever mistakes we may have made we left nobody, either inside or outside our country, in doubt as to where we stand and why we stand there. We are committed to the recognition of the dignity and the fundamental rights of every human being. . . . We do not know whether we will succeed – at the present moment it seems more likely that we might fail – but the real and lasting test of success or failure is not always determined by visible signs.'[60]

There seemed to be an air of resignation about Beyers as he flew back to South Africa in December 1974. Photographers and reporters gathered at Jan Smuts Airport to intercept the man *Die Vaderland* had called 'the most unpopular South African'.[61] As he and Ilse were confronted by the cameras and questions, it was as if he had already guessed the outcome of the CI's final confrontation with the state.

14
The Confrontation Grows, 1975–1977

By January 1975 Beyers Naudé knew it was only a matter of time before the state would act against the CI and use the long-awaited Schlebusch Commission report to justify its move. As a result of earlier reports by the commission, the government had enacted an Affected Organisations Bill, aimed at cutting off foreign funding to organisations involved in anti-apartheid activities.[1] The CI began to make contingency plans in the event of being declared an 'affected' organisation. A new printing company was set up in order to put the CI's publishing initiatives on a better business footing, *Pro Veritate* was streamlined, and Beyers renewed his call for the CI to raise a greater part of its income from South African sources.[2]

He also wrote to CI members, warning them to expect the worst from the Schlebusch report. Summarising the most recent pronouncements of the CI's board of management, Beyers outlined the organisation's support for the struggle for liberation in South Africa. 'Steadfastly adhering to its policy of non-violence in working for radical social change, the Institute seeks to identify itself with the oppressed. Distinguishing between aims and methods used to achieve those aims, the Institute upholds as consistent with the Gospel the goal of a just and non-discriminatory society. . . . As members of the Board of Management we recognise that to spell out our alignment with the oppressed and with the aims of resistance to oppression is to incur the hostility and malice of those who defend exploitative power and privilege in South Africa.'[3]

The full extent of this hostility and malice was spelt out in the Final Report of the Commission of Inquiry into Certain Organisations. The report, tabled in parliament in May 1975, found the CI to be a danger to the state, and in addition contained a scathing attack on Beyers Naudé. It claimed that Beyers and the CI were promoting violence and revolution in South Africa, their main objective being to use racial conflict in order to replace the existing order with a 'Black-dominated socialist system'. The CI was 'linked up' with the World Council of Churches and was 'a completely political body with a political destination'. Foreign organisations exerted undue influence on the CI through financial aid.

The report was hailed by the Afrikaans press and Afrikaner political and church leaders as a vindication of their opposition to the CI. Minister of Justice and Police Jimmy Kruger, referring to 'that celebrated Calvinist Beyers Naudé', declared the report had 'torn the mask of Christianity' from the CI. Black leaders, the liberal English press and overseas supporters, however, took the opposite view. In a full-page commentary on the report the *Cape Times* judged it to be 'about the worst document of its sort we have ever set eyes on, when judged by the criteria of unsubstantiated assertion, guilt by association, unveiled innuendo and jumping to conclusions'. Beyers and the CI's board chairman Colin Gardner described the Schlebusch Commission as a 'patchwork of outright lies, half-truths and facts taken out of context'.[4]

The report, which contained a long, personal history of Beyers Naudé, was riddled with factual errors, contradictions and personal jibes. Although irrelevant to their investigation, the commissioners could not resist referring to Beyers's involvement in the Broederbond exposés, commenting that 'this incident placed a question mark against Dr Naudé's integrity in the minds of Afrikaans-speaking persons'.

The attitude of the commissioners to Beyers Naudé came through clearly in a passage describing his break with the NGK. Claiming that he had founded the CI as a 'substitute' for the NGK, the report stated: 'From then on Dr Naudé turned to the outside world for support for his ideas and philosophy, and at home he also sought contact with organisations such as the Separatist churches and others. In the process he began to turn against his own Church, and did not scruple, for instance, to use his version of the so-called unfrocking process to which he was supposed to have been subjected to make propaganda for the aims of his Institute.

'His opposition to his own Church is evidenced by the fact that, although he had laid down his status as a minister of the Church in terms of Article 11 of the Church Law, he claimed, to suit his own ends, that he had been deprived of it, and according to evidence he still wears his vestments when preaching a sermon, which according to the testimony of experts, is censurable because it is open defiance of the authority of his own Church.'

The report claimed that since the CI was transparently a 'political body', it had not been necessary 'to make an analysis on the principles of canon law or the ecumenical or religious claims of the Institute and its offshoots'. This reluctance to examine the theological basis of the CI did not prevent the commissioners, although lacking a single black member, from making a bold assessment of Black Theology, which Peter Walshe described as a 'virtuoso display of wilful ignorance'.[5] The CI's former Natal director, Manas Buthelezi, found the most positive aspect of the report the 'revelation concerning to what extent the white man can fail to grasp the depth of the black man's soul'.[6]

The commissioners suggested that Black Theology was communist-inspired, and that it was nothing more than the 'theological arm of Black Power' which had been imported to South Africa from the United States. 'Expert evidence was submitted to the commission on the one-sidedness of the "new theology" as set out in the paragraphs above in connection with Black Theology. The evidence of one of South Africa's well-known authorities is so illuminating in this connection that the Commission is submitting it *in toto* as an addendum.' This 'illuminating' addendum spelt out the difference between 'vertical' and 'horizontal' Christian relationships and argued that liberation theology – 'vertical in kind' – had become distorted by its over-emphasis on the social demands of the gospel. In keeping with the secret nature of its inquiries, the commission did not see fit to name this 'well-known authority'. The commissioners were not consistent in this practice, and selectively named witnesses when it suited them, such as the Reverend E. Maqina, a black minister involved in one of the many AICA disputes who, in his evidence, suggested that the CI had misappropriated AICA funds.

In arriving at the finding that Beyers approved 'the use of violence against the existing order . . . while condemning armed defence against terrorists', the report quoted selectively from CI documents and from newspaper reports. The most important 'evidence' which the commissioners used to enforce this claim consisted of inaccurate newspaper reports of his speech in the Netherlands in 1974. While the commissioners eagerly quoted these reports, they made no mention of the subsequent apologies which *Beeld* and other newspapers had carried.

The garbled concluding remarks give some idea of the barbarism of the report. 'The establishment of Black Power, which was deliberately introduced by the UCM as a weapon against the existing order in South Africa, was supported by the above-mentioned planners [Spro-cas 2] as a means of bringing about the desired change, *inter alia* by engineering a revolution, and the actions of the BCP and the PSC, as well as the doctrines of Black Theology, form part of the technique of promoting Black Power. Where, in this report, the Commission expresses disapproval of Black Power, either directly or by implication, it has in mind those aspects of Black Consciousness that have been deliberately developed to foster Black Power, in which process, among other things, innocent Black people are misled and recognised Black leaders and institutions are undermined and denigrated.

'The objectives of Spro-cas 2 have been taken over by the Christian Institute itself, and it is actively supporting and expanding them. This means, among other things, that the Institute has concerned itself, through the PSC, with economic matters, with the aim of discrediting and replacing the capitalist system, as explained above.

'The Christian Institute, among other Dr Beyers Naudé himself and the planners of Spro-cas 2, have pursued these objectives and attempted to achieve them in practice, regardless of the possibility that their actions might lead to the violent overthrow of the authority of the state. In fact, the leaders of the Institute, and in particular the publication *Pro Veritate*, have consistently conditioned public opinion to accept a possible, even an inevitable, violent change in the existing order.

'In the light of your Commission's finding that a Black-dominated socialist state is aimed at, and that violence has been accepted as an element in achieving such a socialist state, it is clear to the Commission that the strategy adopted by the Institute to bring about the desired change is characteristic of revolutionary socialist technique.

'In the light of the cumulative effect of the foregoing findings, the Commission has come to the conclusion that certain activities of the Institute constitute a danger to the state.'[7]

Two days after the Schlebusch report was tabled in parliament the government declared the CI an 'affected' organisation. Yet the blow administered by the state produced an immediate resurgence of support for the CI. The South African Council of Churches and various individual churches reaffirmed their commitment to the CI, while the Catholic Church called on members to make donations to the organisation. Services of dedication were held and donations from local sources poured in. The CI's membership, which had declined to 900 people, climbed back to about 3 000.

Stunned by the body blow, the CI found it difficult to gather the strength needed to soldier on. Apart from financial problems, it had to work hard to maintain the morale of its members amid mounting state surveillance, raids, detentions and bannings. Yet Beyers believed the state action introduced the CI's most significant phase.[8] Although the CI's resources were extremely limited – it had been forced to cut its budget and therefore its personnel and projects – the dedicated staff who remained were steadfastly committed to their mission.

The government's actions forced Beyers to the conclusion that it was almost impossible to use reason and moral persuasion to convince it to abandon apartheid. The most effective way of bringing about change was to support black people in their fight against oppression. The CI, in turn, began to experience greater demonstrations of support from the black community. As Manas Buthelezi put it, the CI was a witness to the redemptive power of the cross: 'Black people can understand this theology because they have always lived it.'[9]

An article in the SACC journal *Ecunews* in June 1975 provided this assessment of the CI's position after it had been declared an affected organisation: 'What is clear by now is that the CI will have enough funds to maintain a vigorous, if somewhat curtailed existence. And that, for the moment, means the CI has won its battle with the authorities. For the significance of the CI has never lain in its projects needing heavy funding, but in its prophetic witness in South Africa as a focus of Christian opposition to apartheid. Even on a reduced budget, the CI can and will continue to perform this function – as it did very effectively in its early years before its activities expanded. Only outright banning is likely to silence the voice of the CI.'[10]

During these turbulent times the CI reviewed its methods of operation. Leading members felt that the CI should shed its 'corporate' image and become more reliant on grassroots structures. This coincided with a feeling – particularly among Cape members of the CI – that there was insufficient shared responsibility and that too often Beyers and the small group around him took all the decisions. Beyers was open to this criticism and agreed that the Cape region of the CI be charged with the task of revising the CI's constitution.[11]

The CI's new constitution, which was finally approved in 1976, emphasised and embodied the principle of decentralisation. Each region in future would take more responsibility for projects, fundraising and administration. The central aim of the CI, as outlined in the constitution, was 'to witness to Jesus Christ as Saviour and Lord, to seek the coming of his Kingdom on earth, to serve the Church in its vocation as the Body of Christ'. In accordance with this, the CI would promote activities and relationships which strengthened the church in its struggle for Christian liberation in southern Africa. The constitution stressed a commitment to building up small communities of people who would, through the witness of their lives, show solidarity with the poor and the oppressed, and try to obey God in their lives. The groups, it was hoped, would contribute to public debate, stressing the biblical demand for social justice, and members would also strive to bring about change in South African society through 'non-violent action'. On an administrative level, the work of the Transvaal region was to be separated from the director's office, leaving Beyers free to concentrate on his 'prophetic ministry', which included reading, writing, speaking and overall coordination.[12]

Apart from the structural changes to the CI, white staff members felt they should adopt simpler lifestyles in solidarity with disadvantaged black South Africans. This was also a practical decision, since after the budget cuts the CI could pay only very modest salaries. In line with this, Beyers and Ilse decided to sell their large double-storey Greenside home. They bought a smaller one in the same suburb, and gave most of the profit they had made to the CI.[13]

In the months after the Schlebusch report was released, Beyers gave a series of public addresses in which he expressed the fear that South Africa was on the brink of violent confrontation. In a speech in Pietermaritzburg in August 1975, he warned whites to take heed of mounting black anger. Looking to the future, he said: 'There are only two forces which will determine the nature and speed of social change in South Africa. On the one hand, the Nationalist Party, if it is able and willing to face the challenge of the fundamental change in the . . . sharing of political power and wealth. . . . On the other hand there is the rising tide of black hopes, aspirations and demands. . . .

'I retain serious doubts of whether the development towards a shared society would take place without serious confrontation which could include some form of violence. If stronger and more concerted support for creating fundamental and rapid peaceful change could be forthcoming from a larger number of bodies . . . then I believe that the transition, though very turbulent, might be reasonably peaceful. . . .

'It is . . . the obligation of all those individuals who truly love their country to do everything in their power to prevail upon the whites to see the light, before the white community pays dearly and unnecessarily for its refusal or blindness to heed and change.'[14]

Beyers sounded an equally sharp warning abroad. Still without a passport, he had been unable to accept an invitation to speak at the Royal Institute of International Affairs in London. In a written address read on his behalf in

December 1975, Beyers called for a national convention between black and white. 'If this call is not heeded in this crisis moment of our history, there is no doubt South Africa will be facing a period where negotiation will be superseded by polarisation, and where reconciliation will be temporarily superseded by increasing hostility,' he said.[15]

While the SACC member churches, the Catholic Church and numerous overseas churches had aligned themselves with the CI during the crisis over the Schlebusch Commission, the NGK fully endorsed its findings. Assessor Koot Vorster expressed the hope that on the basis of the report action would at last be taken against Beyers by the NGK's Parkhurst church – a step the church council refused to consider.[16] Vorster's statement showed that the passing of the years had done nothing to reduce the level of animosity felt by the Afrikaner establishment towards Beyers Naudé. Their loathing was not unconnected to the fact that he continued to concern himself with the affairs of their church – and particularly with the problems faced by many ministers from the NGKA and Sendingkerk.

One issue which aroused great bitterness was the stand Beyers had taken on the cutting of ties between Afrikaans churches and overseas churches and universities. For many years Beyers had pleaded with the NGK and Gereformeerde Kerk not to turn away from the world church movement. But they were uncompromising in their support for apartheid and became increasingly critical of the World Council of Churches. By the mid-1970s Beyers had come to the conclusion that an open approach to the Afrikaans churches would not help to sway them from their political commitments.

The matter came to a head in 1974 when the Free University of Amsterdam began to question seriously its close association with the Potchefstroom University for Christian National Education. For twenty years there had been a regular exchange of staff and students in terms of a cultural agreement which existed between the two universities. For the Free University the question came over time to be posed whether this agreement should end because of Potchefstroom University's strong commitment to the government's race policies. The university was the academic base of the Gereformeerde Kerk and still remained a strong force behind the government's 'Christian National' education policy. In an exchange of correspondence between the two universities, it was clear that Potchefstroom was not willing to compromise in its support for apartheid.[17]

The Free University handed all this correspondence over to Beyers and asked his views on the issue. On the basis of the principles which the Free University had spelt out with regard to racial justice, Beyers declared he had no option but to recommend the agreement be terminated. When the Free University finally announced the termination of the cultural agreement, it said that the letters received from the rector of Potchefstroom, Professor H. J. J. Bingle, with his defence of apartheid, had played the decisive role in its decision.[18] Beeld described Beyers's role in the matter as a 'tragedy'. 'Does Dr Naudé really think that he can help this process with such pinpricks from outside? . . . For the change in attitudes for which he has so passionately pleaded, he is at best irrelevant and at worst a . . . hindrance. This is all his own making, because he has already lost the argument in his own community, and now he is trying to get at them from the outside.'[19] However, it was the NGK which itself completed the process of isolation. In 1974 the church delivered an ultimatum to the Hervormde Kerk in the Netherlands to end its support for the WCC's Programme to Combat Racism. When the Hervormde Kerk refused to do so and once again called on the NGK to reconsider its race policies, the latter announced the 'severing of the close bonds' between the two churches.[20]

Another source of Afrikaner resentment was Beyers's open support for the rebellion which was occurring locally within the NGK 'family' of churches. For decades the white NGK had dominated her racially segregated 'daughter' churches through control of educational resources and church buildings and generally because of her powerful financial position. The relationship between the white and black Dutch Reformed Churches formed a microcosm of apartheid society. The basic principle underlying apartheid was racial separation and white domination – and the same pattern applied in the NGK family.

In 1974 the white NGK's general synod reaffirmed its support for apartheid when it adopted the policy document *Human Relations and the South African Scene in the Light of the Scriptures*. Although the original document had been critical of some of the harsher aspects of apartheid – such as the migrant labour system – the final report supported, on the basis of Scripture, 'autogenous separate development', provided that it was carried out in a 'fair and honourable way, without affecting or injuring the dignity' of any person.[21]

The daughter churches – whose members regarded apartheid as anything but fair and honourable – were becoming increasingly resentful of the white church. Influenced by Black Consciousness and Black Theology, leading churchmen began to ask why white ministers who worked as missionaries in their churches refused to accept full membership and why black ministers were never invited to preach in white pulpits. They also began to question the entire basis of separation which prevailed in the family of churches, encapsulated in the condescending reference to 'daughter' churches, and the NGK's determination to support apartheid at the cost of sacrificing relationships with other churches both inside and outside South Africa.

In 1974, meeting in synod, the *Sendingkerk* cautiously criticised apartheid and called for mixed worship. The NGKA, which was in a very vulnerable position because of its almost complete financial dependence on the white church, took the challenge a step further at its historic synod in Worcester in the Cape in 1975. The significance of the occasion was underlined by the presence of Beyers Naudé and Roelf Meyer, who had been invited as observers. Beyers, who had been warned by an anonymous caller that he would be killed if he attended, spoke to the synod on the need for reconciliation in South Africa. Representatives of the NGK protested against the presence of Beyers at the synod, but the Reverend Ernest Buti – the first black minister to be elected as moderator of the NGKA – dismissed these protests and warmly welcomed both Beyers and Roelf Meyer.[22]

The decisions taken at the NGKA synod were to prove of great significance. Apartheid was condemned as unscriptural and rejected as immoral and unchristian, and a call was issued for unity of the Dutch Reformed Churches. All ethnic divisions within NGKA seminaries (which had been created by the white church) were to be dismantled. Ministers of the white NGK would no longer be permitted to serve the NGKA as missionaries but were welcome to join as full members of the black church and work as brother ministers. The white church was in turn asked to open its doors to black ministers. The synod, ignoring the protests of white NGK representatives, also voted to join the South African Council of Churches.[23]

In an obvious reference to the CI, *Die Kerkbode* criticised several of the Worcester decisions and suggested that 'certain people' were trying to create a rift between the NGK and its daughter church.[24] This attack reflected the concern about the open support the CI had begun receiving from African and Coloured ministers. For years, many black Dutch Reformed churchmen and theological students had played down their sympathy for the CI, since involvement could have cost them their careers. With the change in the political and theological climate in South Africa, black ministers became more willing to take a public stand, and some were now open in their support for the CI. The bond was further strengthened by staff appointments to the CI, such as that of NGKA minister Lucas Mabusela in 1975.

The Reverend Sam Buti, son of the first black NGKA moderator Ernest Buti, spelt out the frustrations experienced by ministers of the daughter churches in a thesis on the subject. 'The Black Dutch Reformed Church's experience in relationship with the DRC [NGK] is in many ways that of rejection and refusal by the white DRC people to accept black people as fellow beings, created in the image of God.'

Referring to the inferior theological education which black ministers received, he said: 'The syllabi of subjects in the Dutch Reformed Church's theological seminaries contain very little relevant material denouncing apartheid as unchristian and evil, [or] encouraging the study of the theology of liberation. For decades no deliberate . . . effort has been made by the DRC to discover the potential of theological, lay, administrative and financial leadership in the younger churches and to . . . encourage the development . . . through advanced study overseas. In fairness towards the Dutch Reformed Church it should be stated that its missionary fervour . . . led to the contribution of large sums of money from the members of the DRC which was . . . used to establish a number of ethnically separated theological schools. But this fervour and the substantial contributions which were thus made have led to a situation of the younger churches being imprisoned in a financial dependence which leads to all other forms of oppression. . . .

'Numerous examples are available where black ministers . . . have been threatened, intimidated, victimized or even have lost their livelihood when they dared to express publicly their opposition to and rejection of apartheid on the basis of the Gospel.'[25]

Beyers was well aware of these problems. He believed that one of the keys to the liberation of the black churches lay in better education, and he used his overseas contacts, particularly with Dutch supporters like Professor Verkuyl, to create opportunities for promising black ministers to study abroad. He was also influential in persuading the Dutch universities to extend the length of time South Africans could study abroad and, where there were only a limited number of places at these universities, to accept African and Coloured students rather than white, apartheid-supporting ministers. The new generation of leaders emerging in the *Sendingkerk* and the NGKA in the late 1970s and the 1980s were products of the Free University of Amsterdam, the University of Kampen and leading universities in the United States. Although many abroad and in South Africa contributed to this education effort, the influence of Beyers Naudé and the CI was central. Beyers's constant promotion of the South African issue – particularly in the Netherlands – made it easier for sympathetic people overseas to raise the necessary funds to sponsor black students and their families.[26] As NGKA minister Elia Thema put it: 'Beyers could be called the father of the external theological programme for the orientation and improvement of the black ministers in the NGK.'[27]

Beyers also played an important role in the emergence of the *Broeder Kring* (BK), the forerunner of the *Belydende Kring*, which consisted mainly of African and Coloured but also a few white ministers of the NGK who wanted to bridge the racial divisions in their church and strive for unity. Although the BK was largely a black initiative, the CI played a significant part in its establishment and Beyers was one of its founder members. Beyers and Sam Buti deposited the first R50 into the BK's bank account in 1974.[28]

Beyers formed many close relationships with ministers of the African and Coloured churches. One of these was with Dr Allan Boesak, a minister from the *Sendingkerk*, who obtained his doctorate from the University of Kampen. Close to Beyers in the early years of his career and active in the CI in its last years, Allan Boesak rose to become moderator of the *Sendingkerk* and president of the World Alliance of Reformed Churches. An excellent speaker and a man of great charisma, Boesak was one of the figures who would take centre-stage in the struggle between church and state in the 1980s. Like so many of Beyers's relationships with strong personalities, there would be moments of personal tension between them. Whatever their personal differences, both were committed to the same political ideals, and this drew them together in numerous initiatives in the 1970s and 1980s.

Beyers was also close to the Reverend Hannes Adonis, lecturer and minister in the *Sendingkerk*. He recalled: 'When I was a minister in Philippi, I invited Beyers to preach in my church and to conduct Holy Communion. Some weeks after that the congregation invited a white minister from the NGK to preach. After this minister left the pulpit, he refused to shake my elder's hand because he was "Coloured." A week later the youngsters of the church came to me and they said that no white minister should ever be allowed in our church. I tried to explain to them that their demand was a form of racism and I said to them: 'What about Beyers?" They said: "We don't have a problem with Beyers. He is not a white man. He is just a man." '²⁹

The incident at Philippi was one of many bitter experiences suffered by black congregations. But not all NGK ministers conformed to this racist mould and many rejected apartheid theology. One such individual was Beyers's brother-in-law, Frans O'Brien Geldenhuys. Geldenhuys believed Beyers had been wrong to leave the NGK and he elected to stay in the church and try to change it from the inside. He was not successful. The story of Frans O'Brien Geldenhuys is one of struggle, compromise and ultimate failure. He worked for several years as director of ecumenical relations in the NGK but fought a losing battle to maintain outside contact as his church turned its back on the South African Council of Churches and the world church community. As a result of self-imposed isolation and because of growing opposition to apartheid overseas, by the mid-1970s the NGK felt cut off and vulnerable. The leadership in the church was thus very amenable when the government offered it secret money to promote the church's message abroad. Unbeknown to Geldenhuys the funding – which stretched over a four-year period – was part of the Department of Information's all-embracing secret programme to 'sell apartheid' abroad.

The scheme ended in disaster when in 1978 the press exposed the 'Information Scandal' and gave details of the secret funding that had been used for numerous propaganda projects. The following year the NGK's role was also revealed. The exposés deeply shook Frans O'Brien Geldenhuys. In his memoirs published in 1982, he reflected on that episode: 'I have a clear conscience about the manner in which I carried out my task. But the further away I stand from events, the clearer it becomes: I lived a lie for four years.'³⁰ He had been shocked to discover the extent of the secret projects and felt that his church had been used as part of the state's propaganda machine. Shattered and disillusioned, Geldenhuys began to face up to the fact that his church was not prepared to budge from its close relationship with the government and he eventually resigned as chief executive officer and director of ecumenical relations of the NGK.

Geldenhuys gives a clue to the symbolic role which Beyers began to fill – to many he had become the forgotten conscience of the NGK. He reflected: 'Shortly after Cottesloe Beyers and I met at a friend's farm near Pretoria and talked things out. We walked through the veld. What next? What was the best way to promote the insights of Cottesloe? Bey felt that he had to make use of the opportunity and found the Christian Institute. He hoped . . . to retain his status as a minister and thought it would still be possible to take part in synods and church decisions as an elder. "You can forget about that, Bey," I told him. "The church will never accept it if you establish an organisation alongside it. I prefer to stay and work from within the church." . . . Twenty years later I resigned as chief executive officer of the NGK, with the bitter realisation that I had not succeeded in moving my church from its complacent stand in favour of apartheid in church and politics. I thought back to that day in the veld outside Pretoria and asked myself: Who was right – Bey or I?'³¹

The Sharpeville shootings on 21 March 1960 had shaken South Africa to the core. Crisis loomed, but the churches still found time to meet at Cottesloe to try to work out a common approach to the underlying problem in South Africa – apartheid. Sixteen years later time had run out for the country and the church. Verwoerd's generation – the children of Soweto – were tired of waiting. On 16 June 1976 their protests and demonstrations were met with forceful police action and South Africa's largest black township erupted. What sparked the unrest was the imposition of Afrikaans as a medium of instruction in black senior primary and junior high schools. Tension had been building for several months over the Department of Bantu Education's insistence that English and Afrikaans should be used equally as mediums of instruction. The Department ignored all pleas and representations from the black community to reconsider the ruling. The SACC, the CI and the SAIRR, through their black staff members, had been told that the situation in Soweto was becoming increasingly unstable. Indeed, the SAIRR warned the government to take action, but its pleas fell on deaf ears.[32]

When on 16 June students from the Naledi and Thomas Mofolo high schools organised a protest march, between 10 000 and 20 000 students converged on the Orlando West High School. The march proceeded peacefully until the children were confronted by police. The police fired teargas into the crowd and the marchers retaliated by throwing stones at them. Police opened fire, killing seven and wounding eighteen. After the first shootings, rioting spread throughout Soweto. Police reinforcements were called in and army troops were placed on standby as buildings and vehicles were burnt.

Horrified by the bloodshed, the CI called on the government to suspend immediately the compulsory use of Afrikaans in black schools. Only hours after word of the violence in Soweto had filtered through to the CI's offices, Beyers sent a telegram to the moderator of the NGK, Dr D. Beukes, pleading with him to intervene: 'In the light of the very serious situation which has developed in Soweto this morning and because of the danger of eruption of large-scale violence, the Christian Institute appeals to you as Moderator and to the Broad Moderature to request the government to immediately terminate the instruction of school subjects through the medium of Afrikaans.'[33]

The SACC also called on the government to take urgent action. 'We are appalled at the authorities' total lack of response and understanding to the aspirations of black people. . . . The fact that the confrontation involved school children has the frightening implication that black grievances are not only a matter of politics, but have become a matter of intense and widespread agony, felt even by children, which could escalate into a national catastrophe.'[34]

The SACC's worst fears were soon confirmed. In the days which followed, police shot and teargassed scores of rioting youths in Soweto, and by the end of the week the official death toll had risen to 176. The unofficial estimate was closer to 300. Demonstrations and violence quickly spread to other townships on the Witwatersrand and around the country as government properties, especially beer halls, administration offices and schools, were burnt down. Police also intervened in scores of funerals for the victims, and on two separate occasions mourners were shot and killed.[35]

On 18 June church leaders gathered at the SACC's headquarters in Diakonia House[36] to listen to an assessment of the situation from Soweto leaders and consider emergency action. Beyers was struck by the sense of helplessness which descended on the meeting, of the vast chasm which separated the white churchmen from their black brothers, as the litany of unresolved grievances and resentments poured out. The church leaders called for a day of prayer, and the SACC, in cooperation with the CI, launched an emergency fund, the Asingeni Fund, to help the victims of the violence. On the same day Beyers and John Rees were served with notices issued by the chief magistrate of Johannesburg, declaring: 'You are hereby warned to please disassociate yourself totally and completely from interfering with the present situation of unrest in the Witwatersrand area.' In an angry reply, Beyers retorted: 'I totally and completely reject any suggestion or inference that I have at any time interfered with the present situation of unrest in the Witwatersrand area, as the contents of the letter of the chief magistrate of Johannesburg implies – or in any other area of our country. I pray that I may be given the strength in this hour of national crisis, in obedience to God, to exercise my Christian ministry, both pastoral and prophetic, to all the people of our land.'[37]

What had begun as a spontaneous protest by black school children developed into a mass uprising. Young people took the lead in rejecting not only Bantu education, but the entire political system in South Africa. In reaction the state resorted to enormous force to quell the protests and by 1977 the death toll in the black townships had risen to more than 700. Thousands were arrested and many were held without charge – including the CI's Transvaal director, Oshadi Phakati. Although the government was forced to back down on its language ruling, mass school boycotts continued well into 1977.

The Soweto uprisings marked a watershed in the country's history and touched almost every facet of South African life, not least the churches. The NGK deplored the loss of life and called for a 'worthy plan of action in which the example of the Lord can be followed', but made no attempt to analyse the issues which had provoked the violence. The English-speaking churches went further and, in statements which emanated from numerous meetings and synods, identified the system of apartheid, complete with its formidable security apparatus, as the cause of the problem.[38] But for South Africa's black community these protests were simply not enough. Increasingly Christians were being challenged to do more than issue statements calling for peace. In the next decade, as black ministers took the lead in the South African Council of Churches and in many of the member churches, they would, by their words and deeds, identify themselves closely with the liberation struggle. However, most white Christians, whose neat suburban lives were far removed from the daily horror of township violence, could not understand why their churches became embroiled in 'politics' and recoiled in alarm.

Exceptional in their beliefs was the small group of white Christians, some in the SACC and some in the CI, who understood and responded to the challenge. Beyers, recalling the confusion and surprise of fellow churchmen during the Soweto uprising, remarked: 'Afterwards, we tried to say to them: "Brothers, now do you realise what we have been trying to warn you about for so long? Whether we like it or not we have to take a decision. Either we have to side with blacks in their struggle for liberation or otherwise we are going to become irrelevant. At the moment we are not on the side of liberation."'

Opting for the 'side of liberation' brought Beyers face to face with the issue of economic sanctions as a means of forcing change. It brought him into close contact with the chief minister of the black homeland of KwaZulu, Chief Mangosuthu Buthelezi. Black homeland leaders had emerged prominently in the 1960s and early 1970s – partly because the crushing of the ANC and PAC had created a leadership vacuum in black politics and because they occupied the only platform on which black views could be safely aired. Although Buthelezi worked within the apartheid system, his strong criticism of government policy led many to believe that he could play an important role in the liberation struggle. As Buthelezi's public utterances became increasingly sharp, so his relationship with the South African government deteriorated, enhancing his credibility, particularly in white liberal circles and also in the eyes of Beyers Naudé. Buthelezi's rejection of the government's offer of independence for KwaZulu at a Sharpeville Day rally in March 1976 received strong support from the CI, and *Pro Veritate* published his address in full.[39]

A figure who played a key role in bringing Beyers and Buthelezi together was businessman and labour consultant Walter Felgate. Felgate did not join the CI but offered his services to Beyers as a consultant on financial, publishing and other matters. Within a short time he appeared to have considerable influence with Beyers, a development frowned upon by the Cape leadership of the CI. Theo Kotze, in particular, did not like Felgate's involvement in the CI, and it was an issue which caused controversy within the organisation.[40] Felgate nevertheless remained on the scene for several years. Influential with Buthelezi, Walter Felgate arranged several meetings between him and Beyers. The focus of their meetings was on economic issues, and they began to examine economic exploitation and investment. Although Beyers never seriously studied socialism or Marxism, the Spro-cas studies had been important in waking him to the realisation that the struggle in South Africa was about class as well as race. Spro-cas had shown, for example, that white incomes, which were among the highest in the world, were at least ten times higher than those of blacks. In a country where the government boasted about the free enterprise system, blacks were not permitted to own land, nor were they permitted to operate businesses or factories in 'white' South Africa, while the immense restrictions and discriminatory measures which applied to black townships made development impossible.[41]

Beyers summed up the views of the CI on economic matters in a speech at the University of Cape Town in June 1976. Calling for a joint study of the economy by black and white South Africans, he said it would not be enough for such a study 'to sing the praises of . . . free enterprise or to warn against the danger of a black socialist . . . system. . . . It has to start with an honest admission of the serious failure of the capitalist system in procuring greater economic justice for the majority of the inhabitants of our country; it has to continue with an honest and critical appraisal of the weaknesses and injustices inherent in all economic systems – capitalist, socialist as well as Marxist, and it has to lead to the evolvement of a system which will bring about a much more equitable sharing in economic wealth.'[42]

For many years Beyers and the CI had refrained from calling for economic sanctions as a way of bringing about change in South Africa. Yet he believed that capitalism had fed on the government's migrant labour policy and homeland system, and that foreign and local investors had done nothing to challenge injustice. Beyers took the first cautious step towards opposing foreign investment in a statement issued jointly with Chief Buthelezi. They declared: 'A radical redistribution of wealth, land and political power is essential for the establishment of a stable and moral society. . . . In South Africa for over a century capitalistic paternalism has produced the conclusive evidence which makes us reject government by minority elite. . . . If the homelands exist to make labour available to maintain the cash economy and standard of living of the elite . . . and to establish an economic buffer zone of homeland economies to protect the central economy and provide benefits for the favoured few, we can come to only one conclusion. Foreign investment in the central economy is devoid of all morality. . . .

'Whites in South Africa have denied blacks access to the central parliamentary decision-making process. They have imposed on blacks a divide and rule policy as though the blacks of the country have no right to speak on issues of national importance. The question of investment is one such issue. We call for a national convention in which the blacks in South Africa can speak for themselves on the matter of foreign investment.'[43]

The cooperation between Beyers Naudé and Chief Buthelezi was shortlived. A year later Buthelezi officiated at the opening of a foreign-funded chemical factory in the homeland. When the CI questioned his action, he replied that he could not deny jobs to the unemployed.[44] On political issues Beyers and Buthelezi also went their separate ways. Buthelezi, who had been a member of the African National Congress's Youth League, became estranged from the liberation movement in the 1980s. Buthelezi resurrected and nurtured the Zulu-based 'National Liberation Movement' Inkatha – and was accused by the ANC and later by the United Democratic Front of perpetuating apartheid structures. Beyers later felt he had made a mistake in working closely with Buthelezi. 'We had hoped that Buthelezi, given his background and his position, would become a major force for political change. But later it became clear that Buthelezi was prepared to go to a certain point but not any further. He was not prepared to step out of the structure which gave him that position of political power.'

The CI became even more explicit in its support for the liberation struggle when its board of management met in Natal in September 1976. Shaken by events in the townships, the CI board declared a new stage in the struggle for liberation had been reached. It called for a national convention between black and white, and offered support for the goals of black political movements, both exiled and those still operating legally, in so far as their aims accorded with 'biblical values of justice, freedom and human responsibilities'. The CI also promised support 'for all peaceful efforts to bring change, including work stayaways, economic sanctions and the discouragement of immigration'.[45]

The CI followed up this resolution with a fuller statement on the issue of investment in South Africa. It declared that the government's insistence on enforcing apartheid had produced a situation where it was difficult to prevent an escalation in violence and confrontation. One of the last remaining avenues of working for peaceful change was through economic pressure. The CI went on to assert that it supported the call against further investment in South Africa because investment in apartheid was 'immoral, unjust and exploitative', and previously neither pressure from investors nor economic growth had helped change the situation. The CI stated that many black organisations opposed foreign investment in South Africa – 'and we believe this would be the opinion of the majority of South African blacks if their voice could be freely heard'.[46]

While the government had already accused the CI of endangering state security, this new stance represented the last straw. Beyers remarked of this resolution: 'I remember so well our discussions and eventually our decision to publicly support the liberation movements. I said to them that we should be aware that with the adoption of this resolution it would be the beginning of the end of the CI as an organisation.'

The resolutions not only outraged the government but naturally provoked criticism from the business community. It also upset a number of white members of the CI and many began to withdraw. Their unhappiness was summed up by a CI member who wrote to cancel his subscription to *Pro Veritate*. 'It seems to me . . . that the Institute has lost patience with the churches so that the tone of voice it now uses has become strident and thus counter-productive. . . . Do you really still love the racialist sinner while hating his sin or do you hate and ultimately condemn him too now? Are you speaking the truth in love? Or in condemnation? We know our problem and so it doesn't really help to rub our noses in it.'[47]

Beyers was saddened by this alienation. 'It was an agonising situation. The more that we supported and expressed support for black aspirations, the more we experienced criticism, alienation and withdrawal of white membership. It was very painful. But by that time I realised it was inevitable, and I foresaw that this would eventually also occur in the so-called multi-racial English churches.'

During this time of mounting tension between the CI and the authorities, the long process of litigation surrounding Beyers's refusal to give evidence before the Schlebusch Commission at last drew to an end. After a series of appeals and counter-appeals, the Supreme Court in Pretoria, in October 1976, finally upheld his conviction and sentence of a R50 fine or thirty days' imprisonment.

Beyers chose to go to jail rather than to pay the fine. Recalling the commitment of all the CI members who had been prepared to suffer prosecution rather than submit themselves to an unjust authority, and thinking of the many prisoners of conscience in South Africa, Beyers was determined to make this symbolic gesture. As he said at the time: 'A fine of R50 is of little significance to me. To go to jail is a little painful, but it allows me, in a small way, to identify myself with the hundreds of blacks in jail.'[48] On 28 October 1976 Ilse Naudé drove Beyers to the Pretoria Magistrate's Court. He was taken to the maximum security section of Pretoria Central Prison, and spent the evening in his cell reading the Book of Amos. He 'slept like a top on a prison bed, and was half way through his lonely walk round the exercise yard in the morning when he was abruptly returned to the pressures and punishments of normal CI life'.[49]

Beyers's minister, Dr Jan van Rooyen, had driven to Pretoria to pay the fine. In justifying his action to the press Van Rooyen said he had paid the fine because most South Africans had forgotten about the Schlebusch Commission and so Beyers's stand was therefore 'irrelevant'. He also feared that Beyers's imprisonment would spur unrest and tension and would give other countries 'a chance to throw more stones' at South Africa. 'This would have caused all the more embarrassment for those who still want to defend us.' He felt it would have widened the rift in the NGK family of churches. 'I believe that I had to do it. . . . It was based on my real love for my church, my country and all the people of my country and also for Dr Naudé to whom I explained my motives during the drive to Johannesburg.'[50] Beyers was upset by this action of his minister, and it caused a rift in their relationship. For a long time Dr Van Rooyen had felt that Beyers was too 'extreme', and he regarded Beyers's decision to go to jail as provocative. The leadership of the CI, on the other hand, supported and sympathised with Beyers. Brian Brown, who by that time was chairman of the CI's newly formed National Council, issued a statement making it clear that Van Rooyen had acted 'without the consent and against the wishes of the prisoner'. 'Apart from his conscientious rejection of the commission, Dr Naudé made no secret of the fact that although his sentence of 30 days was so small, the personal sense of emotional and intellectual identification with the thousands of his fellow citizens who are jailed for their beliefs was very large. But in South Africa, it appears, a man is not even free to stay in prison if he wants to!'[51]

Less than a month after Beyers's brief stay in jail, security police conducted a huge raid on the offices of both the CI and the SACC in Diakonia House in Braamfontein. The raid by about 40 security policemen began at 7 a.m. When Beyers arrived at work a security policeman presented him with a search warrant. For eight hours the policemen searched every room, and confiscated numerous CI documents and pamphlets. They also seized 3 000 copies of *Black Review*, edited by Steve Biko, from the Ravan Press offices, as well as all copies of the SACC's magazine *Kairos*. One woman was detained during the search, and in the course of the day Beyers heard that *Pro Veritate* editor Cedric Mayson had been detained while on holiday in Mossel Bay in the Cape. British-born but a naturalised South African, the former Methodist church minister regarded himself as a 'Christian revolutionary'. Under his influence *Pro Veritate* became increasingly strident in its rejection of white power. Mayson was held without charge for 15 days while other CI staff members, including Oshadi Phakati and field worker Mashwabada Mayatula, were detained for much longer periods. The authorities never bothered to inform the CI or the SACC about the purpose of their search. A few months later, the CI's Cape Town branch was subjected to a similar raid.[52]

As 1977 dawned, anger and discontent continued to simmer in black townships. In spite of the systematic detention and banning of black leaders and publications, the spirit of resistance was kept alive at numerous mass funerals and meetings. Beyers continued to attract strong government criticism. As a director of Ravan Press, he was once again charged with publishing offences – for conspiring with four black journalists to produce an undesirable publication. The charges were eventually dropped.[53]

In a foretaste of what was awaiting the entire leadership of the Christian Institute, Oshadi Phakati was served with a five-year banning order in March 1977. The banning, which confined her to the black township of Mamelodi and the surrounding magisterial district of Pretoria, came as a terrible blow and caused her immense frustration and bitterness. In her years at the CI she had made an important contribution through her community programme work. A member of the Black Parents' Association which had been formed after the Soweto uprising, she was one of the first group of people to be detained under the new all-encompassing Internal Security Act from August to December 1976. After her banning Oshadi Phakati felt she had to choose between going to jail repeatedly for breaking her banning order, abandoning her work altogether or continuing it in another form outside the country. Finally, she fled the country with her son and joined Horst Kleinschmidt in the CI's Netherlands office.[54]

Beyers continued to travel across the country, and a note of desperation began to creep into his speeches. He repeated his fears and warnings again and again. Some colleagues felt that Beyers was wasting his energy, among them Calvin Cook. 'Beyers had moved towards black associations and to that extent he had disappeared from most white consciences. By that stage many regarded Beyers as crying "wolf, wolf", they had heard it all before. In a curious kind of way I felt that his being banned was a way in which he was going to save his soul. I felt that he needed time in quiet and silence to reassess his mission. When you saw him in those days he was desperately tired, and when a person is tired they are sometimes driven to speak when there may not have been anything fresh to say.'[55]

Beyers presented what would be his final report as director of the CI at the organisation's annual general meeting in Johannesburg in September 1977. It was a clear and realistic exposition of the problems confronting South Africa and the churches. 'The situation has developed into a struggle for power, with the majority of whites supporting the military, police and economic power of the government in the belief that this will guarantee their future security, while practically all blacks are convinced that the power of truth, the power of youth, the power of sustained black political aspirations, the power of numbers and of world pressure, will eventually enforce fundamental change and achieve liberation. The implications which this struggle has for the church are staggering and the challenge which this presents to the Christian faith is, I believe, only vaguely realised in our country.'

Beyers argued that the institutionalised brutality of the apartheid system had engendered so much bitterness and hatred that many black leaders were coming to the conclusion that counter-violence was a tragic inevitability. 'In the light of this, the staff and Council of the Christian Institute have increasingly given their support to black initiatives for self-realisation and self-development, whilst at the same time interpreting to the white community the real nature of the vast social and political change taking place in our country. Admittedly – especially with white attitudes moving more and more to the right – such a witness and work antagonises many whites, . . . while for many blacks our non-violent stand and Christian call for reconciliation on the basis of justice becomes irrelevant.'

Turning to the churches in South Africa, Beyers declared it had been wrong to hope that the NGK would eventually put pressure on the government to abandon its race policies. The NGK had rejected the CI and the SACC and was now experiencing opposition from the black Dutch Reformed churches. 'As in the political field, such initiatives for change will emanate from the black community – in this case the black DRC. The CI has always seen as part of its witness its expression of support for such actions, as we believe these to be a more realistic and effective way of bringing about change than to wait for the day in the distant future when eventually and belatedly the white DRC may be willing to stand up and be counted publicly in total rejection of the racial policies of the government.'

Referring to the multi-racial English churches, he said: 'With sincere gratitude we acknowledge the moral support we have received. . . . We are aware, however, that within each church the conservative grouping of the white membership have become increasingly critical of the stance of the CI in supporting black initiatives for change. We have been accused of taking an anti-white stand and a pro-black stand in our expression of Christian solidarity with the oppressed. It is of vital importance that we restate our stand as being neither pro-black nor anti-white but pro-Christ. . . . If our witness, pronouncements and actions are authentically Christian, then we deserve the full and enthusiastic support of the churches. If not, we need the fearless and loving criticism of the church – and not a fearful withdrawal of moral or financial support because we are seen to be too "radical", "outspoken" or too little "diplomatic."'

Looking to the future, Beyers declared the Christian Institute shared the hope of the oppressed and dispossessed that a better day was dawning. It also sympathised with whites who lived with uncertainty and fear. He concluded: 'As South Africa moves into an increasingly uncertain future, Christ is calling His followers to step into the unknown tomorrow with faith and hope and joy – because this is His world and His people and His kingdom. Aware as we are that our country is moving into a period of great suffering, anguish and conflict, we move forward in hope and joy in the certain knowledge that where Christ leads He brings the assurance of the fulfilment of our striving for justice, liberation and recognition of human dignity.'[56]

Two days after his address, on 12 September 1977, Steve Biko died of extensive head injuries and acute renal failure in police custody in Pretoria. Biko, the acknowledged leader of the Black Consciousness movement, had been arrested and detained on many occasions since his banning in 1973 – mostly for contravening his banning order. In August 1976 he was held for 101 days under the Internal Security Act and in 1977 he was detained three times. Arrested by security policemen for the last time on 18 August 1977 he was stripped naked, placed in leg irons, manacled and held in solitary confinement in the Port Elizabeth police cells. On 6 September he was transferred to the security police offices for interrogation. According to medical evidence submitted by Biko's family at his inquest, he had entered the interrogation room 'alive and well but by 7 a.m. on 7 September he was a physical and mental wreck'. According to this evidence, at least three blows would have been needed to inflict the brain damage he suffered. Finally Steve Biko was thrown naked and unconscious into the back of a Land Rover, and driven 1 184 kilometres, from Port Elizabeth to Pretoria Central Prison, where he died within hours.

When news of his death filtered out, the SABC speculated that Biko had committed suicide and went on to claim that the police had 'never been responsible for killing or torturing a single detainee'. Two days after Biko's death, Jimmy Kruger told a National Party congress that Biko's death 'leaves me cold . . . I shall also be sorry if I die.'[57] At the inquest police claimed that Biko had struck the back of his head during a scuffle. In a verdict which lasted three minutes, the magistrate found no one responsible for Biko's death and said the head injury had probably been caused during the scuffle. The magistrate did not deal with any of the arguments or evidence presented by lawyers for the Biko family, but questioned the conduct of the doctors who had examined him.[58]

The CI joined South Africa's black community in mourning the death of Steve Biko. It was appropriate that the last issue of *Pro Veritate*, of September 1977, was dedicated to him. His haunting face stared from the cover of the journal. An emotional editorial paid tribute to him and accused whites of sharing responsibility for his killing.[59]

Beyers was deeply saddened by his death. 'I remember so well that I visited him in Port Elizabeth in July 1977, just before he was arrested for the last time and tortured and killed. We spoke that night about the future: I asked him, "Steve, what do you see the role of whites in South Africa to be?" And he said to me: "There will be a period where blacks will move out on their own. They have to do this, and without it they will never be able to break the shackles of white domination, of white paternalism and of white power." Then he said to me: "After that, there will be a new re-orientation where hopefully black and white will be able to meet each other as equals." I asked him: "Do you believe that you and I will be able to experience that moment?" And he was silent for a moment and then he said: "It may be, but I don't think so."'[60]

15
The Death of the Christian Institute, 1977

At 4.20 a.m. on Wednesday, 19 October 1977, Theo and Helen Kotze were woken by the ringing of the doorbell of their Cape Town home. Security police were there with a warrant stating that the CI and seventeen Black Consciousness organisations had been declared unlawful, and giving them the right to search the house for any documents connected to these bodies.

They began searching the house. At about 5.30 a.m. Theo Kotze suggested that his wife make coffee. In the kitchen the Kotzes' dog – old and deaf – had begun to stir with the activity in the house. Helen Kotze decided to take the dog for a walk. She slipped out of the house with the dog, also taking their contact book which lay on the telephone table.

After a while the police noticed her absence. They asked Theo Kotze, 'Where is your wife?'

'I don't know, perhaps she has taken the dog for a walk.'

'She has got no right to do that.'

'Is she under arrest?' he asked them.

A few minutes later one of the security policemen said: 'Your wife has been gone a long time.'

'Oh, it's a very old dog,' Kotze replied.

Helen Kotze had hurried to a friend's house nearby. There she made a series of telephone calls, alerting family, friends, journalists and lawyers, in South Africa and abroad, to the massive crackdown that was coming.[1]

Beyers Naudé, as he replaced his telephone, was filled with fear as he thought of the consequences for himself and for his country.

In Johannesburg police did not search homes but proceeded directly to the CI's offices in Braamfontein where they waited to pounce on the CI leadership. They were puzzled by the arrival of the first person at Diakonia House that day – not one of the 'radicals' in line for a banning order – but an old lady wearing hat and gloves. She was Violet Walker, a long-time worker at the CI. As was her daily habit she had attended 6 a.m. mass at her church and then proceeded to work. The police questioned her about her suspicious early arrival, then ordered her into the hall in Diakonia House to wait for the arrival of the rest of the staff.

Helen Kotze's quick thinking had ensured that the CI leaders were prepared for their fate. Before he left for work that morning, Brian Brown had repacked his briefcase, filling it with his children's Noddy books, his wife's hand-written recipe book, and a few letters from a 'religious nut' who had taken to sending him unintelligible screeds on the Book of Hebrews. Brian Brown recalled: 'I still remember the relish with which the police marched me off to my office. Then they pounced on my briefcase. An officer started to go through the Noddy books and the recipe book and the stuff on the Book of Hebrews. I could see him moving from expectation, to perplexity and then to seething anger because he realised that he was being taken for a long ride. I suppose it was an instance of how one tried not to let the system get on top of you. You sought to keep one step ahead by using your own defence mechanisms which, denied violence and power, meant that you engaged in humour. It is strange that in the use thereof you were in the ascendancy and very much in control of that situation in those early hours.'[2]

As other CI staff began arriving they were ordered into the hall while Beyers Naudé and Cedric Mayson were escorted to their offices. Then the police began the systematic confiscation of all CI books, documents and furniture.

Raids, bannings and detentions were taking place all over Johannesburg and around the country. Across the road from Diakonia House police had burst into the offices of the Union of Black Journalists searching for suspects and documents 'which advocated violent revolution'. Across town the black newspapers *The World* and *Weekend World* were closed down and their editor, Mr Percy Qoboza, was detained. In Cape Town police had taken Theo Kotze to the Ecumenical Centre in Mowbray to seize all CI documents and possessions.

By the end of the day the state had not only closed down the CI and *Pro Veritate*, but had banned the entire leadership of the CI for five years: Beyers Naudé, Theo Kotze, Brian Brown and Cedric Mayson. Also banned were Peter Randall, by then working at the University of the Witwatersrand but still involved with Ravan Press, David Russell, an Anglican priest and CI member, and Donald Woods, editor of the East London-based *Daily Dispatch*.

The government smashed in addition the entire Black Consciousness movement. Months of systematic detentions and bannings had failed to still black unrest. Anxious to achieve a show of strength on the eve of a white election the government decided to bludgeon its opponents into submission. The Black People's Convention (BPC), the Black Community Programmes (BCP), the South African Students' Organisation (SASO) and many other parent, youth, student and community organisations were declared unlawful in terms of the Internal Security Act. Police also swooped on scores of activists, detaining 70 Black Consciousness leaders.[3]

The extent of this repression could be gauged by the numbers who, by the end of 1977, were in jail or under banning orders. At least 700 people – 250 of whom were under the age of 18 – had been detained, while more than 171 banning orders were in force. In addition, 35 people had been banished to homelands and 440 convicted political prisoners were serving jail sentences.[4]

All the assets of the banned organisations were forfeited to the state – including the CI's Cape Town and Pietermaritzburg buildings. All housing loans which the CI had provided to staff were called in, and many were left without any income. Theo and Helen Kotze resorted to starting a small home-construction business, while local and overseas churches helped Beyers until the German churches provided him with a pension. But their hardships were minimal compared to the immense suffering endured by black families. The detentions and bannings deprived hundreds of families of breadwinners – and it was left to the SACC and welfare organisations to provide emergency help. Scores of prominent black leaders as well as hundreds of students who fled the country also faced a bleak future in exile.

October 1977 represented the end of an era in South Africa. Steve Biko was dead, the Black Consciousness organisations were crushed, and the CI was closed along with them. It was also the end of a difficult yet enriching chapter in Beyers Naudé's life.

His work at the CI, although it spanned only fourteen years, was a highpoint in his ministry and its history is in many ways his story. In a thoughtful assessment of the CI, former member James Cochrane wrote: 'In the end one recognised that this unique body in South African history had been something of a paradox, perhaps a contradiction in itself – a vital failure. . . .

'Many churches and Christian groups have protested against apartheid in its various guises, confessing their guilt, and their rejection of the system. But resistance is more than confession – it implies a practice which goes beyond public statement and liturgical drama. It implies more than a distancing of oneself from a bad system, more than non-cooperation. It implies cooperation with others against that which is deemed to be fundamentally flawed, wrong, unjust, evil. To this point few individual Christians, let alone groups or denominations, were (or are) able to bring themselves.

'The CI gained its unique place in South African church history because it did take the crucial steps. Quite consistently, it also became the first Christian body in South Africa to be totally outlawed. . . .

'It was as if the CI was always trying to catch up with the demands of the very gospel upon which it firmly stood, never able to sit back on its loins in proud achievement. This is not surprising, for it heard the gospel through voices (often screams) that the church has usually tended to mute. It saw the gospel in hands, faces and even twisted bodies that were more usually treated from afar, if even recognised.

'It failed . . . in converting many of those it most often addressed, the powerful and the privileged, in church and out. It did not even entirely convert itself. It reached for the people 'at-the-bottom', seeking a grass-roots base, yet it was built upon gifted, individual personalities. And though its house was built on rock, its walls could not stand the blasting sands of official enmity. . . .

'In its searching struggle to understand and respond to the gospel in South Africa, the ultimate . . . failure of the Christian Institute to achieve what it hoped for is also the deposit of its hope. What it sought and hoped for was more than the CI or its greatest representatives could ever expect to achieve, more than any of us could. But its journey, its battle, and even its death, are the heritage Christians in South Africa must in one way or another all eventually come to terms with. . . .'[5]

Brian Brown, speaking about Beyers and the CI at the time of its closure, said: 'After the CI was closed down, the security police called me down to John Vorster Square in Johannesburg to answer their questions as they were going through the CI's documents. One of the things they were searching for was the "great financial fraud" – there had always been these rumours that Beyers Naudé and presumably others had feathered their nests with the vast sums they had handled. The truth was that the financial lifestyle of the CI and its director was very modest. I would say that one of the enduring accolades that can be given to the CI was that when we were at the mercy of the government, with all of our records open to prying eyes, and with all the restraints imposed on us as an affected organisation, they could not bring a single charge against the CI or any of its personnel.'[6]

For Beyers the CI's first important contribution had been in exposing and destroying the NGK's biblical justification of apartheid. But while the CI may have won the battle intellectually, it failed to win the hearts and minds of Afrikaners. Early CI supporters recognised that in some respects Beyers was fighting a personal battle – and, moreover, they wanted to believe in his mission. Beyers, misjudging the strength of the ideological stranglehold which Afrikaner nationalism exerted on the church, became marginalised and lost a great deal of his influence in the Afrikaner community.

Beyers's early commitment to mission had made him open to establishing contact with black ministers, and it was this commitment, combined with his newly awakened concern for black South Africans, which led to the CI's involvement in the African Independent church movement. Beyers's years of work with these churches – so frustrating and seemingly fruitless at the time – set an example to the churches in South Africa. In handing over funds and cars to AICA ministers Beyers was sometimes accused of being irresponsible to the point of recklessness. But these and other mistakes did not negate the significance of what he and others at the CI tried to achieve. Beyers took these churches seriously and recognised that they were destined to grow spectacularly within the South African church community. The SACC later followed the CI's example in accepting the Independent churches as full members of the body of Christ – and while the Independent churches continued to be fraught with divisions, the recognition they won undoubtedly helped towards developing and strengthening ecumenical links in South Africa.

The Christian Institute also contributed to the development of Christian unity by including right from the outset Roman Catholics on its board of management. Coming out of a Reformed Church, Beyers had been taught to be deeply suspicious of the Catholic Church. His ability to accept Roman Catholics at an early stage in the history of the Christian Institute was a pointer to the openness he would develop with other groups – both Christian and non-Christian.

Beyers realised that in the early years he had been mistaken in believing that the English-speaking, multi-racial churches could play a major role as agents of change in South Africa. He appreciated the courageous stand taken by many individuals in these churches but he was disillusioned with the often racist or paternalistic attitudes of the majority of rank-and-file members and some of their leaders. He came to the conclusion that the CI had to encourage and nurture small groups within these churches that would challenge fellow members to reconsider their obedience to the gospel. In the same way that he had supported the emergence of the *Belydende Kring*, he gave his support to the emergent black caucuses in the English-speaking churches. It was out of these that the black church leadership of the late 1970s and 1980s would emerge – figures such as Archbishop Desmond Tutu, Father Smangaliso Mkhatshwa, Dr Allan Boesak and the Reverend Frank Chikane.

In spite of the tensions evident sometimes between the CI and the SACC member churches, the CI played an important role in prodding the churches to take a stronger stand on challenging the status quo in South Africa. After the release of the *Message to the People of South Africa*, with its fearless attack on the government's race policies, it was the CI, led by Beyers, which played the dominant role in the development of the Spro-cas 1 and 2 programmes. Spro-cas represented a weighty indictment of white South Africa. It spelt out clearly that apartheid was immoral and impractical and that it was possible to develop alternatives. In the same way, the CI gave attention to issues such as conscientious objection, economic exploitation, foreign investment and support for Black Consciousness groups. At a time when many white liberals dismissed Black Consciousness as merely racism in reverse, the CI swallowed its misgivings and came to recognise that blacks held the key to change in South Africa.

In the early years Beyers had been influenced by the history of the German confessing church movement and he had hoped a similar movement would emerge in South Africa. But while the CI performed the function of giving support to courageous individual Christians, a confessing church remained a dream. Some members of the CI looked to Beyers to take the lead on this issue, but Beyers in turn insisted that it was from within the churches that such a movement should come.

Beyers also played a vital role in drawing the attention of the international community to apartheid. At a time when the world community of churches was itself awakening to the issue of racism, Beyers developed a network of contacts with influential church leaders, journalists and politicians to whom he could put across his views. His Reformed background gave him an entrée to the Dutch churches, and his regular trips and numerous addresses and meetings focused the attention of European churches on the South African crisis. His ability to speak Dutch fluently was a great advantage. Similarly his knowledge of German helped him gain influence with the German churches, in spite of the fact that the Germans remained reluctant to put pressure on the South African government. He also won the respect and support of church leaders in the Scandinavian countries, Switzerland and Great Britain, and to a lesser extent in the United

States. The honorary doctorates, the numerous prizes and invitations he received before, during and after his banning were a testimony to his influence abroad.

During the last few years of its existence, the CI had begun to reassess the 'aid' which overseas churches were prepared to give to the CI and other organisations in South Africa. Beyers realised that black South Africans were deeply cynical about the stand of the West towards the Third World. European countries and the United States might condemn apartheid, and their governments and churches might offer financial aid, but they were not prepared to give up their lucrative economic ties with South Africa. In the 1980s churches and many other bodies continued to rely heavily on foreign funding – a sign that this issue had not been fully resolved.

Beyers felt that the CI had also been mistaken in initially regarding South Africa's problems as solely bound up with racial conflict. He came to recognise that at the bottom level it was a struggle between the haves and the have-nots, and that the CI had failed to make any impact on the lives of the poor. 'We needed to show solidarity, first of all with the people at the grassroots, the unskilled or semi-skilled workers, domestic servants, students, the rural peasants and the lesser-educated. This realisation only began to emerge at a later stage where we realised that, to a large degree, the CI, like the churches, had never been able to capture the imagination and the support of the people at this level.'[7] In spite of Beyers's recognition of this principle, he never fully resolved his personal style with a theoretical commitment to 'grassroots' – a problem shared by many others in leadership positions.

Dr Margaret Nash, who served on the Cape and national boards of the CI, commented: 'In the early years of the CI, Beyers was like an ecclesiastical businessman; there were so many companies and trust funds and so on. The whole ethos at the time was very commercial, not in the profit-making sense, but in the use of commercial structures. . . . There was also the endless litigation, there was one case after another, and we finally got to the stage of saying to Beyers: "Why don't you just decide at some point not to fight these?" But it seemed at times as if he enjoyed the fight. . . .

'In one sense he was so far ahead of the rest of us in his thinking, that he built a structure that was top-heavy. The CI was supposed to be democratic, but in fact it was quite dependent on Beyers. We even had a fight about the fact that Beyers always chaired meetings and we said, "Let's have an elected chairperson." Mercifully we won that fight, so that when the CI was banned, Reverend Rob Robertson, who was chairman of the CI's National Council, could at least issue a statement on the banning. . . .

'Beyers is not a saint, he is not a perfect person. He has got his weaknesses and failings, but it is probably true to say that until the emergence of Desmond Tutu and Allan Boesak as national and international church leaders, Beyers Naudé could justly be described as the single most important church person this country has so far produced. His contribution to the ecumenical movement was enormous. Not to the kind of ecumenism of getting irrelevant institutions together to make a larger, irrelevant institution. His was the ecumenism of faithfulness to love and truth and unity. I think we will go on learning, exploring and reflecting on his contribution for many years to come.'[8]

16
Seven Lean Years, 1977–1984

In banning Beyers Naudé the government had hoped to destroy his influence, but instead, at the age of 62, he entered the most significant phase of his life. It is not possible to tell that story in any detail because South Africa is not yet free. Many of the people involved are themselves still compelled to remain silent, awaiting the day of liberation. We can offer little more than a brief glimpse of those years, and a large part of the story must remain untold.

The banning came as a great shock not only to Beyers but to Ilse. This strong, small woman did not pretend to agree with all her husband's political convictions, yet she never faltered in her loyalty to him. In Beyers's public life, Ilse remained in the background, yet this did not diminish her importance in his life. She provided him with a secure and loving base, attending to all the domestic responsibilities and making sure that he kept in touch with his children and their families. Beyers had not always shared his political insights with Ilse and sometimes she found it difficult to relate to his work. However, soon after the CI was formed she had joined the staff and later took responsibility for a Christian exchange programme, the Christian Fellowship Trust. It meant she was on the scene as the CI evolved and this helped her to keep up with changes in his thinking.

Sensitive and prone to depression, Ilse struggled to cope with her husband's seemingly endless ability to meet and talk with the scores of people who flocked to their home each day after his banning. Yet even in her late sixties and seventies she possessed enough energy and strength to adjust to these new circumstances. There were moments of great tension between them, but through prayer and discussion they worked through these difficulties. Their daughter Liesel remarked: 'They had a very vibrant relationship. The circumstances would have created difficulties for any marriage, and my mother did not always find it easy. But they had such an open relationship, a love for one another and a strong commitment to Christianity, and this helped them enormously.'[1]

Personal problems apart, the restrictions created a crisis of conscience for Beyers and the other leaders of the CI. Suddenly this group of Christians who regarded themselves as decent, respectable people found that they were 'beyond the pale'; their activities had been outlawed; they were considered a danger to the state. They were confronted with many unresolved questions and problems: Should they simply abdicate their responsibilities and serve out their banned years in silent resignation? Should the CI continue underground? What should their relationship be with other banned people? Should they leave the country? Which organisations and what methods and goals should they support? What of their relationship with the exiled liberation movements – which had undergone exactly the same experiences seventeen years before?

They struggled for answers to these questions amid intimidation and state surveillance. Their phones were tapped, they were followed, their letters were opened, even their garbage was scrutinised, and they faced the constant threat of prosecution if they were caught meeting together as banned people. The security police visited their homes, and they were also subjected to petrol bomb attacks on their homes and cars.

Even before the CI was banned there had been a great deal of discussion as to whether Beyers or another senior CI leader should leave South Africa and promote the CI's work abroad. Finally it was decided that Theo Kotze, and not Beyers, should leave. He did so with mixed feelings. On the one hand he was attracted by the challenge and excitement of continuing his witness abroad, but he was distraught at the prospect of leaving South Africa. Theo Kotze secretly slipped out of the country in July 1978 and arrived in Europe insecure and unhappy.

As head of the CI's foreign desk in Utrecht, in the Netherlands, he had to deal with bitter political divisions between Horst Kleinschmidt, who by then favoured supporting the ANC, and Oshadi Phakati, who was still committed to the Black Consciousness organisations. Both had added to a difficult situation by making controversial statements on behalf of the CI without the approval of the banned South African leadership. Shortly after the CI had been banned Horst Kleinschmidt, in a speech at the United Nations, called on the international community to throw its weight behind the ANC. Phakati, in a speech in West Germany, declared that the CI favoured violence as a way of bringing change in South Africa. Phakati's statements, which had been made without any consultation with Beyers, created enormous problems for him in South Africa. As a banned person he was unable to explain his position when Jimmy Kruger and government-supporting newspapers used reports of these statements to attack him and to justify the action which had been taken against the CI.[2]

An added problem was the tension created by Walter Felgate's involvement with the CI, and the fact that he had undertaken several trips overseas on Beyers's behalf. Before Theo Kotze's departure he had extracted a promise from Beyers that he would no longer send Felgate abroad as his representative. When Beyers continued to use Felgate as his envoy in breach of this agreement, Theo Kotze, angry and disappointed, decided to pull out of the CI. After discussions with the CI's Dutch supporters, and in the light of the political tensions and the difficulty in communicating openly, it was agreed early in 1979 to close the CI office.[3] The two men later resolved their personal differences, and they agreed that communication problems during this difficult time, more than errors of judgement, were responsible for what had arisen.

Brian Brown, having secured an exit permit for his family, also left the country in 1978. Brown, however, distanced himself from the external CI and moved to Britain where he was later appointed Africa secretary of the British Council of Churches.

At that stage Beyers had also seriously considered leaving the country – believing that he might make a greater contribution to the liberation of South Africa in exile. But Ilse refused to contemplate this. She told him: 'If you feel that it is your duty to go, Bey, then do so, but do not expect me to follow you. I cannot leave South Africa and our children behind.'[4] After long hours of anguished prayer and soul-searching, and because of new possibilities opening up for him in South Africa, Beyers decided to stay.

His initial banning order was for five years. In 1982 it was renewed for a further three years – an action which evoked outrage in South Africa and in the international community, including formal protests by many Western governments. During this time Beyers was named honorary president of the National Union of South African Students, received an honorary doctorate from the University of Cape Town, and was also awarded several international prizes. Among the honours was a human rights award presented by the Bruno Kreisky Foundation of Austria in 1978 and one from the Franklin D. Roosevelt Four Freedoms Foundation in the United States in 1984. He was also invited to deliver numerous addresses abroad, including the first Dom Helder Camara lecture at the Free University of Amsterdam in 1983. He applied on several occasions for permission to travel abroad to attend these functions, but each time this was refused.

Beyers's banning became a major embarrassment to the South African government. Even the Afrikaans churches called for the restrictions to be lifted. In 1982 he was invited by the government to apply for a relaxation of the conditions of his banning. When he refused to do this, the government of its own accord eased some of his restrictions. He was permitted to 'attend social gatherings of more than one person, to enter Black, Coloured and Indian areas, and enter educational institutions, factories, printing works and trade union offices'. Yet he remained restricted, unable to be quoted, to attend political meetings, to address students or to communicate with other banned people.[5]

When Beyers in May 1984 once more applied for permission to travel abroad the Minister of Law and Order, Mr Louis le Grange, again invited him to 'lay before the Review Board any circumstances or facts which, according to your opinion, could justify the withdrawal or easing of the restrictions'.[6]

Beyers wrote a long reply, but unlike Le Grange's letter which had been widely quoted in the press, it could not be published at the time. In his letter Beyers explained that any representation to the Review Board would imply acceptance of the system of bannings and the entire security apparatus which propped up apartheid, and this would amount to a denial 'of my deepest Christian convictions'.[7]

A petition was launched in South Africa for the lifting of his banning order, and numerous international church bodies, trade-union movements and political organisations added their voices to this call. Amid mounting pressure the government finally lifted the banning order in September 1984.

Those seven years as a banned person coincided with the dawning of a new era in South Africa's history. The outlawing of the Black Consciousness organisations had thrown black opposition politics into turmoil. In the years to come the ANC, based on a non-racial and Charterist rather than a Black Consciousness philosophy, emerged as the leading external political movement and the vast majority of those who left South Africa in 1976 and 1977 made their way to the ANC. In the 1980s the ANC stepped up its campaign of sabotage and bombing of mainly government property and installations, while it continued widespread diplomatic initiatives. Many black leaders began to give open support to the Freedom Charter, which called for a non-racial democratic state and a redistribution of wealth.[8] Other major developments were the continuing militancy of students and the huge strides which were made in the trade-union movement.

White politics entered a new phase when in 1978 former Minister of Defence P. W. Botha took over as prime minister and later state president. The government began to devise a new constitution which would concentrate more power in the hands of the executive while co-opting Coloureds and Indians into the system through a racially segregated tricameral parliament. The government's plans sparked a chain of new political developments. Dissatisfied Afrikaners under the leadership of Andries Treurnicht broke away from the Nationalists to form the Conservative Party, committing themselves to returning South Africa to Verwoerdian-style apartheid. The proposed constitution, which completely ignored black political rights, provoked outrage in the black community. In 1983 the United Democratic Front was formed to coordinate mass resistance.[9]

An historic moment of significance to Beyers was the meeting of the World Alliance of Reformed Churches (WARC) in August 1982. The WARC declared apartheid a heresy and voted to suspend the NGK and the Hervormde Kerk from the body until they opened their doors to blacks and supported those suffering under apartheid. Dr Allan Boesak was unanimously elected president of WARC.[10]

Although excluded from direct participation in these political and church developments, Beyers was nevertheless caught up in them. Black and white visitors streamed to his home to share their insights, hopes, frustrations and problems. Overseas visitors, diplomats and journalists knocked on his door – seeking him out for his views, and in this process his influence gradually increased. He spent most of his time giving individual pastoral counselling or participating in small, intensive discussion groups. Far from being shut out, he seemed to be at the centre of political discussion and thought. He not only gave advice and help, he listened – to the insights of black students, trade-union leaders, churchmen and activists – and in this process he was once again converted, as he tried to understand and heed the voices of the people at the grassroots. His perceptions of the problems facing South Africa deepened, and he was left with no illusions about the long and difficult road to freedom in South Africa. Beyers was named as one of the patrons of the United Democratic Front at its formation in 1983 and he regarded its establishment as a major development in the struggle for political liberation.

Many of his friends gained a deeper insight into his personal life during the years he was confined to his home. They discovered Beyers and Ilse's love of music. Beyers had bought second-hand speakers at auction sales and had placed them in various rooms so that he and Ilse could listen to music anywhere in the house. Visitors were accustomed to hearing the strains of a German *lied* as they approached the front door and many times Beyers would hold a discussion while in the background there played the work of one of his favourite classical composers: Mozart, Beethoven, Chopin, Liszt or Schubert.

They also saw the pleasure the couple derived from their garden – which was tended with great care by another familiar figure in the household, the Naudés' long-time gardener, Freddie Makubela. Many visitors were received in Beyers's small, book-crammed study. He collected and consumed vast quantities of reading material, and books, magazines and newspaper articles littered his desk. He received numerous letters, and always complained that his correspondence was not up to date. But most of his friends knew that even if it took many months, they would eventually receive a reply, either typed by a part-time secretary or handwritten by Beyers himself.

There were many momentous events in his life at this time. In 1980 he severed the last formal tie which bound him to Afrikanerdom when he left the NGK to join the Nederduitse Gereformeerde Kerk in Afrika in the black township of Alexandra, Johannesburg. He took the decision in the light of the NGK's refusal to consider unity with black 'daughter' churches. In doing so he upset his wife, who felt he had not fully discussed this decision with her. She found it impossible to follow him out of her church and she continued to worship at the NGK in Parkhurst. Beyers's restriction order at first prevented him from attending services in Alexandra, and so he often joined the small group of black domestic workers in Parkhurst who were permitted to hold a separate service in the NGK's hall on Sunday afternoons. He also frequently attended services at St Antony's – a Presbyterian church in the Johannesburg suburb of Mayfair, which had a multi-racial congregation. He stretched the limits of his banning order by preaching at St Antony's and other churches on many occasions. But he always left the church immediately afterwards as his banning order prevented him from greeting the congregation at the door.

He felt the pain of his restrictions keenly when he had to apply for special magisterial permission to attend funerals in other towns. In those years he mourned the deaths of many people he had loved, such as his youngest sister, Lirieka Badenhorst, his old friend and colleague Fred van Wyk, and AICA minister and former CI colleague, Mashwabada Mayatula. In 1982, Frikkie Conradie, the white co-minister at the Alexandra church and a close friend of Beyers and Ilse Naudé, was killed in a car accident one day before the birth of his first child. When Beyers applied for permission to travel out of Johannesburg to attend the funeral, his application was refused because he was not allowed to enter Alexandra.[11]

His involvement in the political life of the country – manifest through his pastoral counselling, meetings and letter-writing – annoyed the security police. In November 1981 his former colleague Cedric Mayson was detained by security police, and at 5 a.m. on the same day the police carried out a six-hour raid on Beyers's home, confiscating letters, papers and a few banned publications. The action sparked speculation that the police were searching for evidence linking Beyers and others to the liberation movements.[12] After fifteen months in detention Cedric Mayson was charged with treason for supporting the ANC. There was controversy in 1983 when Mayson skipped bail and fled the country. He explained that Beyers and other friends had been subpoenaed to give evidence in his trial and that he had fled the country to save them from jail.[13]

Cedric Mayson appeared to have been under close security police surveillance after his banning in 1977. In July 1981 his banning order was prematurely lifted, and its seems that the motivation for lifting the banning order may have been to gather the necessary evidence against him to charge him with treason. Mayson appeared to fall into this trap. During a trip to Britain he held talks with ANC officials in London. He mailed a note on his discussion to a fictitious person at his son's address in South Africa, and this was intercepted by security police. In November 1981 he was detained, and after 15 months in detention, he appeared in court on charges of high treason. During his trial it emerged that the note intercepted by police had been used as the basis of a 'confession' Mayson had been forced to make. But after Mayson presented evidence to court that he had been tortured, the judge rule the statement as inadmissible as evidence. Mayson was freed on R1 000 bail in March 1983 and fled the country a month later – *The Star*, 11 October 1982, 8 February 1983, 10 February 1983, 12 February 1983, 18 February 1983 and *Rand Daily Mail*, 20 April 1983, SAIRR, *Survey*, 1983, p. 559.

There were many other encounters and events which brought joy and hope, despair and frustration, to the life of Beyers and to those close to him. He is reserved in speaking about these years, insisting that the full story can only be told when all are free to speak without fear. He has made only one major speech about his years as a banned person, at the University of Cape Town in 1985. This chapter ends with an edited version of his address, presenting it as an incomplete, but nevertheless deeply personal account of his experiences.

'. . .The prospect of life under a five-year banning order had to be faced immediately. What should I do? What could I do? There were a number of options and possibilities which I considered: I felt motivated to think about, and possibly write on, theology – liberation theology, to reflect on issues of social justice and on the future of South Africa. Secondly, I could start writing a diary or a book about my life, my ministry in the NG Kerk, my theological and political conversion . . . (both these options would be illegal if it could be proved that they were written with a view to publication). Thirdly, I could continue my ministry in a form of individual pastoral counselling linked to continued study, reading and reflection.

'The decision of what in fact would take place was partly determined by events and developments outside our control – namely the stream of friends and visitors as well as people in need who came to our door, many times unannounced through fear or ignorance of what a banning order and the position of a banned person implied. At times the visitors arrived at all hours of the day or the night. It may sound unbelievable but for the first 12 months after my banning (and beyond that period) the flow of visitors never stopped. At times we had quite a ludicrous situation in our home: A number of people, sometimes three to four at a time, sitting in our lounge (which looked more like a doctor's consulting room than the lounge of a private home) waiting to meet me personally in my small study or in the garden if the weather permitted. Ilse was continually interrupted in her work programme, to answer the doorbell or the telephone, or to serve tea or coffee to visitors or friends. During this time she was still employed in a part-time capacity as the secretary of the Christian Fellowship Trust. Very soon we discovered that our house was in fact serving a threefold purpose: It was the office of a pastoral counsellor, it was the office of my wife and it was a private home.

'Very soon after my banning I made a shocking discovery: There was no way in which I as a human being could live without breaking my banning order. One of the terms of the order prohibits a banned person from participating in any way in any political discussion, even if such discussion is intended to defend or support government policy. For me the choice was rapidly and readily made: I would under no circumstances allow the expression of my Christian convictions, my Christian concern and my judgment on political matters and events from a Christian perspective to be curtailed or restricted by my banning order. If this would lead to me being charged, I would gladly face such a trial.

'It was not easy to comply with every aspect of the banning order. I had to study and memorise the long list of the premises I was not allowed to enter; I had to memorise the municipal boundaries of the Johannesburg Magisterial District to which I was restricted. My wife and I had to live with the awareness that our letters were regularly opened, our phone was tapped and our home was under surveillance. Would we be able to withstand and survive the stress and tension of such a life?

'It was during this period of reflection that, without any conscious effort on my part, I discovered that more and more people were coming to our home for personal counselling or advice. Some of them were white, many of them were black; all of them came with serious personal needs and problems. Some of these were related to the political situation of the country which was affecting their lives, and those of their husbands or wives, their sons or daughters. As I listened to their dilemmas and concerns and reflected on them it became clear to me that this was a demand which people were making upon my time and my life. This was possibly God's way of telling me that he wanted me to offer my service to these people. . . .

'Despite the pressures upon my time and my ministry of pastoral counselling, and despite the serious restrictions which a banning order imposes upon one's life, nothing could deter me from continuing to reflect on the system of banning and detention as a method of suppressing the ideas of opponents of an oppressive regime. I had no need to be convinced about the inhumanity, the illegality and the ethical immorality of a system of banning or detention without trial. I was fully aware, through previous experiences of other banned persons, of the tremendous financial problems which every banning created for the family. If it had not been for a number of awards which I received, and for the continued support being given by churches inside and outside South Africa, it would have been near impossible for us to support ourselves.

'Ilse continued to work in a part-time capacity as secretary of the Christian Fellowship Trust and although her monthly income was relatively small, it enabled her to keep her mind occupied with issues beyond our immediate concerns. This was very important. A banning order also creates tremendous emotional problems between husband and wife, parents and children, the banned family and their friends. It is especially in the sphere of relationships between husband and wife that intolerable tensions occur. My wife and I had to work through these. Under normal circumstances such tensions could be shared with close friends and thereby resolved, whereas in our case I soon realised that the only way to resolve such tensions was for us to face them alone, through prayer, reflection and the honest expression of our feelings. There were times when I deeply pitied my wife for what she had to face up to through my emotional tensions and agonies. At other times we were tremendously enriched by the discovery that we were drawn together through our being forced to face honestly and openly the tensions which had arisen between us.

'There are several aspects of a banning order which I believe should be emphasised. The first is the personal one. People have asked me what I found to be the most difficult aspect of my banning. It is a difficult question to answer. I believe it is the lack of free social intercourse, the prohibition of meaningful political and theological discussion, and the opportunity to relax in the company of a small circle of friends. These were the most distressing aspects of the banning order. Twice we had the opportunity for a period of quiet, withdrawing to the seaside at Onrus near Hermanus, when we were given permission to go on leave. . . .

'I also reflected on the principle of a banning order as part of the legal system of a so-called democratic country. I discovered personally that a banning was an injustice to every banned person. It is a moral judgment on any system which approves and implements such a practice of banning and detention without trial. It is a fundamental violation of the rule of law and the concept of justice. It cannot work and it is counter-productive. It can never stifle or kill the convictions and opinions which in many respects lead to the banning of such a person. It eventually has a serious detrimental effect on the leaders and the community sanctioning and upholding such an evil and inhuman practice. My thoughts time and again turned to the Afrikaner people who had devised and implemented this system and I realised more than ever how they were dehumanising themselves and preparing their own destruction by the justification of such methods in order to maintain their position of political power.

'In fact it reflects a sense of deep insecurity on the part of my Afrikaner people, a desperate effort to retain their power and authority, a false attempt to ensure their identity and their ideological chauvinism. Many of them have tried to justify this practice morally by arguing that extreme measures are required in terms of national crisis. My question is: How long must that crisis continue before such a practice is discontinued? I have become increasingly concerned about the fact that our people had in fact adapted themselves to all kinds of facetious arguments in defence of the indefensible, and that this unethical approach has penetrated and affected every relationship and outlook of the Afrikaner *volk*.

'But there was also the practical side of a banning order. It has to do with facing one's feelings of anger, frustration and vindictiveness which arise. I had to make a crucial decision with regard to these feelings: Would I allow these feelings to take root in my life, or would I do everything in my power to ensure that no such feelings would corrode my inner life and freedom? I requested Ilse to be on the lookout for any signs of such expression of anger or bitterness and to help me to discover this. This she did faithfully, and for this I thank God, and as far as I know both of us have been able to live through this period and to conquer any feelings of bitterness, hatred or revenge which otherwise would have destroyed us.

'I consciously refused to allow the banning order to accomplish its intended goal.

1. It would not rob me of the opportunity to think, reflect and plan for the future.

2. It would not rob me from sharing and passing on my insights, analyses, discoveries of new values to other people – even if this could only be done one at a time. Such discovery of precious thoughts and new truths were like small seeds which I was sowing all the time, certain in my faith that the explosive power of truth would let it take root and grow in the hearts and minds of many of those with whom I associated during this period.

3. It would not stop me loving people and trying to understand them better, deepening my concern for their hopes, their joys and their suffering, therefore becoming more sensitive to such joys and suffering.

4. It would not stop me from growing as a human being and as a Christian.

5. It would not rob me of my inner freedom, my peace of mind, my joy of living, loving and sharing. All this brought me to the firm conclusion: Through God's grace I would never allow this banning to break my spirit, to distort my freedom of mind or my concern for justice.

6. It would never rob me of the deep conviction, inspired by my Christian faith and my sense of justice, as I discovered time and again through the pronouncements of the Old and the New Testament that freedom will come to our land, that the system of apartheid will eventually crumble and disappear, and that our country and our people will be free.

'Through all these years there was constant contact between myself and others. One by one they came, black and white, old and young, early in the morning and late at night. Many times such visits made it very difficult for Ilse and myself to have any private time to ourselves. But in and through this experience I gained tremendous insight into the life, the needs, the hopes and fears of many different people.

'I reflected more deeply than ever before on the rise and the crisis of the Afrikaner people: On their sense of joy and satisfaction at having attained their political ideals, but also on the tragedy that they were now inflicting – in many ways the same injustices on the black community as the British had inflicted on them. Time and again I asked myself: When will the moment arrive when our people will discover that God's justice would not allow injustice to sustain a system of oppression such as the Afrikaner had instituted and was now desperately trying to uphold?

'I reflected on the English liberal tradition of our country and saw the agony and the confusion in the minds of many English-speaking white South Africans at not being able to understand why they were being viewed with increasing suspicion by blacks and why liberalism was being rejected.

'I reflected on the ascendancy of black aspirations, the struggle within the black community to find ways and means of achieving their goals of political liberation, the serious tensions and conflicts within black society, and the frustration and suspicion among themselves.

'I reflected on the situation facing the student community, both black and white, and the struggle of the students to discover for themselves what the future would be that they would have to face. I became increasingly aware of the growing frustration in the black student community which I knew would eventually lead to increasing resistance, rejection and eventual revolution.

'I reflected on the growth of black political power and the emergence of black trade unions as an eventual process of change in the situation which we face. To me this was a totally new experience, as my theological training had in no way brought me to any knowledge, understanding or interpretation of the position of the worker and of Christian responsibility towards their needs. I tried to read as much as possible about the emergence of the trade union movement throughout the world and of the justification of worker demands in the light of the gospel. . . .

'I also reflected on the position of the churches in our country. I followed with deep interest and concern the events in the South African Council of Churches. . . . I followed the development within the *Broeder Kring*, later termed the *Belydende Kring*, and the increasing urge and longing of many to create a confessing community of all Christians, of all confessions, classes and races. . . . I agonised about the future of the three Dutch Reformed Churches, especially the NG Kerk to which I belonged until 1980. In October 1978 the national synod of the NG Kerk met in Bloemfontein and considered an urgent plea for unification. This plea was rejected with a large majority and that decision was the final turning point in my resolution to terminate my membership of the NG Kerk and to join the black NG Kerk in Afrika. . . .

'As the years passed, I discovered that there was a turning of the tide in the struggle for liberation in South Africa. The presentation and acceptance of the new constitution had brought about a totally new situation. The National

Forum was convened and soon afterwards the UDF emerged, as a basis for massive resistance against the new constitution, led by students, youth, black trade unions, women's groups, civic organisations and many grassroots people. A new determination to achieve liberation was born; a growing impatience to destroy the present system was emerging; the old sense of resignation on the part of the adult black community was being overtaken by a new determination on the part of the young people to stand up and to initiate new moves towards liberation. This movement was gaining momentum day after day and I became increasingly aware that nothing would stop it. I sensed the tragedy of the majority of whites in South Africa who, having through all these years excluded themselves through lack of interest or concern, would fail to understand what was happening and would eventually be exposed to one shock after the other. I reflected on the efforts at reform and realised that we were facing a tragic failure because what was undertaken was too little, too diffident, too slow and too late.

'While all these thoughts and feelings were still occupying my mind, Wednesday, 16 September 1984 arrived. I was discussing the situation in South Africa with three church visitors from Germany when three figures passed the window in front of the lounge of our home. I could only see the outline of these figures but I immediately knew they were security police. I wondered what I had again done to incur the further displeasure of the government. By the time I reached the front door Ilse had already invited them in. I accompanied them to my study. I stood with these three men in front of me.

"Is there anything that I can do?" I asked them.

"Yes," they said, "we have a letter from the Minister of Law and Order which we are required to deliver to you."

"Could I know the contents?" I asked.

"The Minister is lifting your banning order."

'I stood there speechless and silent. I thanked them for delivering his letter, greeted them and accompanied them to the door. I entered the kitchen and said to my wife: "You won't believe it, my banning order has been lifted!"

'My seven lean years were over – the longest and leanest of my life. No, I am wrong. Upon reflection I realise that in all probability they were the most difficult, but certainly the most enriching experience of my life because this banning brought to fruition many latent insights, feelings, visions and hopes. I thank God for what He was able to convey to both Ilse and myself through this period. . . .'[14]

17
Pilgrimage of Faith

Beyers emerged from his banning order unbowed. He felt attuned to the aspirations of black South Africans and was determined to give his all in the fight for political liberation. As he entered his seventieth year the signs of crisis in South Africa were everywhere. Black resistance had reached unprecedented levels and in July 1985 the government declared a state of emergency, cracking down on political dissent.

During his banning Beyers's political influence had intensified rather than dulled. Unbanned, he was even more driven than before, and many of his friends and family questioned whether he was not pushing himself too hard. Nevertheless, his handling of those banned years made possible a new career – as caretaker general secretary of the South African Council of Churches between 1985 and 1987, in a most difficult and sensitive phase of the history of the church. His appointment to this post was sudden and surprising, and followed the award of the Nobel Peace Prize to the incumbent general secretary, Desmond Tutu, and his elevation as Bishop of Johannesburg. The transformation in Beyers's life was drastic – one moment banned and restricted, the next back at the centre of the church struggle. While serving the SACC Beyers developed heart problems. He postponed surgery because of his heavy commitments, but by November 1986 he had no choice but to undergo an operation to correct two leaking valves. His doctor advised him not to go back to work until mid-February, but in his usual committed and determined fashion he was back at his desk early in January 1987.

In the wider political sphere there was an escalation in conflict during his tenure at the SACC. The violence which he had so often warned of was now a reality in South Africa. There were mass detentions, army occupation of the townships, and numerous attacks on anti-apartheid activists. There was also an escalation in the ANC's armed struggle in the form of bomb blasts and landmine explosions. In the black townships, street or defence committees were formed at the height of the turbulence. For the church, the merits of violence or non-violence were no longer a matter of academic debate; battles were raging in the townships, bombs were exploding in white areas. White and black

Christians were deeply divided, and the question which faced church leaders was how to minimise bloodshed.[1] Beyers never changed his view that violence was wrong and counter-productive, but he believed the conflict was the inevitable result of apartheid and he refused to judge those who had taken up arms against white rule. But he also believed that there was no turning back from a new South Africa and that its people would finally be forced to resolve their differences around the conference table. He believed the ANC was destined to play a central role in negotiations. At a time when government propaganda against the ANC reached its height, he threw his considerable influence behind the drive for negotiations and meetings with the ANC. From 1985 there was a trickle and then a stream of black and white South Africans travelling across the border to meet with the exiled leaders of the ANC, a trend which coincided with the ANC's growing stature in the international community.

Much of Beyers's work was being carried out behind the scenes, but in public he was uncompromising in his support for black initiatives. He supported the *Kairos Document* – which challenged the churches, if they were serious about reconciliation, to reconsider their theology. The *Kairos* signatories, for example, argued that the counter-violence of the oppressed could not be condemned in the same way as the violence of the oppressor. Beyers also added his voice to the call from leading churchmen, black organisations and trade unions for civil disobedience and for economic sanctions against South Africa as a means of pressurising the government into ending apartheid. In some quarters in South Africa, Beyers came in for bitter criticism for supporting sanctions, not only from old enemies, but from many old liberal white friends. Alan Paton was one of many who, while maintaining affection for Beyers, could not support his stand on sanctions and disinvestment.[2] In the NGK, several theologians, who had been shamed by Beyers's banning, had hoped that he would emerge from his banning somewhat chastened and willing to return to his church.[3] They did not understand the change and growth in his thinking or why he ignored their appeals to return to the Afrikaner fold.

An event of symbolic importance in Beyers's life occurred in 1987. All of 24 years after his white church deprived him of his status as *dominee*, he once again officially assumed this title when he was ordained as a minister of the black Nederduitse Gereformeerde Kerk in Afrika. In the crisis enveloping South Africa, Beyers had become a committed political activist, yet he always regarded himself as first and foremost an *evangeliedienaar* – a minister of the gospel. It was highly appropriate that at a time when he was gaining the status of one of the 'elder statesman' in the liberation struggle, he was welcomed and accepted as minister in a church born of apartheid. The numerous problems experienced by the NGKA, mainly related to its economic dependence on the white NGK, continued to absorb a great deal of Beyers's time and energy in the late 1980s.

It has not been the intention in these final chapters to provide any detailed analysis of the past decade of his life, and his involvement with many other projects forms another story still to be written. We can mention that his work included serving as a trustee on the board of several anti-apartheid organisations.

He also travelled widely, but in common with many anti-apartheid activists, he often experienced difficulties in getting a passport. Passport applications were often delayed and, when issued, were granted for short time-periods only. He nevertheless made many trips abroad as an official guest of numerous governments, and church and political groups. He preached on a guest basis at churches all over the country, including his Alexandra church.

One of the remarkable features of Beyers Naudé has been his accessibility to people – and it is on this level that he has been at his greatest and also his weakest. In his advancing years he continued to make himself available to people, and showed equal respect for the humble and the mighty in society. People continued to stream to him, and on a normal working day he might easily see ten or more people, including foreign visitors, workers, diplomats, churchmen, the unemployed, students, trade unionists, housewives and political activists.

His story is unfinished and his full contribution – particularly in the latter years – can only be clarified in the light of history. We conclude by asking: What is special about Beyers Naudé?

A unique combination of features has made him a person of note, a man admired and supported by many but also rejected by some. His background, personality and Christian convictions are all part of the make-up of a person who has made an extraordinary contribution to the struggle against apartheid.

For many there is something mysterious about a man who came from the womb of Afrikaner nationalism to fight for the creation of a non-racial democracy, and his background is crucial to the contribution he was able to make. The recognition he received and the particular impact he has made was only possible because he was born a white Afrikaner and became a leading *dominee*. He defied the rules and mores of his society when he broke free of his *volk*. His pedigree and background would on the surface seem to have precluded or made unlikely any radical changes in his life, yet radical changes occurred.

The respect he won should also be considered in the context of the specific era in which he began to question apartheid. In the early 1960s – after the banning of the two major black organisations and the jailing of their leaders – opposition to apartheid was anything but a popular cause, especially for white Afrikaners. Those were the golden years of supreme white confidence, when criticism of Afrikanerdom's racial blueprint was considered nothing less than traitorous. Sustained by his faith in God, Beyers had the courage to reject apartheid, to declare a new understanding of South Africa and to hold to it through years of vilification by his church and society. Not many prophets live to see the day when their views are vindicated by history. But in the late 1980s white leaders of the NGK publicly acknowledged their guilt for their complicity in apartheid and Beyers witnessed their confessions.[4]

It is difficult to define human personality, especially in such a complex man. Undoubtedly his achievements are linked to his character, intelligence and faith. It is easier to like rather than to dislike Beyers Naudé. Even one of his fiercest critics described him as a 'very lovable' person. People find him charming, and he has a genuine warmth and concern for others. Some of his friends say this works both ways: he has an ability to attract individuals, and over the years many people have served him with devotion. His friends and family also speak of his twinkling sense of humour, a welcome attribute in a man who devotes most of his time to serious issues. Beyers has a grit-like determination and has employed every ounce of it in his fight for justice. It has infuriated his enemies, and even his friends have despaired at his stubbornness and his sometimes reckless commitment to people and projects. A voracious reader, he is also a man of deep intelligence who can charm an audience with simple Afrikaner sincerity. Yet he is not considered an outstanding theologian – a fact mentioned by several white theologians, annoyed at and perhaps jealous of the honour he has been accorded.

But the central strand of his make-up is the rocklike Christian faith which he shares with Ilse. It was this faith which led him to question apartheid and it has sustained him on a lifelong political and spiritual journey.

Beyers has been called a prophet, the conscience of white South Africa. He made history because of his courage and his actions, and he will undoubtedly be remembered as one of the great church figures in a particularly turbulent period of South Africa's history. His many contributions are the story of this book, and we mention only a few.

He challenged the Afrikaner establishment's claim that apartheid was in any sense a moral or Christian policy. He stimulated debate in the Afrikaans and the English-speaking churches about their responsibility in an unjust and unequal society. He promoted the ecumenical ideal of church and Christian unity through his own faithfulness to the truth. He served as an example to both blacks and whites that Afrikaners, like any other people, have the capacity to change. Through this, he gained the trust of numerous black organisations and leaders. Along with others, he served as an important leader, helping to shape the struggle against apartheid.

A neat summary of his contributions does not really do justice to him. Like all of us, his life has been a process of change. Beyers's two main points of focus were his own Afrikaner people and the oppressed black communities, even though, ironically, for many years it was from the liberal English-speaking white community that he attracted the most support and admiration. But finally, it is from the black and Afrikaner communities that we still see the greatest extremes in response, and these are evident in reactions his life has provoked. Many Afrikaners still regard him as a hopeless left-wing radical, a man who betrayed his people. Most black South Africans believe he is a patriot, a symbol of hope, a sign that people can change. Not all Afrikaners would go so far as to call him a traitor. The less harsh view, expressed in one Afrikaans newspaper, is that he is a 'half-tragic figure, an honourable and sincere person, who, like a hero in a Greek tragedy, was led by forces outside of his control to a situation which he did not want but from which he could not escape'.[5]

One of Beyers's oldest friends in the NGK, Ben Marais, gave an inkling of the view of 'a man led astray' when he remarked: 'Beyers and I were very good friends and spent five years together at Stellenbosch. I supported him and Albert Geyser when they wanted to launch the Christian Institute. But when they were named as handing over Broederbond documents to the *Sunday Times*, I knew they would become political targets. It was the end of the CI as far as Afrikaners were concerned. I was glad the Broederbond stuff was no longer secret, but I regretted the way Beyers and Albert had handled it. They should not have done it secretly and then tried to get away with it. . . .

'The day Beyers was unbanned I wrote him a letter and told him that I rejoiced that he was free. I said to him: "Beyers, use every opportunity God gives to witness for what you believe, but don't be used by other people." Even before he had my letter, I read that he had flown down to the British Consulate in Durban to identify with the UDF leaders who were hiding there. I wrote him several other letters but he did not reply. . . . More recently I spoke to someone involved in a political trial and he called Beyers a traitor to his people. . . . But if you ask me today, I still like to believe that Beyers is not a traitor in the ordinary sense of the word. He acts according to his convictions, but I disagree with his methods.'[6]

But there is another perception about Beyers among Afrikaners. Dr Frederik van Zyl Slabbert, who symbolises the new, questioning voice of Afrikanerdom, commented: 'Beyers's impact has to be seen against the background of where he has come from – a member of the Broederbond, a pillar of the establishment. Beyers left mainstream Afrikanerdom at a time when most would have looked towards retirement or higher office. That is when he stopped, reversed and changed direction. And he did it with a high degree of moral integrity. Whatever else is the view of Beyers from within the Afrikaner establishment, he essentially raises a stark moral issue for them. And it is precisely in that context that he symbolises for blacks the fact that Afrikaners can change.'[7]

The Reverend Peter Moatshe, a minister of the black NGKA, encapsulated that hope when he remarked: 'We see Beyers as a brother, as a father. He makes you realise that colour does not count, it is not colour which makes us different, but racist attitudes. Beyers has been received by all quarters of the black community. He has proved beyond doubt that he is a man of God. He is a symbol, a sign of hope, and I think the respect we give him will remain. What he stands for is people. It is for life. It is for a new future in South Africa.'[8]

There are many who argue that history is not about individuals or 'great men' or women, but about ordinary people, their experiences and contributions to change. Some say, particularly in the context of the South African struggle, that it is wrong to recognise one person, especially a white person, when the oppressed people have borne the brunt of the suffering. While there are merits in this argument, South Africa's history has also been shaped by the role of its leaders – and loved or hated, Beyers Naudé will certainly be remembered as a leader. How does one define a 'great person of history'? Great people are remembered mainly for the good or bad they have done, for the effect their lives have had on society. It has been said that Beyers is a great person because he personifies the spirit of his times yet also anticipates the future. He is a prophet, he is ahead of his people, yet he is not so far ahead that he is lost to them.[9] Many seemingly great figures soon fade from prominence, and are remembered only in outline, reduced to historical caricature. Yet the impact of some remains, and the question is: how will history judge Beyers Naudé?

Beyers will be remembered for his vision and involvement in numerous anti-apartheid organisations, and even in his old age he has maintained an astonishing level of commitment and involvement. Many of the people who stream to see him say there will never be another Beyers Naudé.

Perhaps more important than his immense practical contribution, Beyers has functioned as an important symbol. His life has been seen as 'the miracle and mystery of the road to Damascus, of the reality of conversion and transformation'.[10] He is a sign of hope that people can change, a promise of the new South Africa. He is part of the first fruits of a new society – a white Afrikaner who believes in his country's future led by black South Africans. When you strip away the symbolism and stand by the man, you see an imperfect human being, a man who has had his share of failures and contradictions. In spite of these failings, his greatness remains. It is located in his boundless optimism, in his faith that the Kingdom of God will one day reign on earth and in his own country.

After all the words have been written, all the dates and facts described, all the opinions catalogued, we still know so little about the man. No book can do justice to the complexities of a human life. It is especially difficult to give any answers when Beyers Naudé is still an active player in the fast-moving South African drama. Beyers, in his long and painful journey of change, carved a new route in South African history, and there are numerous markings along the way which must still be explored. Even his closest colleagues have difficulty in explaining his influence. Many of them have noted that only a part of his life and activity has been on the surface – the rest has been dedicated to less perceptible goals.

How does Beyers Naudé see his life? His answer is very simple: 'It has been a pilgrimage of faith.'

An intentionally undertaken journey to find truth & a real place in God, Community & Life

References

All quotations by Beyers Naudé, unless otherwise indicated, are taken from a series of interviews conducted with him by the author between 1987 and 1989.

1 The Banning of Beyers Naudé, 19 October 1977
1. This account based on: C.F.B. Naudé, 'My Seven Lean Years', speech at the University of Cape Town, 8 May 1985, and C.F.B. Naudé interview with R. Bilheimer, May 1986, Rochester, New York. Excerpts of the filmed interview appeared in Worldwide Documentaries' biographical documentary, 'A Cry of Reason: Beyers Naudé – An Afrikaner Speaks Out'.

2 Born into Afrikaner Nationalism
1. *The Graham's Town Journal*, 2 Feburary 1837.
2. M. Jordaan, *Jozua Naudé as Kultuurdraer en Kultuurleier* (Unpublished M.A. thesis, University of Pretoria, 1986), p. 10.
3. Jordaan, *Jozua Naudé*, p. 10.
4. Jordaan, *Jozua Naudé*, p. 20.
5. J. Naudé, *Vechten en Vluchten van Beyers en Kemp* (Rotterdam, 1905).
6. Naudé, *Vechten en Vluchten*, p. 55.
7. C.F.J. Muller, *500 Years. A History of South Africa* (Pretoria, 1981), p. 361.
8. J. Naudé letter to 'Jozua, Bey en Frans', 31 May, 1948, and C.F.B Naudé interview with C.Ryan, 1988.
9. J. Naudé interview with C. Ryan, 1988.
10. Jordaan, *Jozua Naudé*, p. 40.
11. R. O'Brien Geldenhuys interview with C. Ryan, 1988.
12. C.F.B.Naudé–Ryan interview.
13. Jordaan, *Jozua Naudé*, p. 78.
14. Jordaan, *Jozua Naudé*, p. 121.
15. C.F.B. Naudé–Ryan interview.
16. *The Star*, 10–15 May 1915.
17. C.F.B. Naudé–Bilheimer interview.
18. Jordaan, *Jozua Naudé*, p. 149.
19. Jordaan, *Jozua Naudé*, pp. 80–150.
20. C.F.B. Naudé–Ryan interview.
21. Jordaan, *Jozua Naudé*, p. 159.
22. Jordaan, *Jozua Naudé*, pp. 160–170.

23. I. Wilkins and H. Strydom, *The Super-Afrikaners. Inside the Afrikaner Broederbond* (Johannesburg, 1980), pp. 35–52.
24. Commission of Inquiry into Secret Organisations (Pretoria, 1965) p. 4, and Jordaan, *Jozua Naudé*, p. 183.
25. R. O'Brien Geldenhuys–Ryan interview.
26. C.F.B. Naudé interview with P. Randall, 1982.
27. R. O'Brien Geldenhuys–Ryan interview.

3 The Shaping of a Young Nationalist, 1921–1939

1. R. O'Brien Geldenhuys–Ryan interview.
2. Jordaan, *Jozua Naudé*, p. 17.
3. C.F.B. Naudé–Ryan interview.
4. C.F.B. Naudé–Ryan interview and R. O'Brien Geldenhuys–Ryan interview.
5. C.F.B. Naudé–Ryan interview and J. Naudé–Ryan interview.
6. C.F.B. Naudé–Ryan interview.
7. C.F.B. Naudé–Ryan interview and R. O'Brien Geldenhuys–Ryan interview.
8. C.F.B. Naudé–Ryan interview and R. O'Brien Geldenhuys–Ryan interview.
9. C.F.B. Naudé–Ryan interview.
10. C.F.B. Naudé–Bilheimer interview.
11. R. O'Brien Geldenhuys–Ryan interview.
12. C.F.B. Naudé–Ryan interview and R. O'Brien Geldenhuys–Ryan interview.
13. C.F.B. Naudé–Randall interview.
14. Jozua Naudé sermon, June 1921.
15. R. van Graan, Graaff-Reinet 1786–1986, *Lantern*, July 1986.
16. Jordaan, *Jozua Naudé*, p. 224.
17. Jordaan, *Jozua Naudé*, p. 236.
18. C.F.B. Naudé–Ryan interview.
19. Jordaan, *Jozua Naudé*, pp. 217–236.
20. R. O'Brien Geldenhuys–Ryan interview.
21. C.F.B. Naudé–Ryan interview.
22. R. O'Brien Geldenhuys–Ryan interview.
23. C.F.B. Naudé–Ryan interview.
24. R. O'Brien Geldenhuys–Ryan interview.
25. C.F.B. Naudé–Bilheimer interview.
26. W.A. de Klerk, *The Puritans in Africa – A Story of Afrikanerdom* (London, 1975), p. 107.
27. De Klerk, *The Puritans*, pp. 108–109.
28. C.F.B. Naudé–Ryan interview.
29. C.F.B. Naudé–Ryan interview.
30. C.F.B. Naudé–Bilheimer interview.
31. C.F.B. Naudé–Bilheimer interview.
32. C.F.B. Naudé–Ryan interview.
33. C. Villa-Vicencio, 'A Life of Resistance and Hope', in C. Villa-Vicencio and J. W. de Gruchy (eds), *Resistance and Hope. South African Essays in Honour of Beyers Naudé* (Cape Town, 1985), p. 5.
34. Villa-Vicencio, 'Resistance and Hope', p. 5.
35. C.F.B. Naudé–Randall interview.
36. C.F.B. Naudé–Ryan interview.
37. C.F.B. Naudé–Ryan interview.
38. Villa-Vicencio, 'Resistance and Hope', p. 6.
39. *Pro Libertate*, 15 May 1932.
40. J. Naudé–Ryan interview.
41. I. Naudé interview with C. Ryan, 1988.
42. I. Naudé–Ryan interview.

43. I. Naudé–Ryan interview.
44. C.F.B. Naudé–Ryan interview and C.F.B. Naudé–Randall interview.
45. *Pro Libertate*, 15 June 1932.
46. C.F.B. Naudé–Ryan interview and I. Naudé–Ryan interview.
47. J.H.P. Serfontein, *Brotherhood of Power* (London, 1979), p. 34.
48. J. Naudé–Ryan interview.
49. C.F.B. Naudé–Ryan interview.
50. *Pro Libertate*, 15 May 1932.
51. C.F.B. Naudé–Ryan interview.
52. C.F.B. Naudé–Ryan interview.
53. J. Naudé–Ryan interview.
54. C.F.B. Naudé, *Die Waardering van Poësie. Enkele aspekte van die vraagstuk, toegelig met voorbeelde uit die Afrikaanse poësie* (Unpublished M.A. thesis, University of Stellenbosch, March 1936).
55. C.F.B. Naudé–Ryan interview.
56. D.J. Bosch, 'The Roots and Fruits of Afrikaner Civil Religion', in J.W. Hofmeyr and W.S. Vorster (eds), *New Faces of Africa: Essays in Honour of Ben Marais* (Pretoria, 1984), p. 15.
57. The full resolution said: 'The Synod considers it desirable and scriptural that our heathen [black] members be received and absorbed into our existing congregations wherever possible; but where this measure as a result of the weakness of some, impedes the furtherance of the cause of Christ among the heathen, the heathen congregation, founded or still to be founded, shall enjoy its Christian privilege in a separate building or institution.' As quoted in J. Kinghorn (ed), *Die NG Kerk en Apartheid* (Johannesburg, 1986), p. 76.
58. Z.E. Mokgoebo, *Broederkring – A Calling and Struggle for Prophetic Witness within the Dutch Reformed Church Family in South Africa* (Unpublished M.A. thesis, Faculty of New Brunswick Theological Seminary, New Jersey, 1983), Section 1, p. 130.
59. J. Durand, 'Afrikaner Piety and Dissent' in *Resistance and Hope*, p. 42.
60. Kinghorn, *Die NG Kerk en Apartheid*, p. 86.
61. Bosch, 'The Roots and Fruits', p. 32.
62. F. Regehr, *Perceptions of Apartheid – The Churches and Political Change in South Africa* (Scottdale, 1979), p. 151.
63. F.E. O'Brien Geldenhuys, *In die Stroomversnellings – Vyftig Jaar van die NGK* (Cape Town, 1982), pp. 1–11.
64. O'Brien Geldenhuys, *In die Stroomversnellings*, pp. 3–11.
65. Villa-Vicencio, 'Resistance and Hope', p. 8.
66. C.F.B. Naudé–Ryan interview.
67. C.F.B. Naudé–Randall interview.
68. C.F.B. Naudé–Randall interview and O'Brien Geldenhuys, *In die Stroomversnellings*, p. 11.
69. Durand, 'Afrikaner Piety', pp. 46–7.
70. Durand, 'Afrikaner Piety', p. 46.
71. C.F.B. Naudé–Ryan interview.
72. Serfontein, *Brotherhood*, p. 43.
73. D.T. Moodie, *The Rise of Afrikanerdom – Power, Apartheid and the Afrikaner Civil Religion* (London, 1975), pp. 119–201.

4 Early Ministry – Living with Apartheid, 1939–1954

1. I. Naudé–Ryan interview.
2. I. Naudé–Ryan interview.
3. Serfontein, *Brotherhood*, p. 35.
4. Serfontein, *Brotherhood*, pp. 130–140.
5. C.F.B. Naudé–Ryan interview.
6. Serfontein, *Brotherhood*, pp. 132–133.

7. C.F.B. Naudé–Ryan interview.
8. C.F.B. Naudé–Ryan interview.
9. Kinghorn, *Die NG Kerk en Apartheid*, p. 91.
10. Regehr, *Perceptions of Apartheid*, p. 151.
11. B. Marais interview with C. Ryan, 1988.
12. J. Naudé letter to 'Jozua, Bey and Frans', 31 May 1948.
13. N. Smith interview with C. Ryan, 1988.
14. I. Naudé–Ryan interview.
15. C.F.B. Naudé–Randall interview.
16. *Die Vaderland*, 19 July 1951.
17. B. Marais, *Die Kleur Krisis en die Weste* (Pretoria, 1952).
18. *Die Kerkbode*, 10 December 1952.
19. C.F.B. Naudé and W. de W. Strauss, *Kerk en Jeug in die Buiteland en Suid Afrika* (Pretoria and Cape Town, 1955).

5 Awakening and Sharpeville, 1955–1960

1. C.F.B. Naudé–Randall interview.
2. Regehr, *Perceptions of Apartheid*, p. 148.
3. I. Naudé–Ryan interview.
4. T.R.H. Davenport, *South Africa: A Modern History* (Johannesburg, 1977), p. 270.
5. M. Nash, *Black Uprooting from 'White' South Africa. The Fourth and Final Stage of Apartheid* (Johannesburg, 1980), pp. 1–23.
6. B. Marais–Ryan interview.
7. B. Marais–Ryan interview.
8. Nico Smith later joined the Broederbond, but resigned in disillusionment many years later.
9. N. Smith–Ryan interview.
10. C.F.B. Naudé–Bilheimer interview.
11. I. Naudé–Ryan interview.
12. L. Naudé interview with C. Ryan, 1988.
13. H. Naudé interview with C. Ryan, 1989.
14. L. Naudé–Ryan interview.
15. Villa-Vicencio, 'Resistance and Hope', p. 8.
16. B.B. Keet, *Whither South Africa?* (Stellenbosch, 1956), pp. 19–85.
17. *Die Kerkbode*, 15 February 1956.
18. J.W. de Gruchy, *The Church Struggle in South Africa* (Cape Town, 1979), p. 61.
19. De Gruchy, *The Church Struggle*, p. 61.
20. R.T.J. Lombard, *Die Nederduitse Gereformeerde Kerke en Rassepolitiek. Met Spesiale Verwysing na die Jare 1948–1961* (Pretoria, 1981), p. 170.
21. Lombard, *Die Nederduitse Gereformeerde Kerke*, pp. 150–153.
22. C.F.B. Naudé–Randall interview.
23. C.F.B. Naudé interview with André du Toit, Hermann Giliomee and Rykie van Reenen, 1984.
24. C. le Roux interview with C. Ryan, 1988.
25. Davenport, *South Africa*, pp. 274–275.
26. C.F.B. Naudé–Bilheimer interview.
27. C.F. B. Naudé–Du Toit, Giliomee, Van Reenen interview.
28. C.F.B. Naudé–Randall interview.
29. D. Bosch interview with C.Ryan, 1988.
30. C.F.B. Naudé–Bilheimer interview.
31. W. Jonker interview with C. Ryan, 1989.
32. *Maandbrief van die NG Gemeente Aasvoëlkop*, 1 March 1960, vol. 1, no. 1.
33. C.F.B. Naudé–Ryan interview.

34. Davenport, *South Africa*, p. 280.
35. South African Institute of Race Relations, *A Survey of Race Relations in South Africa, 1959-1960* (Johannesburg, 1961), pp. 39–49.
36. SAIRR, *Survey, 1959-1960*, p. 52.
37. Davenport, *South Africa*, p. 285.
38. SAIRR, *Survey, 1959-1960*, pp. 60–89.

6 Cottesloe, December 1960

1. SAIRR, *Survey, 1959-60*, p. 122.
2. K. Kritzinger interview with C. Ryan, 1988.
3. *Maandbrief van die NG Gemeente Aasvoëlkop*, 1 May 1960, no. 3.
4. Davenport, *South Africa*, pp. 291–293.
5. The Natal and Orange Free State churches were not members of the WCC.
6. 'Statement on the Riots in South Africa', by members of the NG Kerk moderatures, 1960.
7. De Gruchy, *The Church Struggle*, p. 63.
8. De Gruchy, *The Church Struggle*, p. 64.
9. A.H. Luckhoff, *Cottesloe* (Cape Town, 1978), p. 17.
10. World Council of Churches, *Mission to South Africa, April–December 1960*, Department of Historical Papers, University of the Witwatersrand Library, Johannesburg: Fred van Wyk Collection, A.D. 1752.
11. Minutes of first Planning Committee Meeting, 19 July 1960, Van Wyk Papers.
12. Luckhoff, *Cottesloe*, pp. 35–36.
13. Letter from the Minister of Interior, T. Naudé, to the Moderature of the NG Kerk, 22 September 1960, Van Wyk Papers.
14. WCC, *Mission*, Van Wyk Papers.
15. Luckhoff, *Cottesloe*, p. 73.
16. Luckhoff, *Cottesloe*, pp. 47–48.
17. Luckhoff, *Cottesloe*, p. 48.
18. Regehr, *Perceptions of Apartheid*, p. 190.
19. Report of the Study Committees of the NG Kerk of Transvaal, pp. 34–40, Van Wyk Papers.
20. Regehr, *Perceptions of Apartheid*, p. 189.
21. WCC, *Mission*, Van Wyk Papers.
22. C.F.B. Naudé–Du Toit, Giliomee and Van Reenen interview.
23. Statement issued by the Hervormde Kerk delegation at Cottesloe, Van Wyk Papers.
24. Statement of the World Council of Churches Consultation, Cottesloe, Johannesburg, 7–14 December 1960, Van Wyk Papers.
25. Regehr, *Perceptions of Apartheid*, p. 193.
26. Statement by the NG Kerke of the Cape and Transvaal at Cottesloe, Van Wyk Papers.
27. C.F.B. Naudé–Du Toit, Giliomee and Van Reenen interview.
28. Luckhoff, *Cottesloe*, p. 95.

7 The Storm after Cottesloe, 1961–1962

1. Luckhoff, *Cottesloe*, p. 126.
2. Luckhoff, *Cottesloe*, pp. 79–105.
3. Luckhoff, *Cottesloe*, p. 106.
4. C.F.B. Naudé, 'Afrikaans Churches in Danger of Confusion', *Dagbreek en Sondagnuus*, 18 December 1960.
5. Luckhoff, *Cottesloe*, p.107.
6. Luckhoff, *Cottesloe*, p. 116.
7. Wilkins and Strydom, *The Super-Afrikaners*, p. 296.
8. Luckhoff, *Cottesloe*, p. 120.

9. Lombard, *Die Nederduitse Gereformeerde Kerk*, p. 244.
10. *Maandbrief van die NG Gemeente Aasvoëlkop*, 1 March 1961, vol. 2, no. 3.
11. Luckhoff, *Cottesloe*, p. 123.
12. Handelinge, Transvaal Synod, 5 April 1961 and following days, pp. 351–364.
13. International Commission of Jurists (eds), *The Trial of Beyers Naudé. Christian Witness and the Rule of Law* (London, 1975), p. 65.
14. Luckhoff, *Cottesloe*, p. 139.
15. Luckhoff, *Cottesloe*, p. 140.
16. Luckhoff, *Cottesloe*, pp. 141–142.
17. C.F.B. Naudé–Bilheimer interview.
18. C.F.B. Naudé–Bilheimer interview.
19. C.F.B. Naudé–Du Toit, Giliomee and Van Reenen interview.
20. Luckhoff, *Cottesloe*, p. 152.
21. *Rand Daily Mail*, 25 August 1961.
22. *Pro Veritate*, 15 May 1962.
23. J.W. de Gruchy, 'A Short History of the Christian Institute', in *Resistance and Hope*, p. 15.
24. C.F.B. Naudé sermon, Aasvoëlkop, Sunday 27 May 1962.
25. Letter from C.F.B. Naudé to W. Landman and A. van Wijk, 6 August 1962, Van Wyk Papers, and G. Kotze interview with C.Ryan, 1988.
26. Letter C.F.B. Naudé–Landman and Van Wijk, Van Wyk Papers.
27. Minutes of the Meeting held on 1 November 1962 to discuss the proposed Christian Institute, Van Wyk Papers.
28. Proposed Christian Institute Report, Van Wyk Papers.

8 Leaving the Fold – Christian Institute Established, 1963

1. I. Naudé–Ryan interview.
2. Acta van die Vierde Vergadering van die Suid-Transvaalse Sinode van die NG Kerk, Pretoria, op 26 Maart 1963 en volgende dae.
3. W.D. Jonker, *Huldigingsuitgawe, Maandbrief van die NG Gemeente Aasvoëlkop*, October–November 1963.
4. Acta van die Vierde Vergadering van die Suid-Transvaalse Sinode van die NG Kerk.
5. *Maandbriewe van die NG Gemeente Aasvoëlkop*, February to September 1963.
6. Letter from Fred van Wyk to C.F.B. Naudé, 29 March 1963, Van Wyk Papers.
7. Letter from C.F.B. Naudé to F. van Wyk, 19 April 1963, Van Wyk Papers.
8. A. Benjamin interview with C.Ryan, 1988.
9. *Pro Veritate*, 15 May 1963.
10. Letter on the Christian Institute issued by Mrs J.S. Lubbe, 3 July 1963, Van Wyk Papers.
11. Constitution of the Christian Institute of Southern Africa, Van Wyk Papers.
12. *Die Transvaler*, 16 August 1963.
13. W. Jonker–Ryan interview.
14. J. van Rooyen interview with C.Ryan, 1988.
15. *The Star*, 27 August 1963.
16. *The Star*, 30 August 1963.
17. *The Star*, 5 September 1963.
18. *The Star*, 6 September 1963.
19. C.F.B. Naudé–Bilheimer interview.
20. C.F.B. Naudé–Bilheimer interview.
21. C.F.B. Naudé, 'My Decision', 23 September 1963.
22. *Die Transvaler*, 23 September 1963 and H. Serfontein, 'Beyers Naudé', *Ecunews*, March 1985.
23. *The Star*, 25 September 1963.
24. *Die Kerkbode*, 9 October 1963.

25. *The Star*, October 1963.
26. W.D. Jonker, *Huldigingsuitgawe, Maandbrief van die NG Gemeente Aasvoëlkop*, October–November 1963.
27. C.F.B. Naudé, 'Flame of Fire and Sledgehammer', 3 November 1963.
28. G. Kotze–Ryan interview.
29. C.F.B. Naudé–Bilheimer interview.
30. F. van Zyl Slabbert interview with C. Ryan, 1988.
31. C.F.B. Naudé–Ryan interview.
32. Christian Institute budget for first year, Van Wyk Papers.
33. *Die Kerkbode*, 16 October 1963.
34. *The Star*, 18 November 1963.
35. C.F.B. Naudé–Randall interview.

9 Broederbond exposés, 1963
1. B. Marais–Ryan interview.
2. *Sunday Times*, 21 April 1963.
3. *Sunday Times*, 21 April 1963.
4. Wilkins and Strydom, *The Super-Afrikaners*, pp. 293–294.
5. Wilkins and Strydom, *The Super-Afrikaners*, pp. 301–302.
6. Serfontein, *Brotherhood of Power*, p. 244.
7. *Sunday Times*, 10, 17, 24 and 31 March 1963.
8. *Sunday Times*, 21 April 1963.
9. Wilkins and Strydom, *The Super-Afrikaners*, p. 312.
10. *Sunday Times*, 21 April 1963.
11. *Dagbreek en Sondagnuus*, 28 April 1963.
12. *Sunday Times*, 5, 12, 26 May, 2 June and 22 September 1963.
13. Wilkins and Strydom, *The Super-Afrikaners*, pp. 303–305.
14. C.F.B. Naudé statement and letters, as quoted in the *Rand Daily Mail*, 20 November 1963.
15. Broederbond statement issued 20 November 1963, as quoted in the *Rand Daily Mail*, 21 November 1963.
16. Albert Geyser statement issued on 20 November 1963, as quoted in the *Rand Daily Mail*, 21 November 1963.
17. C.F.B. Naudé–Du Toit, Giliomee and Van Reenen interview.
18. H. Naudé–Ryan interview.
19. C.F.B. Naudé–Bilheimer interview.

10 A New Ministry Unfolds, 1963–1965
1. Report by R. de Villiers, *The Star*, 20 December 1963.
2. *Die Transvaler*, 16 October 1965.
3. D. van Zyl interview with C. Ryan, 1988.
4. Letter from F. van Wyk to C.F.B. Naudé, 30 April 1964, Van Wyk Papers.
5. Letter from C.F.B. Naudé to F. van Wyk, 15 May 1963, Van Wyk Papers.
6. *Pro Veritate*, 15 June 1964.
7. *The Star*, 11 and 12 February 1963.
8. *Die Vaderland*, 24 June 1964.
9. *The Star*, 13 August 1964.
10. Various reports in *The Star* and *Die Transvaler*, May 1964 to May 1965.
11. *The Star*, 1 February 1964.
12. *Die Kerkbode*, 1 January 1964.
13. List of members on Board of Management, elected August 27 1964, Van Wyk Papers.
14. Christian Institute minutes of the Board of Management of 27 August 1964, Van Wyk Papers.

15. Martin West interview with C. Ryan, 1988.
16. C.F.B. Naudé–Randall interview.
17. *Pro Veritate*, 15 September 1966.
18. M. West, *Bishops and Prophets in a Black City* (Cape Town, 1975), p. 145.
19. *Pro Veritate*, 15 October 1966.
20. M. West–Ryan interview.
21. Christian Institute memorandum: 'Some Notes of the Financial Needs of the Christian Institute', 1967, Van Wyk Papers.
22. D. van Zyl–Ryan interview.
23. *Die Transvaler*, 10 March 1965.
24. *Die Kerkbode*, 17 March 1965.
25. *Pro Veritate*, 15 June 1965.
26. Various reports in *The Star*, May–June 1965.
27. C.F.B. Naudé, Director's Report for the Christian Institute, 1964–5.
28. E. C. Helmreich, *The German Churches under Hitler. Background, Struggle and Epilogue* (Detroit, 1979).
29. *Pro Veritate*, 15 July 1965.
30. *Pro Veritate*, 15 October 1965.
31. *Die Kerkbode*, 4 August 1965.
32. *Pro Veritate*, 15 November 1965.
33. *Pro Veritate*, 15 December 1965.
34. De Gruchy, *The Church Struggle*, p. 107.
35. *Die Transvaler*, 7 August 1965, *The Star*, 10 August 1965 and *Die Vaderland*, 10 August 1965.
36. *Rand Daily Mail*, 30 July 1965.
37. Open Letter to Ministers of the Dutch Reformed Church, November 1965, Van Wyk Papers.

11 Years of Struggle at the Christian Institute, 1966–1968

1. C.F.B. Naudé–Randall interview.
2. SAIRR, *Survey, 1966*, p. 98.
3. *Pro Veritate*, 15 March 1966.
4. *The Star*, 23 February 1966, and C.F.B. Naudé–Ryan interview.
5. M. West–Ryan interview.
6. D. van Zyl–Ryan interview.
7. C.F.B. Naudé, Director's Report of the Christian Institute, August 1965–July 1966.
8. Director's Report, 1965–1966.
9. C.F.B. Naudé–Randall interview.
10. De Gruchy, *The Church Struggle*, pp. 115–116.
11. Christian Institute of Southern Africa, Minutes of meeting of Board of Management, 27 September 1966, Van Wyk Papers.
12. A.J. van der Bent (ed), *Breaking Down the Walls. World Council of Churches Statements and Actions on Racism, 1948-1985* (Geneva, 1986), p. 15.
13. De Gruchy, *The Church Struggle*, p. 117.
14. J. Verkuyl, J. Bos, and B. van Kaam interviews with C. Ryan, 1988.
15. *The Star*, 6 July 1966.
16. J. Bos–Ryan interview.
17. Memorandum on 'The Christian Institute and the NG Kerk', Van Wyk Papers.
18. Handelinge, second Meeting of the General Synod of the NG Kerk, Bloemfontein, 13 October 1966 and subsequent days.
19. Memorandum on 'The Christian Institute'.
20. Memorandum on 'The Christian Institute'.
21. *Die Kerkbode*, 2 November 1966.

22. Memorandum on 'The Christian Institute'.
23. *Trouw*, 1 November 1966.
24. *The Star*, 5 November 1966.
25. *The Star*, 15 December 1966.
26. Statement by Parkhurst Church Council, 1967, Van Wyk Papers.
27. *The Star*, 20 June 1967, *The Star*, 14 August 1967 and Statement by Parkhurst Church Council, as contained in memorandum on 'The Christian Institute' and *The Star*, 23 February 1968.
28. *Pro Veritate*, 15 August 1967.
29. T. Kotze interview with C. Ryan, 1988.
30. *Sunday Times*, 3 December 1963.
31. *The Star*, 15 February 1967.
32. *The Star*, 22 February 1965.
33. *Pro Veritate*, 15 January 1967.
34. Various reports in *The Star*, 15 February 1967 to 20 March 1967.
35. SAIRR, *Survey, 1967*, p. 11 and *Survey, 1968*, p. 20.
36. C.F.B. Naudé–Ryan interview.
37. *The Star*, 7 May 1968.
38. O' Brien Geldenhuys, *In die Stroomversnellings*, p. 75.
39. World Council of Churches, *Breaking down the Walls*, p. 15.
40. *Rand Daily Mail*, 27 July 1968.
41. Christian Institute Memorandum on the Reformed Ecumenical Synod, 6 September 1968, Van Wyk Papers.
42. P. Walshe, *Church versus State in South Africa: The Case of the Christian Institute* (Maryknoll, 1983), p. 80.
43. J. Cochrane, book review of Peter Walshe's *Church versus State*, in *South African Outlook*, pp. 12–14, January 1984.
44. C.F.B. Naudé–Randall interview.
45. J. Rees interview with C. Ryan, 1989.
46. J. W. de Gruchy and W. B. de Villiers (eds), *The Message in Perspective* (Johannesburg, 1968), p. 10.
47. De Gruchy and De Villiers, *The Message in Perspective*, p. 14.
48. De Gruchy, *The Church Struggle*, pp. 120–121.
49. Walshe, *Church versus State*, p. 62.
50. As quoted in De Gruchy, *The Church Struggle*, pp. 118–119.
51. C. Cook, Address to annual general meeting of the Christian Institute, October 1968. Tielman Roos, a prominent lawyer, Nationalist and cabinet minister in the 1920s, formed his own, unsuccessful political party in 1933. Robey Leibbrandt, was a prominent member of the *Ossewabrandwag* and a supporter of Nazi Germany who committed acts of sabotage against the South African government during the war.

12 The Challenge of Black Consciousness, 1969–1972

1. Cedric Mayson interview with C. Ryan, 1988.
2. H. Ngada interview with C. Ryan, 1988.
3. Els te Siepe interview with C. Ryan, 1988.
4. West, *Bishops and Prophets*, pp. 152–153.
5. C.F.B. Naudé, 'Memorandum on the Relationship between AICA and the Christian Institute', 1972, Van Wyk Papers.
6. West, *Bishops and Prophets*, p. 161.
7. B. Brown interview with C. Ryan, 1988.
8. CI Memorandum: 'Evaluation of the Christian Institute of Southern Africa', August 1970 and Minutes of the CI Board of Management meeting, 18 February 1969, Van Wyk Papers.

9. *The Argus*, August 23, 1969 and B. Engelbrecht interview with C. Ryan, 1988.
10. B. Engelbrecht–Ryan interview.
11. J. Rees–Ryan interview.
12. Report on *Pro Veritate* by Roelf Meyer, for the Annual General Meeting of the CI, 9 September 1972.
13. T. Kotze–Ryan interview and Walshe, *Church versus State*, p. 73.
14. Christian Institute Memorandum: Budget 1969 to 1970, Van Wyk Papers.
15. *The Star*, 2 November 1970.
16. C.F.B. Naudé–Randall interview.
17. *Pro Veritate*, 15 August 1969, p. 3.
18. *Die Vaderland*, 15 July 1969.
19. C.F.B. Naudé–Randall interview.
20. Walshe, *Church versus State*, pp. 104–105.
21. P. Randall (ed), *A Taste of Power. The Final Coordinated Spro-cas Report* (Johannesburg, 1973), p. 99.
22. Z. Mbali, *The Churches and Racism. A Black South African Perspective* (London, 1987), p. 50.
23. Randall, *A Taste of Power*, p. 36.
24. P. Randall (ed), *Apartheid and the Churches, Report of the Spro-cas Social Commission* (Johannesburg, 1971), p. 161.
25. C.F.B. Naudé Director's Report of the Christian Institute, 1969.
26. *Pro Veritate*, 15 April 1970.
27. *Pro Veritate*, 15 March 1970.
28. *Pro Veritate*, 15 October 1988.
29. B. van Kaam–Ryan interview and J. Verkuyl–Ryan interview.
30. K. Groenendijk interview with C. Ryan, 1988.
31. C.F.B. Naudé–Ryan interview.
32. *Die Burger*, 7 April and 29 April 1970.
33. Minutes of the Ulvenhout Consultation, pp. 12–16, Van Wyk Papers.
34. *Pro Veritate*, 15 October 1970.
35. De Gruchy, *The Church Struggle*, p. 129.
36. Elisabeth Adler, *A Small Beginning. An Assessment of the First Five Years of the Programme to Combat Racism* (Geneva, 1974), p. 15.
37. *The Star*, 5 September 1970.
38. *Pro Veritate*, 15 October 1970.
39. *Rand Daily Mail*, 2 October 1970.
40. De Gruchy, *The Church Struggle*, p. 133.
41. *Pro Veritate*, 15 January 1971.
42. SAIRR, *Survey, 1972*, p. 95.
43. Cosmas Desmond, *The Discarded People* (Middlesex, 1971).
44. *Pro Veritate*, 15 April 1972.
45. *Pro Veritate*, 15 March 1971.
46. *Die Vaderland*, 10 August 1971.
47. *Pro Veritate*, 15 November 1970.
48. *Rand Daily Mail*, 26 October 1970, *The Star*, 26 October 1970 and *Pro Veritate*, 15 November 1970.
49. C.F.B. Naudé, 'Apartheid is Morally Unacceptable', *Ster*, 13 November 1970.
50. C.F.B. Naudé, 'Black Anger and White Power in an Unreal Society' (Edgar Brookes Lecture delivered at the University of Natal, Pietermaritzburg, on the 19th May, 1971).
51. D. van Zyl–Ryan interview.
52. De Gruchy, *The Church Struggle*, p. 154.
53. *Pro Veritate*, 15 July 1971.

54. *Pro Veritate*, 15 April 1972.
55. Walshe, *Church versus State*, pp. 81–83.
56. Walshe, *Church versus State*, p. 95.
57. Mbali, *The Churches and Racism*, p. 58.
58. C. Villa-Vicencio interview with C. Ryan, 1988.
59. E. Thema interview with C. Ryan, 1988.
60. C.F.B. Naudé, 'Apartheid Morally Unacceptable'.
61. Randall, *A Taste of Power*, p. 6.
62. Randall, *A Taste of Power*, p. 129.
63. C.F.B. Naudé–Randall interview.
64. *Pro Veritate*, 15 January 1972.
65. Walshe, *Church versus State*, p. 131.
66. Walshe, *Church versus State*, pp. 140–149.
67. S. Nolutshungu, as quoted in P. Randall, 'Spro-cas Revisited', in *Resistance and Hope*, p. 168.
68. Walshe, *Church versus State*, pp. 152–153.
69. Walshe, *Church versus State*, p. 154.
70. C.F.B. Naudé–Bilheimer interview.

13 State Pressure Intensifies, 1972–1974

1. SAIRR, *Survey, 1972*, p. 48.
2. *Rand Daily Mail*, 6 May, 8 May, 9 May 1972, *The Star*, 6 May, 8 May 1972.
3. *Die Vaderland*, 8 May 1972.
4. *Sunday Express*, 21 May 1972.
5. *Dagbreek en Sondagnuus*, 16 October 1966.
6. *The Star*, 14 May 1968.
7. C.F.B. Naudé sermon in Utrecht at the Peace Week Programme, 19 September 1971.
8. *The Star*, 8 May 1972.
9. *Rand Daily Mail*, 20 September 1972.
10. *Die Vaderland*, 20 September 1972.
11. Walshe, *Church versus State*, p. 93 and *Pro Veritate*, 15 October 1972.
12. SAIRR, *Survey, 1972*, p. 52 and *The Star*, 7 February 1972.
13. SAIRR, *Survey, 1973*, pp. 24–25.
14. SAIRR, *Survey, 1972*, p. 53.
15. SAIRR, *Survey, 1973*, p. 27.
16. Rick Turner wrote an important work for the Spro-cas Economics Commission, *The Eye of the Needle*, which was banned by the government. He was later assassinated and his murderers have never been found.
17. B. Brown–Ryan interview.
18. SAIRR, *Survey, 1973*, p. 29.
19. Brian Brown, Theo Kotze, Roelf Meyer, Beyers Naudé and J. E. Phakati, *Divine or Civil Disobedience?* (Johannesburg, 1973), pp. 8–13.
20. C.F.B. Naudé–Randall interview.
21. B. Brown–Ryan interview.
22. SAIRR, *Survey, 1973*, pp. 33–36.
23. SAIRR, *Survey, 1974*, p. 39.
24. *Die Vaderland*, 1 October 1973.
25. *The Star*, 3 October 1973.
26. "Summary of Action taken against the CI and Spro-cas between August 1973 and January 1974', 1974, Van Wyk Papers.
27. A. N. Allott, 'The Legal Background' in *The Trial of Beyers Naudé*, p. 17.
28. A Allott, *State Law and the Christian Conscience in South Africa*, supplement to *Christian Institute News Digest*, June 1974.

29. *Rapport*, 18 November 1973.
30. International Commission of Jurists, *The Trial of Beyers Naudé*, pp. 18–131.
31. P. Randall (ed), *Not without Honour. Tribute to Beyers Naudé* (Johannesburg, 1982), p. 37.
32. Walshe, *Church versus State*, p. 176.
33. *CI News*, December 1973 and Walshe, *Church versus State*, p. 174.
34. SAIRR, *Survey, 1973*, p. 282.
35. C.F.B. Naudé–Randall interview.
36. Walshe, *Church versus State*, pp. 162–163.
37. O. Phakati interview with C. Ryan, 1988.
38. C.F.B. Naudé–Ryan interview.
39. SAIRR, *Survey*, 1975, pp. 64–65, *The Star*, 17 April 1976, *Die Vaderland*, 15 April 1976 and *Die Transvaler*, 15 April 1976.
40. H. Kleinschmidt interview with C. Ryan, 1988.
41. T. Kotze–Ryan interview.
42. J. Rees–Ryan interview.
43. C. Villa Vicencio–Ryan interview.
44. H. Kleinschmidt–Ryan interview.
45. *Pro Veritate*, 15 December 1973.
46. B. Brown–Ryan interview.
47. De Gruchy, *The Church Struggle*, p. 138.
48. C.F.B. Naudé, Speech on the Hammanskraal Resolution, 6 September 1974.
49. D. Bax interview with C. Ryan, 1988.
50. SACC National Conference, 1974, Motion on Conscientious Objection.
51. SABC Current Affairs, Transcript, 5 August 1974.
52. SAIRR, *Survey, 1974*, p. 62.
53. C.F.B. Naudé, Speech on Hammanskraal, 1974.
54. C.F.B. Naudé address at the service of United Christian Witness re the Defence Further Amendment Bill, St Mary's Catholic Church, Pietermaritzburg, 15 September 1974.
55. *Die Vaderland*, 5 August 1974 and *Rapport*, 4 August 1974.
56. Graduation Programme, University of the Witwatersrand Graduation Ceremony, April 1974.
57. *Beeld*, 11 November, 15 November 1974.
58. *Beeld*, 19 November 1974.
59. *Beeld*, 25 November 1974.
60. C.F.B. Naudé, 'Christian Involvement in the Struggle for Human Rights and Justice', address in reply to receiving the Reinhold Niebuhr Award, 1974.
61. *Die Vaderland*, 19 December 1974.

14 The Confrontation Grows, 1975–1977

1. SAIRR, *Survey, 1974*, pp. 25–26 and p. 62.
2. C.F.B. Naudé Director's Report of the CI, August 1973–July 1974 and Minutes of the meeting of the CI Board of Management, 7 and 8 December 1974, Van Wyk Papers.
3. C.F.B. Naudé letter to CI members, 3 February 1975.
4. *The Cape Times*, 4 June 1975, H. Suzman interview with C. Ryan, 1989, and Davenport, *South Africa*, p. 309.
5. Walshe, *Church versus State*, p. 176.
6. M. Buthelezi, 'Black Theology and the Le Grange–Schlebusch Commission', speech at the CI's annual general meeting, 5 September 1975.
7. L. le Grange (chairman), *Final Report of the Commission of Inquiry into Certain Organisations. Christian Institute of Southern Africa* (Pretoria, 1975), p. 165.
8. C.F.B. Naudé, Director's Report of the Christian Institute, 1 August 1974–31 July 1975.
9. Manas Buthelezi, 'The Significance of the Christian Institute for Black South Africa', speech given at CI rally, 26 October 1974.

10. *Ecunews*, 2 June 1975.
11. Letter from C.F.B. Naudé to M. Nash, 23 July 1976.
12. Christian Institute Memorandum: 'Proposed Restructuring in Transvaal', 1975.
13. *The Star*, 27 July 1977.
14. C.F.B. Naudé, 'A Glimpse into the Future of South Africa', address delivered to the Convocation of the University of Natal at Pietermaritzburg, 22 August 1975.
15. *Sunday Tribune*, 28 December 1975.
16. *Rand Daily Mail*, 30 May 1975 and *Die Transvaler*, 30 May 1975.
17. C.F.B. Naudé, 'Memorandum insake die Huidige Kultuurverdrag tussen die Vrije Universiteit van Amsterdam en die Potchefstroom Universiteit vir CHO', 24 September 1974.
18. *The Star*, 11 October 1974.
19. *Beeld*, 11 October 1974.
20. Walshe, *Church versus State*, p. 187.
21. Dutch Reformed Church, *Human Relations and the South African Scene in the Light of the Scripture*, Offical translation of the report *Ras, Volk en Nasie en Volkverhoudinge in die Lig van die Skrif,* approved and accepted by the General Synod of the Dutch Reformed Church, October 1974 (Cape Town–Pretoria, 1975).
22. Walshe, *Church versus State*, p. 189.
23. SAIRR, *Survey, 1975*, p. 31.
24. *Die Kerkbode*, 2 July 1975.
25. Samuel Palo Ernest Buti, *Black Experience and the Struggle for Liberation in the Relationship Between the White Dutch Reformed Church and the Black Dutch Reformed Church* (Unpublished thesis submitted in partial fulfilment for the degree Master of Theology to the Faculty of Princeton Theological Seminary, Princeton, New Jersey, 1982), pp. 66–74.
26. Mokgoebo, *Broederkring*, p. 120, H. Adonis interview with C. Ryan, 1988 and J. Verkuyl–Ryan interview and B. van Kaam–Ryan interview.
27. E. Thema–Ryan interview.
28. Mokgoebo, *Broederkring*, pp. 119–132.
29. H. Adonis–Ryan interview.
30. O'Brien Geldenhuys, *In die Stroomversnellings*, p. 76.
31. O'Brien Geldenhuys, *In die Stroomversnellings*, pp. 59–61.
32. SAIRR, *Survey, 1976*, p. 57.
33. Copy of telegram from C.F.B. Naudé to Rev Beukes, Moderator of the NGK, 16 June 1976.
34. Statement issued by the SACC, 16 June 1976.
35. SAIRR, *Survey, 1976*, pp. 51–87 and Walshe, *Church versus State*, pp. 205–207.
36. Beyers Naudé played a central role in the purchase of Diakonia House. He served on an ecumenical committee which, by 1971, had secured the necessary funds, mainly from the Lutheran and Reformed Churches in Germany (EKD), to buy a building in Braamfontein. Diakonia House, which housed the SACC, CI and other church organisations, was later sold. A new building, Khotso House, was bought with the proceeds of the sale but it was bombed by unknown persons in 1988.
37. C.F.B. Naudé, handwritten statement, 17 June 1976.
38. De Gruchy, *The Church Struggle*, pp. 173–175.
39. *Pro Veritate*, March 1976 and *The Star*, 28 May 1976.
40. T. Kotze–Ryan interview.
41. Randall, *A Taste of Power*, pp. 23–24.
42. C.F.B. Naudé, 'The South Africa I Want', Speech at the University of Cape Town, 3 June 1976.
43. *Pro Veritate*, March 1976.
44. *The Star*, 30 May 1977.

45. Resolution Adopted by the Annual General Meeting of the Christian Institute of Southern Africa at Edendale, Natal on 18 September 1976.
46. Christian Institute Statement on Investment in South Africa, 22 October 1976.
47. *Pro Veritate*, December 1976.
48. *Rand Daily Mail*, 29 October 1976.
49. *Pro Veritate*, December 1976.
50. *Rand Daily Mail*, 30 October 1976.
51. *Pro Veritate*, December 1976.
52. Randall, *Not without Honour*, p. 39, Walshe, *Church versus State*, p. 214, *Rand Daily Mail*, 26 November 1976 and *The Star*, 23 March 1977.
53. *The Star*, 11 October 1977.
54. O. Phakati–Ryan interview.
55. C. Cook interview with C. Ryan, 1988.
56. C.F.B. Naudé, Director's Report of the Christian Institute, July 1976 to August 1977.
57. Walshe, *Church versus State*, p. 220.
58. SAIRR, *Survey*, *1977*, pp. 159–164, and SAIRR, *Survey*, *1978*, pp. 119–121.
59. *Pro Veritate*, September 1977.
60. C.F.B. Naudé–Bilheimer interview.

15 The Death of the Christian Institute, 1977

1. H. Kotze interview with C. Ryan, 1988, based on her diary of these events, and T. Kotze–Ryan interview.
2. B. Brown–Ryan interview.
3. *Rand Daily Mail*, 19 October, 20 October 1977, *The Star*, 19 October, 20 October 1977, *The Argus*, 19 October, 20 October 1977.
4. SAIRR, *Survey*, *1978*, pp. 106–107, and IDAF, *Prisoners of Apartheid. A Biographical List of Political Prisoners and Banned Persons in South Africa* (London, 1978), pp. 4–164.
5. Cochrane, review, *South African Outlook*, January 1984.
6. B. Brown–Ryan interview.
7. C.F.B. Naudé–Randall interview.
8. M. Nash interview with C. Ryan, 1988.

16 Seven Lean Years, 1977–1984

1. L. Naudé–Ryan interview.
2. *Trouw*, 12 November 1977, *Rand Daily Mail*, 17 August 1978, *The Citizen*, 10 August 1978.
3. T. Kotze–Ryan interview.
4. C.F.B Naudé, 'My Seven Lean Years'.
5. *The Star*, 10 December 1982.
6. Letter from L. le Grange to C.F.B. Naudé, 22 May 1984.
7. Letter from C.F.B. Naudé to L. le Grange, 6 June 1984.
8. Tom Lodge, *Black Politics in South Africa since 1945* (Johannesburg, 1983), pp. 339–343.
9. SAIRR, *Survey*, *1983*, pp. 57–61.
10. SAIRR, *Survey*, *1982*, pp. 565–566.
11. *The Star*, 5 March 1982.
12. *The New York Times*, 4 February 1982.
13. Cedric Mayson appeared to have been under close security police surveillance after his banning in 1977. In July 1981 his banning order was prematurely lifted, and its seems that the motivation for lifting the banning order may have been to gather the necessary evidence against him to charge him with treason. Mayson appeared to fall into this trap. During a trip to Britain he held talks with ANC officials in London. He mailed a note on his discussion to a fictitious person at his son's address in South Africa, and this was intercepted by security police. In November 1981 he was detained, and after 15 months in detention, he appeared in

court on charges of high treason. During his trial it emerged that the note intercepted by police had been used as the basis of a 'confession' Mayson had been forced to make. But after Mayson presented evidence to court that he had been tortured, the judge ruled the statement as inadmissible as evidence. Mayson was freed on R1 000 bail in March 1983 and fled the country a month later – *The Star*, 11 October 1982, 8 February 1983, 10 February 1983, 12 February 1983, 18 February 1983 and *Rand Daily Mail*, 20 April 1983, SAIRR, *Survey, 1983*, p. 559.

14. C.F.B. Naudé, 'My Seven Lean Years'.

17 Pilgrimage of Faith

1. Frank Chikane, 'Where the Debate Ends', in C. Villa-Vicencio (ed), *Theology and Violence. The South African Debate* (Johannesburg, 1987), pp. 304–305.
2. 'Beyers Naudé in Conversation with Alan Paton', *Leadership SA*, vol. 3, no.4.
3. B. Engelbrecht, 'The Outcast Dominee. Let the church welcome him back, and listen to what he has got to say', *Sunday Times*, 30 September 1984 and B. Marais–Ryan interview.
4. *Sunday Star*, 12 March 1989.
5. *Die Vaderland*, 25 November 1982.
6. B. Marais–Ryan interview.
7. Frederik van Zyl Slabbert–Ryan interview.
8. P. Moatshe interview with C. Ryan, 1988.
9. Villa-Vicencio, 'Resistance and Hope', p. 12 and C. Villa-Vicencio–Ryan interview.
10. M. Nash letter to C. Ryan, 6 September 1989.

Index

Abolition of Passes and Coordination of Documents Act, 36
Adonis, Hannes, 175-176
Affected Organisations Act, 167
African Independent churches, 102, 125-126, 159, 189
African Independent Churches Association, 103-104, 106, 114, 124-128, 142, 189
African National Congress, 51, 54-55, 129, 136, 165, 179, 194, 196, 198, 204, 205
African National Congress Youth League, 180
Afrikaanse Nasionale Studentebond, 22-23
Afrikaner Broederbond, 10, 22, 24, 26, 31-33, 35, 37-39, 42-43, 49, 61, 64, 67, 69, 71-75, 78, 81, 85-95, 101, 112, 155, 168, 197-198
Afrikanerkring, 64
All Africa Conference of Churches, 76, 165, 168
Allott, Antony, 155
Anglo American Chairman's Fund, 145
Azanian People's Organisation, 196
Bantu Education Act, 36
Bantu Laws Amendment Act, 92
Baragwanath Hospital, 158
Baptist Church, 122
Barmen Confession (1934), 107
Barnard, A. C., 75
Barth, Karl, 37, 152
Bavinck, J. H., 37
Bax, Douglas, 163-165
Beeld, Die, 165, 168, 172-173
Belydende Kring, 175, 202
Berkhof, H., 37
Beukes, D., 67, 75, 177
Beyers, Christiaan Frederik, 6, 8

Biko, Steve, 132, 141, 145, 147, 151, 182, 185-187
Bilheimer, Robert, 55, 57-58, 65, 67-69, 71, 76
Bingle, H. J. J., 172
Black Community Programme, 146-147, 151, 157, 160, 169, 187
Black Consciousness movement, 124, 129, 132, 136, 140-144, 146-147, 158-159, 169, 173, 185, 186, 182-188, 190, 194, 196
Black Parents' Association, 183
Black People's Convention, 142, 146-147, 151, 187
Black Review, 147, 182
Black Theology, 143
Black Viewpoint, 147
Bloomberg, Charles, 88, 94
Boesak, Allan, 175, 190-191, 196
Bos, Jone, 114, 135
Bosch, David, 48
Boshoff, G., 49
Botha, Louis, 8
Botha, P. W., 163, 196
Brink, André, 133
Brink, Bertie, 49
British Council of Churches, 106, 155, 195
Broeder Kring, 175, 190, 202
Brown, Basil, 101, 112
Brown, Brian, 125, 127, 129, 151, 153-154, 159, 162, 182, 187, 189, 195
Brunner, Emil, 37
Bruno Kreisky Foundation Award, 195
Burger, A. J. V., 74
Burger, Die, 27, 63, 76, 135
Burnett, Bill, 101, 112-113, 131
Buthelezi, Manas, 151, 158, 168, 169
Buthelezi, Mangosuthu, 179-180
Buti, Ernest, 173

Buti, Sam, 174
Cape Times, 27, 149, 168
Catholic Church, 170, 172, 189
Chikane, Frank, 190
Christian Council of South Africa, 59, 101, 103, 112-115, 121
Christian Fellowship Trust, 192, 199
Christian Institute of Southern Africa, 1-3, 55-56, 72-73, 76-84, 92-104, 106-122, 124-131, 133-139, 141-6, 149-151, 153-155, 157-162, 164-172, 174-184, 186-195, 207
Church of the Province of South Africa, 45, 54-59, 61, 64, 137-138, 150
Cochrane, James, 120, 188, 189
Cook, Calvin, 121-122, 183
Collier, Mark, 129
Commission of Enquiry into Certain Organisations, 149-157, 167-172, 178, 181-182
Commissions Act, 155
conscientious objection, 162-164
confessing church movement, 107-108, 149, 190
Conradie, Frikkie, 197-198
Conservative Party, 196
Cottesloe Consultation, 55-57, 59-69, 71-72, 75, 78-79, 137, 150, 176-177
Cronje, Geoff, 25
Cronje, U. J., 18
Curtis, Neville, 146, 151
Daily Dispatch, 187
Dagbreek en Sondagnuus, 63, 76, 89
Davies, John, 121
Davison, Colin, 138
De Beer, David, 138
De Beer, Zach, 133
De Blank, Joost, 54-56, 61, 98
De Bruin, Hannes, 50
Defence and Aid Fund, 138
De Gruchy, John, 108, 113
De Klerk, Jan, 96
De la Rey, Koos, 8
Desmond, Cosmas, 129, 138
De Villiers, Bruckner, 115, 129, 134
Divine or Civil Disobedience?, 152-154
De Wet Strauss, W., 38
Diederichs, N. J., 25
Discarded People, The, 138
District Six, 110-111
Du Plessis, Danie, 81
Du Plessis, Johan, 26-27

Du Preez, A. B., 65-66
Du Toit, André, 133
Du Toit, E. J., 31
Ecunews, 170
Engelbrecht, Ben, 78, 100-101, 106, 109, 115, 117, 121, 128-129
Federasie van Afrikaanse Kultuurvereniginge, 22, 28
Felgate, Walter, 179, 194
ffrench-Beytagh, G.A., 138-139
Final Report of the Commission of Enquiry into Certain Organisations, 167-170
Fischer, Bram, 111
Franklin D. Roosevelt Four Freedoms Foundation award, 195
Freedom Charter, 51, 196
Freemasons, 42-43
Free University of Amsterdam, 25, 116, 172, 175, 195
Frelimo, 157, 159
Gandhi, Mahatma, 166
Gardner, Colin, 151, 168
Genadendal, 21, 28, 30-31, 33
Gereformeerde Kerk, 40, 45-46, 68, 71, 120, 134, 172, 196
Gereformeerde Kerk (Netherlands), 25, 113-114, 134, 155
Gereformeerde Kerk (Netherlands) Lunteren synod, 134-135, 139
Gericke, Kosie, 112, 116, 134
German Evangelical Church, 107
Geyser, Albert, 68, 71-72, 77, 86-90, 93-95, 101, 118-119, 128, 207, 208
Graaff, Sir De Villiers, 150
Greyling, Chris, 48
Groenendijk, Kor, 135
Group Areas Act, 36, 47, 49, 92
Hervormde Kerk, 55, 58, 60, 63, 65, 67, 71, 82, 87, 89, 93, 118-119
Hervormde Kerk (Netherlands), 114, 116, 165, 173
Hervormer, Die, 118
Hertzog, J. B. M., 15, 17, 23, 29
Hoofstad, 163
Hope, Anne, 128-129
Huguenot College, Wellington, 7
Human Relations and the South African Scene in the Light of the Scriptures, 173
Hurley, Denis, 146
Immorality Act, 92
Information scandal, 176

Inkatha, 180
Institute for a Democratic Alternative for South Africa, 83
Internal Security Act, 183, 185, 187
International Commission of Jurists, 155
Jansen, Mrs E. G., 34
Jonker, Willie, 50, 68, 74, 76, 78, 82, 100
Kahn, E., 165
Kairos, 182
Kairos Document, 205
Kairos working group, 135
Keet, B. B., 27, 36-37, 45, 78, 84, 116
Kemp, Jan, 6
Kerkbode, Die, 27, 37, 45, 56, 67, 69, 81-82, 84, 101, 105, 108-109, 116-117, 174
Khoapa, Bennie, 133, 145-147, 151
King, Martin Luther, 98, 122, 163, 166
Kleinschmidt, Horst, 129, 146-147, 159-160, 162, 183, 194
Kleur Krisis en die Weste, 36-37
Knox, John, 152
Kotze, Helen, 2, 129-130, 149, 161, 186-188
Kotze, L. M., 155-156, 161
Kotze, Theo, 2, 129-131, 138, 149, 151, 159, 161, 186-188, 194
Kriegler, J. C., 155-156
Krige, Uys, 24
Kritzinger, Klippies, 53
Kruger, Jannie, 49
Kruger, Jimmy, 1, 70, 150-151, 168, 185, 194
Kruger, Paul, 5, 114
Kuyper, Abraham, 25, 40
Landman Commission, 120
Landman, Willem, 49, 55, 57, 61, 71, 119-120
Langenhoven, C. J., 9, 24
Lategan, D., 26, 27
Leenhardt, Franz, 37
Le Grange, Louis, 150, 195
Le Roux, Charl, 46
Leibbrandt, Robey, 123
Lions, 89
Lombard, R., 46
Luckhoff, Johann, 35, 37
Lutheran Church, 158
Mabata, J. C. M., 101-102
Mabusela, Lucas, 174
Mafuna, Bokwe, 142
Mahabane, E. E, 102

Makubela, Freddie, 197
Malan, D. F., 10, 24, 33
Malan, D. G., 26, 28
Malan, François, 47
Malherbe, Margaret, 98
Malukazi, Z. J., 102
Mandela, Nelson, 54, 129
Maqina, E., 127, 169
Marais, Ben, 35-37, 42-43, 45, 58, 78, 207-208
Mayatula, Mashwabada, 183, 197
Mayson, Cedric, 124, 182-183, 187, 198
Mbali, Zolile, 143
Meer, Fatima, 133
Meiring, A. J., 55, 66
Message to the People of South Africa, The, 121-122, 130-131, 190
Methodist Church, 50, 72, 77-78, 96, 129-131, 141-142
Meyer, P., 25, 49, 88
Meyer, Roelf, 100, 105, 129, 154, 173
Mindolo Consultation on Race Relations (1964), 98-99, 118
Mines and Works Amendment Act, 17
Mkhatshwa, Smangaliso, 190
Moatshe, Peter, 208
Mohono, S. A., 102
Moore, Basil, 138, 141-143
Moulder, James, 101, 103
Myeza, Lindy, 125
Nash, Margaret, 151, 191-192
National Party, 4, 10, 17, 24, 26, 28, 32-35, 42, 64, 67, 94, 151, 171, 185
National Union of South African Students, 22-23, 139, 142, 150-151, 154, 157, 195
Native Laws Amendment Act, 45
Natives Resettlement Act, 47
Naudé, Adriana, 5, 7-11, 13-19, 23, 28, 30, 44, 117
Naudé, Christiaan Frederick Beyers: birth 8; childhood, 12-14, 16-19; university, 20-29, marriage, 28-29; ministry in the NGK, 30-83; clash with Broederbond, 86-95; ministry at the Christian Institute, 96-192; banned years, 193-203; unbanning and general secretary of the SACC, 204-205
Naudé, Hermann, 34, 44, 80, 95
Naudé, Hymne (Weiss) 28

Naudé, Ilse, 1-2, 21-23, 27, 30, 34, 36, 39-40, 43-44, 50, 73-74, 80, 82-83, 94-95, 115, 117, 150, 192, 195, 197, 200-201, 203, 207
Naudé, J. François, 30, 50
Naudé, J. F. (Joos), 13, 16, 18-23, 27, 29
Naudé, Johann, 30, 50
Naudé, Jozua François, 4-19, 23, 25, 30-32, 35, 149
Naudé, Liesel, 36, 44, 80, 94
Naudé, Lirieka (Badenhorst), 197
Naudé, Reinet (O 'Brien Geldenhuys), 16
Naudé, Tom, 56
Nederduitse Gereformeerde Kerk, 3, 5, 8-9, 13-18, 23-27, 29-38, 40-43, 45-46, 48-51, 53-61, 63-72, 74-79, 82, 84-85, 88, 94-101, 105-106, 108-109, 113-117, 119-120, 122, 124, 126, 128-130, 134, 137, 139, 155-157, 172-178, 182, 184, 189-191, 197-198, 202, 205-207
NGK Federal Council, 26, 45-46, 65
NGK Federal Mission Council, 34, 36
NGK in Afrika, 25, 134, 144, 172-175, 197, 202, 205, 208
NGK *Jeugvereniging*, 36, 37, 38, 40, 45
NGK Reformed Church in Africa, 25, 53
NGK *Sendingkerk*, 17, 25, 31, 40-41, 120, 172-173, 175
NGK Sendingsinstituut, Wellington, 31
NGK Theological Seminary, Stellenbosch, 7, 20, 24, 26-28, 35
Netherlands Missionary Council, 113
Ngada, Harry, 125
Niebuhr, Reinhold, 152, 161
Nolutshungu, Sam, 147
O'Brien Geldenhuys, Frans, 27, 49, 56, 68, 79, 176, 177
O'Leary, Eoin, 153
Oosthuizen, A., 82
Ossewabrandwag, 32, 33
Ou Paaie, Die, 26
Pan-Africanist Congress, 52, 54, 129, 136, 179
Paton, Alan, 133, 205
Phakati, Oshadi, 129, 154, 158, 178, 183, 194
Pityana, Barney, 142, 147, 151
Plea for Understanding, A, 119
Pont, Adriaan, 118-119, 122
Population Registration Act, 36, 92
Poqo, 54

Potchefstroom University for Christian National Education, 40, 172
Programme for Social Change, 146, 169
Progressive Federal Party, 83
Progressive Party, 94, 151, 159, 164
Prohibition of Mixed Marriages Act, 36
Pro Liberate, 23, 68
Pro Veritate, 3, 68-70, 74-78, 80-81, 86-88, 97-98, 100, 106-109, 111, 117-118, 128-129, 136-138, 149, 169, 179, 181-183, 185, 187
Qoboza, Percy, 187
Randall, Peter, 110, 120, 127-128, 131-132, 141, 144-145, 147, 151, 157, 158-160, 187
Rand Daily Mail, 76, 163
Rand Ecumenical Study Circle, 50, 68, 78
Ravan Press, 147, 157, 159, 182-183, 187
Rees, John, 121, 128-129, 160, 166, 178
Reeves, Ambrose, 56, 57
Reformed Church of America, 119
Reformed Ecumenical Synod, 46 (Potchefstroom), 120, 134 (Lunteren)
Reformed Independent Churches Association, 126
Reinhold Niebuhr prize, 164-165
Retief, Piet, 4
Reservation of Separate Amenities Act, 36
Rhodes University, 142
Robertson, Rob, 191
Roos, Tielman, 123
Rotary, 89
Round Table, 89
Royal Institute of International Affairs, 171
R. R. Wright School of Religion, Evaton, 104
Ruiterwag, 89
Russell, David, 146, 187
Sakharov, Andrei, 165
Schlebusch, Alwyn, 150
Schlebusch Commission, see Commission of Enquiry into Certain Organisations
Schumann, D. E. W., 24, 27
Schutte, Jan, 71
Serfontein, Hennie, 94
Sharpeville massacre, 52-54, 56, 58-59, 176-179
Sidebotham, G., 55
Slabbert, Frederik van Zyl, 83, 133, 208

Index

Smit, A. P., 49
Smith, J. D., 109
Smith, Margaret, 57
Smith, Nico, 35-36, 43
Smuts, J. C., 7-8, 15, 23, 29, 35
Snijders, H. J. C., 74
Snyman, Dwight, 26
Sobukwe, Robert, 129
Soeklig, Die, 26-27
South African Broadcasting Corporation, 49, 88-89, 93, 164, 185
South African Council of Churches, 59, 103, 110, 113, 120-122, 126, 130-131, 135-138, 143, 145, 154, 161, 162-163, 170, 172, 174, 176-179, 182-183, 188-190, 204
South African Council of Churches: Hammanskraal conference (1974), 163
South African Defence Force, 162-163
South African Institute of Race Relations, 48, 55, 97, 116, 120, 128, 131, 150, 154, 177
South African Party, 15, 23
South African Students' Organisation, 140, 141-142, 146-147
Soweto uprising (1976), 177-179
Special Project for Christian Action in Society (Spro-cas 2), 145-146, 159, 169, 190
Spiritualist Churches Association, 125
Star, The, 76
Strassberger, Elfie, 129
Stellenbosse Student, Die, 23
Ster, 144
Study Project on Christianity in an Apartheid Society (Spro-cas), 130-133, 136, 138-139, 143-145, 147, 151, 155, 159, 179, 190
Sunday Times, 57, 74, 76, 88-90, 93-94, 207
Suppression of Communism Act, 36, 106, 151, 157
Suzman, Helen, 151
South West African People's Organisation, 136
Swart, Gert, 47, 50, 68
Taste of Power, A, 144-145
Terrorism Act, 157, 160
Te Siepe, Els, 103, 125-126
Thema, Elia, 144, 175
Times, The, 148
Tip, Ilona (Kleinschmidt), 154
To the Point, 158
Totius, 24
Transvaler, Die, 63, 70, 76-77, 96
Treurnicht, A. P., 58, 101, 109, 116-117, 199
Trollip, Mr Justice, 118
Trouw, 114, 116
Turner, Rick, 133, 151
Tutu, Desmond, 133, 190-191, 204
Ulvenhout consultations (1969), 135-137
Umkhonto we Sizwe, 54
Union of Black Journalists, 187
United Democratic Front, 180, 196-197, 203, 208
United Party, 29, 35, 151, 154
University Christian Movement, 141-143, 150, 169
University of Cape Town, 179, 195, 198
University of Chicago, 165
University of Kampen, 175
University of Kampen, Theological Seminary, 116
University of Pretoria, 35, 38, 50, 87, 118
University of the Witwatersrand, 89, 128, 165
University of Stellenbosch, 19-22
Vaderland, Die, 76, 132-133, 138, 148, 149, 154, 166
Van den Bergh, Hendrik, 89-90
Van der Merwe, A. J., 49, 55, 61-62
Van Loggerenberg, Nico, 126
Van Reenen, Rykie, 156
Van Rensburg, J. F. J., 32
Van Rooyen, E. E., 26-27
Van Rooyen, Jan, 78, 100, 106, 117, 182
Van Selms, A., 87
Van Wijk, A. J., 65, 67, 71, 77
Van Wyk, Fred, 55, 57, 68-69, 71-72, 76-77, 97-99, 101, 109, 113, 115, 128-129, 197
Van Zyl, Danie, 101, 103-104, 128, 141, 147, 157
Venter, A. J., 100
Vereeniging, Treaty of, 6, 35
Verkuyl, J., 113-114, 116, 135, 175
Verwoerd, H. F. 20, 42, 46, 49, 53, 64, 73, 88, 137
Villa-Vicencio, Charles, 20, 45, 144, 161
Visser 't Hooft, W. A. 59
Volkstem, De, 9

Vorster, B. J., 20, 65, 73, 106, 122, 137, 150, 153, 164, 165
Vorster, J. D., 65, 112, 116-117, 134-135, 137, 172
Wage Act, 17
Walker, Violet, 186
Walshe, Peter, 132, 142, 147, 157, 168
Webb, J. B., 55, 72, 77-78, 97
Weekend World, 3, 187
Wentzel, Ernie, 133
West, Martin, 102-104, 112, 126-127
Whither South Africa?, 45
Wilgespruit Fellowship Centre, 153
Williams, G. O., 154
Wilson, Francis, 133
Winter, Colin, 138
Women's Association of the African Independent Churches (WAAIC), 125-126
Woods, Donald, 187
World, The, 3, 187
World Alliance of Reformed Churches, 196
World Alliance of Reformed Churches, Nairobi Assembly, 135
World Council of Churches, 38, 54-56, 59, 63-67, 87, 119-120, 136-137, 139, 163-164, 167
World Council of Churches' Conference on Church and Society (1966), 113
World Council of Churches, Uppsala Assembly (1968), 119
World Council of Churches Programme to Combat Racism, 113, 136-137, 143, 148, 164, 173
ZANU, 136
ZAPU, 136